Praise for
Identical Strangers

"The mesmerizing result of both hard-won wisdom and breathtaking serendipity, *Identical Strangers* is a compelling read and an astonishing story. With honesty and precision, Schein and Bernstein use their extraordinary circumstances to explore some of life's most universal questions, such as 'Where do personality quirks end and genetic traits begin?'"

—MEGHAN DAUM, author of *My Misspent Youth* and *The Quality of Life Report*

"*Identical Strangers* is the incredible real-life story of a miracle: Two women, sharing the same DNA, the same prehistory, find each other. More than a fascinating science lesson, this story is about the human connection that unites families no matter the odds. A riveting, heart-touching story you'll never forget."

—DARIN STRAUSS, author of *The Real McCoy* and *Chang and Eng*

"[An] absorbing chronicle." —*Wired*

"Transfixing . . . fascinating." —*Publishers Weekly*

IDENTICAL
STRANGERS

IDENTICAL

STRANGERS

A MEMOIR OF TWINS
SEPARATED AND REUNITED

ELYSE SCHEIN | PAULA BERNSTEIN

RANDOM HOUSE TRADE PAPERBACKS NEW YORK

2008 Random House Trade Paperback Edition

Copyright © 2007 by Paula Bernstein and Elyse Schein
Reading group guide copyright © 2008 by Random House, Inc.

Published in the United States by Random House Trade Paperbacks,
an imprint of The Random House Publishing Group,
a division of Random House, Inc., New York.

RANDOM HOUSE TRADE PAPERBACKS and colophon are trademarks
of Random House, Inc.
RANDOM HOUSE READER'S CIRCLE and colophon are trademarks
of Random House, Inc.

Originally published in hardcover in the United States by Random
House, an imprint of The Random House Publishing Group,
a division of Random House, Inc., in 2007.

Library of Congress Cataloging-in-Publication Data
Schein, Elyse
Identical Strangers: a memoir of twins separated and reunited / Elyse
Schein   Paula Bernstein
        p.   cm.
    ISBN 978-0-8129-7565-9
    1. Schein, Elyse–   2. Bernstein, Paula–   3. Twins—New York
(State)—New York—Biography.   4. Sisters—Family relationships.
5. Sisters—New York (State)—New York—Biography.   6. Brooklyn
(New York, N.Y.)—Biography.   7. Paris (France)—Biography.
8. Oklahoma—Biography.   I. Schein, Elyse, 1968–   II. Title.
    CT275.B56545A3 2007
    306.875092—dc22
    [B]   2007014488

Printed in the United States of America

www.randomhousereaderscircle.com

11

Book design by Lauren Dong

ELYSE:

    For Tyler

PAULA:

    To Marilyn and Bernard Bernstein,
without whom this story couldn't be told

Imagine that a slightly different version of you walks across a room, looks you in the eye, and says hello in your voice. You discover that she has the same birthday, the same allergies, the same tics, and the same way of laughing. Looking at this person, you are able to gaze into your own eyes and see yourself from the outside. This identical individual has the exact same DNA as you and is essentially your clone.

We don't have to imagine. After being adopted as babies and raised by different families, we met for the first time at age thirty-five, after discovering we were twins.

While we grappled with this revelation, our natural instinct was to chronicle our mutual discovery. In the first three months following our reunion, we exchanged thousands of e-mails, comparing favorite films, books, and foods. We soon discovered some uncanny similarities, as well as some surprising differences.

As we immersed ourselves in the task of getting to know each other, we couldn't help but conduct our own informal study of the influence of nature vs. nurture. We wondered which aspects of our personalities were forged by our genes and which parts were influenced by environment.

What started out as an idea to write a personal essay about our reunion became a common project that would unite us for the next two years. As we investigated our biological family and explored the reasons for our separation, we unearthed some unpleasant truths about the adoption agency that placed us. We were disturbed to learn that we were not separated because of fate or circumstances, but rather because of a now long-abandoned theory that twinship imposes a burden on both children and their families. For a time we, along with a number of other sets of separated twins and triplets, were followed by researchers participating in a secret study of identical siblings.

Many of the most memorable twin stories—from literature like *The Prince and the Pauper* to popular classics like *The Parent Trap*—revolve around separated twins who find each other. These narratives tap into a fundamental interest in the nature of self. The timeless story poses the question: what is it that makes each human being unique?

This question has fascinated scientists since 1875, when Charles Darwin's cousin, the British anthropologist Sir Francis Galton, conducted the first known twin study. After comparing a small group of identical and fraternal twins, Galton concluded, "Nature prevails enormously over nurture." Since that time, separated identical twins—born with the same DNA, but reared in different environments—have provided researchers invaluable insight into the eternal question of nature vs. nurture. After Mengele's monstrous experiments on twins in Nazi concentration camps during World War II, the studies dwindled. The idea that behavior was inborn was generally frowned upon and even considered racist.

Today, most adoption agencies forbid the practice of separating twins, regarding it as potentially unhealthy. Lawrence Wright, Pulitzer Prize–winning author of the book *Twins: And What They Tell Us About Who We Are,* estimates that fewer than three hundred separated twin pairs have been identified in the world. Unlike us, the majority were raised in part by biological relatives, knew of their twinship, or had contact with each other over the years.

Twins have been seen on sonogram images in the womb kissing, punching, and embracing. Clearly, the powerful connection between twins begins even before birth. Nevertheless, having shared the womb for nine months, when we met we were strangers.

IDENTICAL
STRANGERS

Chapter | One

ELYSE: My mother, my adoptive mother, my *real* mother, died when I was six, but throughout my childhood I believed she watched over me from above. I held the few images that remained of her in my mind like precious photographs I could animate at will. In one, she sat before her dressing table, lining her charcoal eyes, preparing to go out with my dad one Saturday night. The scent of her Chanel No. 5 is enchanting.

I can still see her. She catches a glimpse of me in the mirror and smiles at me, standing in the doorway in my pajamas. With her raven hair, she looks like Snow White. Then, after her death, she seemed to simply disappear, like a princess banished to some far-away kingdom. I believed that from that kingdom, she granted me magical powers.

When I jumped rope better than the other girls in my Long Island neighborhood, I knew it was because my mother was with me. When I went out fishing with my dad and brother, my mother helped me haul in the catch of the day. By sheer concentration, I could summon her force so that my frog won the neighborhood race.

Since I wasn't allowed to attend my mother's funeral, her death remained a mystery to me. When other kids asked how she had died, I confidently announced that she had had a backache. I later learned that her back problems had been caused by the cancer invading her spine.

Along with my mother's absence came an awareness of my own presence. I remember standing in complete darkness in front of the bay windows in our house shortly after her death. Alone, except for my reflection, I became aware of my own being. As I pulled away from the glass, my image disappeared. I asked myself, *Why am I me and not someone else?*

· | ·

Until autumn of 2002, I had never searched for my birth parents. I was proud to be my own invention, having created myself out of several cities and cultures. In my ignorance surrounding my mother's death, I amplified the importance of the few facts I had accumulated—she was thirty-three when she died, which I somehow linked to our new home address at 33 Granada Circle. It was probably no coincidence that when I reached the age of thirty-three, after one year in Paris, the urge to know the truth of my origins grew stronger. Turning thirty-three felt the way other people described turning thirty. I felt that I should automatically transform into an adult.

I had recently starting wearing glasses to correct my severe case of astigmatism, which had allowed me to see the world in a beautiful blur for several years. All the minute details I had been oblivious to were suddenly focused and magnified. But even if it meant abandoning my own blissful vision of the world, I was ready to face the truth.

I was working in the unlikeliest of places, as a temporary receptionist in a French venture capital firm in the heart of Paris's business district. Of course, the desire to eat something other than canned ratatouille for dinner had played a part. I assured myself that I wasn't like the suburbanites who commuted every day in order to pay for a satellite dish and a yearly six-week vacation to the south of France.

Initially I had amused myself by observing French business decorum. As the novelty wore off, I entertained myself with the front desk computer. Assuming a businesslike pose, I sat for hours alternating between answering the phone and plugging words and topics into various search engines. I typed in old friends' names and discovered that my classmates from SUNY Stony Brook were now philosophy professors and documentary directors. One had even edited the latest Jacques Cousteau film.

Meanwhile, bringing espressos to hotshots in suits, I was beginning to doubt that my particular path would somehow lead me to realize my own dream of directing a cinematic masterpiece. After college graduation, I had migrated to Paris, leaving New York and my boyfriend behind to pursue the life I imagined to be that of an auteur film director. My Parisian film education consisted of regular screenings at the cinémathèque and the small theaters lining the streets near the Sorbonne. Sitting in a dark cinema, I returned to the safety of the womb, united with an international family of strangers.

I wanted to go far away, to become someone else. In the French tongue, my name, "Stacie," sounded like "Stasi," the word for the East German secret police. Wanting a name that could be pronounced in any language, I took Elyse, my middle name. I couldn't change my name entirely, though, for as far away as I wanted to wander, I always wanted to be easily found.

My family still called me Stacie, but not in person because I hadn't seen them in four years. My schizophrenic brother could barely leave his house, much less get on a plane. My absence was convenient for them. I criticized their überconsumerism, while they couldn't understand my reluctance to join them in civilization. Though they would have bailed me out if I couldn't pay my $215/month rent, I wouldn't ask them to. My relationship with my father and my stepmother, Toni, consisted of a biweekly call to Oklahoma, where we had moved when I was eleven.

"Is everything okay?" they would ask.

"Yeah. Is everything okay?" I would echo back.

"Everything's okay. The same." *The same* meant that my nephew was still causing mayhem. My family adopted my nephew Tyler as an infant, when my brother, Jay, and his then girlfriend abandoned him. Struggling with the onset of schizophrenia, Jay and Darla, a seventeen-year-old high school dropout, were in no position to raise a baby. Though I never saw them do drugs, I'd heard rumors that Darla sniffed paint while she was pregnant.

Since the moment I snuck into the hospital room and watched Tyler enter the world, I have felt like his guardian angel. I even considered smuggling him into Canada to raise him as my own. Now the child in whom I had put so much hope had become an ornery teenager. The apple had not fallen far from the tree: Tyler had begun to use drugs. Disagreeing with my parents on how to handle him, I was excluded from his life.

· | ·

The hum of the computer filled the silent office. Monsieur Grange had ordered me not to disturb him in his important meeting, so I was able to hide behind my polite mask while making contact with the outside world via the Internet.

On a whim, I typed in "adoption search" and the die was cast.

Countless sites appeared. I sorted through them until I found what seemed to be the most reputable, the New York State Adoption Information Registry. Unlike some states and other countries where adoption records are open to adoptees, New York seals adoption records; they can only be opened by petitioning the court. The Adoption Registry allows biological parents, children, and siblings to be put in contact, if all parties have registered.

Maybe my birth parents were simply waiting for me to register and I would soon be reunited with the mysterious and formidable characters who had shadowed my life. Perhaps, after searching for many years, they had been unable to find me. On the other hand, as a temp, I certainly was not at the pinnacle of my minor artistic success, and the thought of disappointing these imaginary figures was daunting. Maybe they would reject me again. Or perhaps they wouldn't be fazed at all, having come to peace with their decision years ago. I would be a hiccup in their reality. The scenarios and possible repercussions of my inquiry multiplied infinitely in my mind, a million possible futures.

I filled in a form requesting identifying and nonidentifying information about my birth parents and sent it to the registry in Albany.

PAULA: In one of my earliest memories, I am sitting on the brick stoop in front of my grandma's row house in the East Flatbush section of Brooklyn. My pale, skinny legs crossed Indian-style, I peck away at a black manual typewriter. Doing my best to sit up straight and look grown-up, I practice "playing piano." When I press too many keys at once, the metal spokes of the typewriter jam together and I fear that I've broken it.

I like to think that my childhood fascination with the typewriter was an early indication of my eventual career as a writer. More likely, it was simply the closest thing to a toy that I could find in my grandma's house that balmy summer afternoon. No doubt, I also dwell on the memory because it is one of the few that involve my grandmother, who died two years later.

She was the only grandparent I had the chance to meet; the others had died before I was born. Growing up, I grilled my parents with questions about these phantoms and envied friends with grandparents who showered them with attention, not to mention gifts.

I now see that there was another element of my grandparent obsession: they were a link to a past that did not include me. The only evidence I had that they had ever existed were the photos my parents preserved in musty old scrapbooks in the attic. Since all of their pictures were in black and white, I reasoned that my dead grandparents had lived in a time before the world had turned to color. Unlike most kids, I couldn't study these grainy old photos looking to find a resemblance to myself.

How were these antiquated strangers related to me? Just because

I considered my adopted parents my "real parents," did that automatically make their parents my grandparents?

Despite the conventional wisdom that "blood is thicker than water," I had always believed that family is something you create rather than something you are born into. "Never forget for a single minute,/You didn't grow under my heart—but in it," read part of a poem my mother clipped from a "Dear Abby" column and pasted into the inside cover of my baby book.

One fall afternoon, soon before my sixth birthday, I snuggled close to Grandma on her stiff twin bed at the nursing home where she spent the last year of her life. By today's standards, she was relatively young at seventy-one, but at the time, she seemed ancient. Calmly, she cupped my tiny hand in her bony one as we sat there in silence for what felt like an eternity. Although we didn't exchange words, her eyes said good-bye.

Since my mother didn't have biological children and my aunt never married or had children, my grandmother's genes would die with my mother and her sister. Still, I am certain that my grandma never felt any less connected to me because I wasn't her genetic descendant.

Now, as an adult, I'm back in Brooklyn, not far from where my mother was born and raised and my grandfather owned a kosher butcher shop. But, along with my grandmother, the rest of my mother's family has long since died or moved South. "You're moving to Brooklyn?" my mom asked incredulously when I informed her of our plans to move to Park Slope. For her, the suburbs were the Promised Land. Why would we want to settle in the place she had worked so hard to leave?

ELYSE: Six months after I wrote to the adoption registry, I received the only information about my birth mother I ever expected to have. The registry wrote me that they had contacted Louise Wise Services, the adoption agency I knew had handled my case, and requested that they send nonidentifying information to me. As a consolation prize, they enclosed a form listing my birth mother's various attributes, of which only nationality (American) and age (28) are filled in.

I quickly calculated the years: my birth mother would now be in her mid-sixties rather than in her early fifties. I had envisioned her in my mind's eye as a pregnant teenager living on the fringes of New York's subterranean society when she'd given me up. So I could safely eliminate the majority of my fantasy birth mother candidates: She wasn't Edie Sedgwick, who was rumored to have had a fling with Bob Dylan at the Factory in 1967 . . . a possibility that had always left me wondering. And since, at age twenty-eight, my birth mother would presumably have been old enough to raise a child, extraordinary circumstances must have caused her to give me up.

Returning to America after a three-year stint as a film student in Prague, I myself had experienced the first pangs of nature's call to procreate, at the age of twenty-eight. Before then, I had convinced myself that as an artist, I was required to choose between family and film. I chose the illusory world of film. In the fairy-tale city of Prague my dream to turn colored lights into images finally came true. I had been selected to study in the international program at the prestigious film school FAMU. I packed my bags convinced that there was no return.

When my 16mm short film, *Je Vole Le Bonheur* (I Steal Happiness), was received with acclaim and accepted to the Telluride Film Festival in 1996, I felt my choice had been vindicated. I was as satisfied as a proud mother, having given birth to the creation inside me. But the satisfaction was not complete.

Though I espoused my theory of sacrifice, inwardly I longed for a partner and a child. I also suspected that even if I never conceived, someday a wayward and abandoned child would somehow enter my life. I imagined that my gay best friend, John, would help me raise it.

In 1968, my birth mother was obviously unprepared to raise a child. No matter what noble intentions she may have had in providing me with nurturing parents, my birth mother gave me up. The letter was proof that she was clearly not looking for me now.

I resign myself to the fact that even such basic characteristics as her height, weight, and eye color would always remain a mystery.

· | ·

I am shocked to arrive home one wintry day in February, six months after the adoption agency had been asked to provide me with information, to find a certified letter from Louise Wise Services. Is there some new revelation they suddenly want to share? Is my birth mother looking for me? Wanting to linger over the moment, I pour myself a drink and light a cigarette while staring at the envelope.

I savor the last minutes of expectation and then delicately open the letter. Impatiently scanning it, I immediately zero in on the third sentence, the words "You were born at 12:51 p.m. as the 'younger' of twin girls born to a 28-year-old Jewish single woman."

The sentence seems totally unreal, yet at the same time confirms my deepest suspicions. It is as if past and present converge and resonate with meaning. Elation buzzes through my body.

Breathless, I grab for the phone to call a close friend to meet. My first instinct is to share the news. I want to show Jean-Claude the letter to confirm that I am not dreaming.

Over a beer at our local Belgian pub on Boulevard Montparnasse, empty the middle of this winter afternoon, Jean-Claude, a fifty-five-year-old literary aficionado, shares my amazement at the novelistic elements of my discovery. Though we usually drink wine together on evenings after I tutor him in English, he is equally at ease at the pub, overdressed in an elegant suit, guzzling down a pint of rich Belgian amber. His eyes widen in childlike wonderment as I describe the details of the letter to him.

My twin dwells in the abstract. There are still so many questions to be answered: Are we fraternal or identical twins? What would it be like to look at myself? Is that why I have always gazed at my reflection in mirrors and shop windows? Jean-Claude and I laugh at the prospect of her living a parallel life, just down the street from me in Paris, perfecting French, just like me. How many times have we crossed each other's path? I am reminded of one of my favorite films, Krzysztof Kieslowski's *La Double Vie de Véronique*, where, on a visit to Poland, a young French woman coincidentally encounters her double.

"Why were we separated?" I ask rhetorically. The particularly vibrant winter afternoon light illuminates Jean-Claude's puzzled expression. He looks at me as if this is a riddle he cannot fathom, a philosophical conundrum he is left to ponder.

"It's like *The Two Orphans,* the nineteenth-century serial by Adolphe d'Ennery!" he exclaims, making one of his usual esoteric references. "They are looking to unravel the mystery of their origin."

On our second beer, I move my ashtray and lay the letter out on the wooden table so we can go over it together.

"It says that my, um, our birth mother—it's strange to say 'our'!—was 'very intelligent with a high IQ who earned excellent grades in an elite high school,' " I read aloud as Jean-Claude and I pore over the letter together.

"She was very intelligent!" Jean-Claude says excitedly. "That's not a surprise!"

" 'She entered college on a merit scholarship but emotional problems interrupted her attendance,' " I continue. " 'She had a history of voluntary hospitalizations for emotional problems.' "

"Emotional problems?" Jean-Claude asks, "Like depression?"

" 'Secondary sources noted that your mother's diagnosis was schizophrenia, mixed type, which was successfully treated with medication.' "

I look to Jean-Claude for consolation and he answers my silent question by saying "But you are okay," and takes my hand in his.

The letter claims that my birth mother's schizophrenia was successfully treated. But, since my brother continues to struggle with the disease, I know there is no miracle cure for schizophrenia—and there certainly wasn't one in 1968—so I am reluctant to accept her diagnosis. Mixed-type schizophrenia would probably be more accurately diagnosed today as bipolar disorder or manic depression.

Even if she is a mad genius, I would still like to find her.

I wonder about the hereditary factors in mental illness and how they have affected my own emotional stability. Debilitated by depression my junior year of college, I could barely make it out of bed and considered dropping out. Had my twin sister suffered from this illness? And if my twin had indeed succumbed to madness, could I tolerate seeing a deranged, exaggerated version of myself? I fear if I confronted a bleary-eyed stranger with my features. I could not face seeing the life I had barely managed to escape.

Jean-Claude and I ruminate over these possible scenarios. What if my twin is dead? I almost died when I had an extreme allergic reaction to the antibiotic Bactrum, a sulfa drug, when I was fourteen. What if she hadn't survived after having a similar reaction to the drug? Or what if looking at her was like looking at myself, but without the mild, raised scars from the resulting chemical burn that have become so familiar to me? What if I find her, as I am driven to do, only to be rejected by a spoiled Jewish American Princess who frowns upon my years of wandering bohemia?

The vision that scares me the most is that she has conquered her solitude and has settled down with a soul mate and a child. If I witness her domestic bliss, will I regret having opted for a liberated but solitary existence? Considering these possibilities sometimes leads Jean-Claude and me to pensive silences. We also celebrate my enlightenment about the facts of my life. Though I anticipate that finding my twin will be a long and arduous journey, I am tranquil knowing at last that the loneliness I have always felt is not of the usual existential kind; it has a name now.

"*C'est le début d'une nouvelle vie,*" Jean Claude says. It is indeed the beginning of a new life. And yet, I feel the knowledge that I have a twin had always been underneath the surface of things.

· | ·

In a book at the library, I find an image of twins nestled together in their mother's womb. As a fetus first opening my eyes at the gestational age of six months, I must have encountered my twin looking back at me.

In addition to the traumatic separation from their mother at birth, psychologists believe, twins also experience a brutal rupture from their twin, with whom they have shared an intimate relationship in the womb, negotiating for nutrients and space.

Though consciousness in the womb has not been scientifically proven, many people claim to have a memory of a lost twin. One reason may be that researchers estimate that 12 to 15 percent of us began life in the womb as a twin. Yet only one in eighty twin conceptions survive to full term.

Early in a pregnancy, a second or third embryonic sac may appear on ultrasound tests, only to disappear later. In such cases, these embryos are partially reabsorbed by the mother or by the other twin, or they are just shed entirely. Without complications in the pregnancy, these aptly named "vanishing twins" sometimes go unnoticed, often leaving no trace. Since twins are more likely to be left-handed (20 percent of twins, compared to 10 to 12 percent of the total population), some twin experts speculate that many left-handers could be the remnants of a twin pregnancy.

In rare cases, two embryos merge and one twin incorporates the other; the result is called a chimera. In Greek mythology, the Chimera possesses the head of a lion, the body of a goat, and the tail of a serpent. Unlike the gruesome creature for which it is named, the human chimera may only be detected through DNA or blood tests that reveal two blood types in a single person.

And yet, since identical twins share a blood type, it is virtually impossible to determine in a singleton birth if there was originally an identical twin in the womb with her.

PAULA: Dwarfed by the maze of packed cardboard boxes that surround me, I wonder how my husband and I managed to amass so much junk. Piles of books and garbage bags filled with old clothing beckon to be rummaged through and sorted.

We've been in our new apartment in Brooklyn for just over a month and today is the day I have set aside to create some order out of the chaos. The ascetic life is looking good as I envision a sleek, Zen-like apartment with minimal furniture. But reality—especially with a toddler—is a lot messier.

It's the sort of brutally cold early February day when you can see your breath. Despite the weather, my husband, Avo, has bundled up our daughter, Jesse, and carted her off to the nearby playground so I can focus on the task ahead of me. I've declared Jesse's second birthday, just two weeks away, as my unofficial deadline for clearing out the moving boxes.

In addition to showing off Jesse's newfound skills of walking and talking, the event will also serve as an unofficial judgment day. When Avo and I decided to flee the funky East Village for family-oriented Park Slope, Brooklyn, we knew our more eccentric friends might not get it. Jesse's party will be the first opportunity for our Village friends to inspect our new digs and to give us an earful about how we'd sold out.

I had pretty much had my fill of the bohemian life. As a journalist and film critic, I regularly attended film premieres, art openings, and late-night parties. Before I got married, my roommate and I had earned a reputation for throwing raucous parties, which attracted an eclectic mix of indie filmmakers, aspiring photographers, and grunge musicians. I remember one particularly lively bash where a prominent German film director and his drag queen date made their dramatic entrance just as a troupe of fully costumed Shakespearean actors were exiting.

Avo and I had viewed raising a kid in the East Village as a badge of coolness. Unlike other parents who wimped out by bringing their children up in the suburbs (where I had grown up), we were proud to be living on the edge. Rather than cart Jesse around in a minivan, we traveled by bus or subway. Instead of a backyard, Jesse relied on seedy Tompkins Square Park for her fresh air.

But, however much we cherished our lifestyle, we had now been forced to come to terms with the fact that we were on the verge of outgrowing our six-hundred-square-foot walk-up apartment. Since we planned to start work on producing a little sister or brother for Jesse sometime soon, we would need more space. Known for its Victorian town houses and liberal denizens, Park Slope, we rationalized, would be the East Village but with less graffiti and more greenery.

After moving on Christmas Eve, we rang in the New Year eating take-out pizza by the fireplace. Now that we're here, my greatest fear is that I'm going to become a New York City cliché: the Park Slope mom. In the East Village, parenthood made us seem brave. In Park Slope, we are soldiers in an army of parents each marching to orders barked by minisergeants in strollers. Children are the unofficial entry ticket to this neighborhood, where double strollers bottleneck the sidewalks and nursing moms and haggard dads wearing BabyBjörns dominate the cafés.

I've tried hard to balance the stay-at-home-mom life with freelance writing, but switching gears is more challenging than I thought it would be. Occasionally, I manage to put aside the dirty diapers to write articles for various newspapers and magazines. Aside from making some extra cash, it's also an insurance policy that I won't lose my mind entirely to mommy stuff.

As I line Jesse's bookshelves with her favorite Winnie-the-Pooh and Maurice Sendak books, it strikes me that we are creating the home where Jesse will form her first memories. I hope we can give her the stability that my parents provided for me. As a teenager, I found their normality oppressive, but while I was growing up, it was comforting to know that I could rely on them to behave like the supportive parents I saw on my favorite TV show, *The Brady Bunch*. I could always count on my mother to contribute to the school bake sale, conjure up creative Halloween costumes, and volunteer to be the Brownie leader. Dad always caught his commuter train and made it home in time for dinner with the family, which my mom dutifully had on the table promptly at six p.m.

Since I can't cook or sew and don't have much interest in being a den leader, I'm resigned to the fact that I won't live up to *Brady Bunch* standards of motherhood. The only thing I hope to emulate is the unflagging sense that my parents would always be there for my brother and me when we needed them.

ELYSE: "I feel like I've lost a twin," I had often said to friends, after film school, out in San Francisco, whenever I faced a particularly difficult bout of depression. I had always assumed that my profound loneliness stemmed from the early death of my mother and the loss, in some sense, of my older brother to schizophrenia. My friends thought it was just the potent Humboldt County weed speaking. But my stoned suspicions had been right—literally. Those other later losses echoed a first and most dramatic separation from a twin sister.

I am grappling not only with the realization that I have been separated from my twin, but also with the fact that I was, as the letter clearly stated, adopted at six months rather than shortly after birth, as I had always thought. My parents had lovingly recounted the story of my adoption without ever getting into the exact details. It didn't help that my mom was no longer around to repeat the story, and my dad's memory is rather spotty.

In fact, I had assumed that my brother's late adoption, at six months, had contributed to his schizophrenia. The knowledge that I had also languished in parentless limbo for months makes me pity the orphaned infant I once was. My vision of the past is slowly shifting, this new fact making the others fall like dominoes.

Since I received the letter, my mind has been so consumed with the discovery of my twin that thoughts of finding my birth mother have been relegated to the back burner. Back in 1988, when returning to Long Island for college, not far from where I had been adopted, I wondered if without even knowing it I might someday pass the woman who gave birth to me. I wished for a sign, hoping that some imaginary spectators would call out to alert me, "That's her!"

Like the baby bird in the children's book, I cracked out of my shell in front of every kind woman wondering, "Are you my mother?" " 'Yes, I know who you are,' said the baby bird. 'You are a bird and you are my mother.' "

Or would I instinctively know her by her bushy hair and doelike eyes? The concept of kin eluded me. Do people related by blood recognize each other on some basic primal level?

Returning home now to my small flat on boulevard Raspail, I stare at myself in the mirror and try to imagine that somewhere out in the world I have a sister who resembles me. In constantly looking at my own reflection, have I been inadvertently looking for her—my doppelgänger?

The notion of the double had always fascinated me. At college, I had taken an entire class centered on self-reflexivity in cinema. It was this class that motivated me to become a director. Watching Ingmar Bergman's *Persona*, in which a mute actress and her nurse fuse identities at a secluded seaside town, I was mesmerized. My emotions were mirrored in the nurse's question "Is it possible to be two people at the same time?"

Now that the concept of the doppelgänger has become strangely relevant, I start to read whatever I can find at the local library. *Doppelgänger* comes from the German words *doppel*, meaning "double," and *gänger*, "goer" or "walker," but is commonly rendered in English as "double" or "look-alike." I remembered reading Freud's 1919 essay, "The Uncanny," in which he describes the phenomenon of the double as encountering something very familiar that becomes frightening.

Seeing one's double is often construed as a bad omen, which portends death. In fact, the poet Percy Shelley drowned in a river shortly after seeing his doppelgänger appear on his balcony. In folklore, doppelgängers are similar to vampires in that they cast no shadow and have no reflection in a mirror or in water. They provide advice to the person they shadow, which can be misleading or malicious. In many cases, once someone has viewed his or her own doppelgänger she is doomed to be haunted by images of that ghostly counterpart.

In Edgar Allan Poe's short story "William Wilson," written in 1839, the eponymous protagonist encounters a classmate who eerily shares his name and birth date. Tormented by his double, whom he believes to be a saboteur, Wilson kills him in a climactic duel. Likewise, in Dostoyevsky's novella The Double, the protagonist's doppelgänger threatens to ruin his good name and usurp his position in society.

As I daydream about my newfound twin somewhere out in the world, I wonder why the idea of twinship has such a dark cultural legacy. Finding out I have a mysterious lost twin only exponentially increases the gothic overtones.

Just last month, my friend Laurent had chanced upon a sculpture that, he felt, bore an uncanny resemblance to me. While he was wandering through a small museum in Montparnasse, the sculpture The Polish Woman, who appeared to be one of my ancestors, had startled him out of his Sunday reverie. On Laurent's insistence, I visited her at the Bourdelle Museum the following Sunday. Expecting to see her at every turn, I walked with anticipation through the stately museum. As I passed through a gathering of monumental Greek gods, she came into view. Though she was just a small bust made of clay, the resemblance was remarkable; we had the same mane of thick hair and the same mischievous smile.

Until now, I had based my life on a fallacy: that I had been born alone. Rocking myself to sleep at night, the stuffed bear I bought myself the first day of college nestled against my chest, I repeated like a mantra, "I am alone. We are all born alone." I could no longer be lulled by that lie, though I would never be able to truly replace what I had lost. Was my twin the "we of me" that I had been unconsciously searching for all my life?

PAULA: Even after they learn the basics of how babies are made, most children remain incredulous that such an unseemly physical act could have been responsible for their arrival into the world. Eventually, they come to terms with the fact that their parents must have had sex at least once in order to procreate. But since I was adopted, I had no proof that my parents had ever had intercourse. Perhaps, I reasoned as a child, they had adopted my brother and me because they were leading a celibate life and therefore were unable to produce children of their own.

I was caught off guard one night when I was nine years old and my extended family had gathered in the dining room for a Rosh Hashanah dinner. Blithely ignorant of the adult conversation around me, I froze when one comment demanded my attention. "I remember when you were pregnant," Aunt Marilyn, my father's sister, said casually to my mother. I studied my mom's face for a reaction, but found none. Why didn't she correct Aunt Marilyn and remind her that Steven and I were adopted? I fiddled with the kasha varnishkes on my plate, but couldn't bring myself to eat any more. My brain was struggling to make sense of what Aunt Marilyn had said. I visualized a younger version of my mother with a full belly and a pregnant glow. What had happened to the baby inside her?

After dinner, I approached my mother as she was scraping the dinner plates clean.

"Mom, can you come to my room? I have something I want to talk to you about," I said in as mature a voice as I could muster.

I studied the bright, floral pattern on my bedspread as my mother made room for herself on my platform bed.

"Aunt Marilyn said something about your being pregnant. I

didn't know you were ever pregnant," I said tentatively. I hugged my favorite stuffed animal, an oversized bunny rabbit who wore a goofy felt smile.

"Yes, I was pregnant a couple of times, but I had miscarriages."

My eyes welled up with tears, which I soaked up with the sleeve of my burgundy velvet dress. I wasn't sure exactly what a miscarriage was, but I gathered that it wasn't good.

"The doctors couldn't find a medical reason for it, but I knew I couldn't go through another miscarriage," my mom said softly. "Your dad and I always felt comfortable with the idea of adopting. Now I'm glad that I had the miscarriages or else I might never have had you."

It hurt to hear that if it weren't for my mother's miscarriages, my parents wouldn't have adopted me. Aside from my celibacy theory, I must have subconsciously wanted to believe that adoption was their first choice.

I don't remember a specific moment when I was told I was adopted. I like to think that I always knew. It was never presented as a secret, just a fact. My older brother and my childhood best friend had also been adopted, so it seemed commonplace to me. None of my classmates seemed to think that being adopted warranted much of a reaction—I was neither taunted, nor handled with kid gloves.

Since it was such a banal topic, my adoption wasn't something my family discussed much, with one notable exception. I routinely egged my parents on to tell the sob story of my early days.

"When you were born, you weighed only four pounds and eleven ounces. By the time we brought you home at five months, you still weighed less than ten pounds. You had a layer of dirt caked onto the soles of your feet that we had to scrape off. Dad would proudly show your picture around his office, but people must have thought that you looked like a concentration camp survivor. To us, you were beautiful." My mom lovingly recited the tale, like a favorite bedtime story.

"What did the doctor say about me again?" I wanted every last detail, every time.

"The doctor who examined you surmised that your foster parents boiled your formula for so long that it had lost all its nutrients, which explained your inability to digest food and your malnutrition. He told us, 'Don't get too used to her.' "

The pediatrician's flip dismissal of my chances for survival must have devastated them at the time, but my parents' innate optimism was apparently enough to fatten me up. They quickly managed to compensate for my early months of neglect.

This heart-wrenching tale of a pathetic orphan and the parents who rescued her from certain death and nursed her back to health seemed so incongruous with my comfortable suburban upbringing that I returned to it again and again. I was no longer that starving abandoned baby, but I loved to romanticize my humble beginnings—especially in the comfort of our four-bedroom house in manicured Westchester County. I might have been wearing a Benetton sweater and Calvin Klein jeans, but I came from dirt. I was tough.

It always seemed surreal to me that I had had another identity before my parents adopted me. The social worker at Louise Wise told my parents that I had been called Jean at the foster home. Perhaps because it represented the time before I had a real family, I despised the name Jean, which sounded so homely to me. I was grateful my parents had decided to call me Paula.

However much I liked to imagine that my rocky start in life made me a more hard-edged person than my pampered peers, it simply wasn't true. If anything, I was more sensitive, more prone to cry when a friend snubbed me for another playmate or when I failed to get a grade I felt I deserved. My parents rarely had to punish me, because most of the time I was harder on myself than they would ever be.

Like most adoptees, I occasionally fantasized about my biological family. When I was seven, I sat glued to *The Sonny and Cher*

Comedy Hour, convinced that the glamorous stars were my parents and that their blond daughter, Chastity, who was about my age, had stolen my birthright to be onstage.

I also felt a kinship with Little Orphan Annie, especially since she also had curly red hair. At nine I barricaded myself in my room after school to sing along to my *Annie* record for hours, mouthing the words to "Maybe." I studied my reflection in the mirror as I imagined my birth parents living a romantic life a world away from mine: "Betcha they're young, / Betcha they're smart, / Bet they collect things like ashtrays, and art!"

I dreamed that one day I would star in *Annie* on Broadway and that my birth parents would come to see me perform and realize how wrong they had been to give me up since I was clearly such a special, talented child.

ELYSE: I have no idea how I will go about finding my twin. I start by looking up the Louise Wise adoption agency on the Internet. Though I've always known this was the agency I was adopted from, I never researched it until now. The first thing I find is the tragic story of Michael Juman, who, like my brother and me, was also adopted from Louise Wise. Coincidentally, Michael was born the same year as my brother and also suffered from schizophrenia.

When Michael searched desperately for information about his birth mother in hopes of understanding the root of his malady, his psychologist contacted Louise Wise, and was denied Michael's medical history from his file. Finally able to locate his birth mother's name in the 1965 birth registry at the New York Public Library, Michael set out to find her so that she could provide insight into his illness and help him find a cure. Michael managed to track down a biological cousin, who informed him that his birth mother had been a lobotomized mental patient.

In 1991, the Juman family filed suit against Louise Wise for fraud and wrongful adoption. It's disturbing to read that Michael

Juman's severe schizophrenia led to his early demise—in 1994, he died from an accidental medication overdose at the age of twenty-nine. Two years later, the court ordered Louise Wise to provide Michael's family with his file. It showed that his birth mother met his birth father, who was also schizophrenic, at a mental hospital.

Unlike most people, adoptees have two birth certificates. One is issued at the time of their birth and lists their birth parents' names. A second birth certificate, which is issued at the time of their adoption, lists their adoptive parents' names. Only a handful of states (Alabama, Alaska, Kansas, Oregon, and New Hampshire) currently provide adoptees who have reached the legal age access to their birth certificates. In the rest of America, an adoptee who would like the original birth certificate must petition the court and plead extenuating circumstances; petitions are rarely granted.

Before the 1930s original birth certificates were available to adoptees and both sets of parents. But, in an effort to deter biological parents from interfering with adoptions during the postwar adoption boom, most states sealed the records. In doing so, they also denied adoptees access to their original birth certificates.

If I manage to locate my original birth certificate, which is supposedly numbered the same as the one I received at the time of my adoption, would my twin's certificate be filed just one page away? When I had applied for French citizenship last year, the certified birth certificate I'd requested from the city's vital records department to accompany the application listed the hospital's name, along with the hour of my birth, a fact I had never previously known.

Seeing my mother Lynn's swirled script on the birth certificate had been a surprise. I felt comforted seeing her name on the official document, as if she were accompanying me on my quest for a new nationality. Her death at thirty-three had circuitously led me to discover the truth about my twin. I long to share this revelation with her, my real mother. If only there were a registry that could reunite me with her.

When she had written me, the director of postadoption services at Louise Wise had enclosed a sibling registration form to send in to the New York State Registry, where I had made my initial request. As she provided me with no other feasible lead, I decide to begin there, though I realize that the chance of a reunion is nearly zero unless my twin somehow also knows of my existence. Perhaps, I think, the agency can do no more than hint and they know that my twin, also looking for her birth parents, has registered. My mind is racing. Is it possible that my birth mother kept my twin and only abandoned me? Why were we separated?

As elation is overtaken by confusion, I call my dad in Oklahoma. Though we live thousands of miles apart and have differing ideas, especially about how to handle my nephew, we share a mutual respect. I find it unlikely that he would have known the truth all along without revealing it to me, but I have to be sure.

"Hello?" By chance, I catch him at a rare moment when he is not busy at work.

"Dad, I got a letter from Louise Wise."

Silence. Having offered to help me search for my birth mother when I turned eighteen, Dad knows the significance of this name.

I continue. "Are you busy? Are you sitting down?"

"Yeah. What's up?"

"I have a twin." I can picture his clear baby-blue eyes on the other end of the line.

"We have to find her," Dad says, without a pause, as if this conversation had been scripted thirty-five years ago. Though I can tell by his voice that it is a shock to him, I am taken aback by his lack of hesitation. The fragile tenor of his voice speaks volumes. "It's wrong to separate twins."

My father is indignant that Louise Wise hadn't offered both twins to him and my mother. He had trusted the agency, which he held in such high regard. Though Dad was not responsible for separating me from my twin sister, an illogical feeling of guilt weighs upon him. He must realize the magnitude of my dual losses—the loss of a twin, compounded by the death of my mother when I was so young.

Even if my twin is alive and well, I know in my heart that I need to follow my own life's design. I can't renounce the first thirty-five years of my life to live in a hypothetical tandem. I am reeling in reverie about my twin, but I will try to focus on my own path, which at the moment means preparing for the CAPES, the notoriously difficult French teacher's exam.

My father and I decide to track down my twin and plan a trip to New York, during my spring break, just two months away. It has been a long time since we have been back to New York together.

Chapter | Two

ELYSE: I am trying to act as if my life hasn't changed, but the world looks different now that I know I have a twin: the truth has empowered me, but I am also frightened of where it may lead me. I am reminded of my friend Joseph, who, wanting to share the exhilaration of skydiving with me on my thirtieth birthday, managed to overcome his fear of heights. As the small single-engine plane ascended thirteen thousand feet over the California desert, we clutched each other's hands in solidarity. When the plane reached the clouds, we leapt, one after the other, surrendering ourselves to the air. Landing on firm ground, he looked around jubilantly, surprised that the world had remained the same.

Now I am leaping again.

Arriving in New York in April after three years in Paris, I feel like a foreigner in the city of my birth. In my travels, I have lost touch with my friends from college. My only friend left in New York is Joseph, whom I met while waiting tables at a French bistro in San Francisco, and who has kindly offered to let me stay with him. With his dark brooding looks, Joseph could be mistaken for a Mexican movie star or a sheik in an old silent movie. Though he has a boyfriend, he dotes on me like a lover. Through his eyes, I see my own bright reflection.

The steady stream of rain outside Joseph's small apartment on Avenue B is a soothing presence. My father is scheduled to arrive next weekend to help me find my twin but I am ready to begin the search now.

The task of finding my twin seems unbelievably daunting. Sitting on the pull-out bed, which takes up the whole apartment, I sort through sheets of paper, each representing a possible lead.

When Katherine Boros, the director of postadoption services at Louise Wise, wrote me that I had a twin, she did not add a polite "Call me if you have any questions," so I figure the agency can't assist me any further in my quest. I decide not to call Katherine until I am sufficiently armed with backup plans, so I work my way through my list of numbers. I was born at Staten Island Hospital, so I contact their vital records department. Hoping to elicit sympathy from the faceless administrative employee on the other end, I explain my absurd situation. Though the hospital worker has a kind voice, she transfers me to another employee who puts me on hold.

Each person gives me other numbers to call, as if reluctant to be the one to tell me that my search is hopeless. There is no recognized protocol for finding a missing twin, and I am put on interminable hold by the Department of Vital Records.

I finally hang up and dial the number for Louise Wise Services. When they answer I ask for Katherine Boros. This is the first time in my life that I have ever directly contacted the agency.

"Aha!" Katherine exclaims when she locates my file. "You must be an extremely calm person. I was expecting you to call right away."

"Why didn't you let me know I could call you?" I want to shout at her. Katherine sent me on a wild goose chase by mailing me the sibling registry form, though she must have known that my twin couldn't have registered if she didn't know I existed. But I am determined to enlist Katherine's help, so I resolve to quell my anger and win her over. I have never exploited my mother's death before, but now I am prepared to use almost any tactic to obtain information about my twin.

"It is extremely important that I find her. My adoptive mother died when I was six. My brother is schizophrenic. I am all alone," I say, deliberately trying to sound as pathetic as possible.

She immediately responds, "Well, your sister contacted us for nonidentifying information in 1987." That means that she wanted to know our birth mother's medical history without wanting to know her identity. I am surprised that my sister contacted the agency yet didn't want to know about her birth family. How would she respond to me now?

Katherine continues, "I will try to locate her."

"You will?" I ask, incredulous. Could it really be this easy? I feel like Dorothy in *The Wizard of Oz*. If only I had clicked my heels together sooner.

PAULA: It is April 13, 2004, and, as I do every Tuesday this spring, I spend the morning at Jesse's "Power Play" class, beaming proudly on the sidelines as she bounces up and down with a gaggle of other toddlers on a trampoline the size of an Olympic swimming pool.

A bubble machine, a ball pit, colorful foam mats, and top-notch gymnastic equipment have transformed an abandoned warehouse in a seedy part of Brooklyn into a toddler wonderland. It's bliss watching the expression of unadulterated pleasure on my daughter's face during the split second she is suspended in the air, her long blond hair flying above her head, her tiny mouth agape.

With her cobalt blue eyes, her rubber-band-thin lips, and a strong chin that curves up slightly, she looks like a miniature version of Avo. Still, I remain convinced that the almond shape of her eyes, her proud, high forehead, and her perky ski-slope nose were my contributions. All parents scrutinize their child's features for signs of themselves, but it is especially important to me that Jesse's face bears some proof that I bore her. In addition to being my firstborn child, she is also the first biological relative I have ever known.

I had always treasured the fact that as an adoptee I wasn't a "chip off the old block" and that I was, as a result, a truly unique individual, one who defied comparisons to generations that had come before. Yet once Jesse entered the world, partially formed by my DNA, I took comfort in knowing that someone else shared my genes.

Arriving home harried and sweaty from pushing Jesse's stroller up the five steep blocks from her gymnastics class, I am so fixated on not letting the cat out as I unlock the apartment door that I barely notice the sound of the phone.

Eventually, the ringing registers in my sleep-deprived mommy brain. I drop my diaper bag on the floor, free Jesse from the stroller, and wind my way through a maze of stuffed animals and toddler toys to reach the phone. The caller ID reads "Louise Wise Services," the adoption agency where my parents adopted me thirty-five years ago. My parents always spoke reverentially of the prestigious Jewish adoption agency, which had the God-like powers of bestowing children on worthy couples. I wonder why they would be contacting me after all this time.

Before I can begin to ponder the limitless possibilities, I answer, and a woman with a thick Eastern European accent inquires, "Is this Paula Bernstein?"

"Yes," I say warily.

"This might sound like a crank call, but it's not. Were you adopted?"

"Yes," I answer, even though she still hasn't introduced herself.

Jesse starts to fuss. I turn on the TV and hand her a couple of apricots, and she stays glued to the set until I hang up the phone.

"Back in 1987, you contacted our agency looking for information about your biological family, but you didn't want any identifying information. Why not?"

The question—I'd been getting it since I was a little girl: Don't I want to know who my "real parents" are? The slack-jawed, incredulous look I'd get when I told people that I had no interest in searching irked me. My adoptive parents—not the two strangers who haphazardly created me and then gave me up—were my real parents, I insisted. In the debate over nature vs. nurture, I always defended nurture, perhaps a bit too vehemently. I felt so strongly about the issue that after I became a journalist, I wrote a personal essay for *Redbook* about how my birth parents didn't influence my identity.

"I have no craving for biological relatives, and the way I see it, I've got enough loving friends and family," I had written in *Redbook* back in 2000. "Although I have no desire to find [my birth mother], I often wish that I could plant a thought in her brain: The child you bore is healthy and happy; you did the right thing."

An element of fear has, no doubt, contributed to my decision not to search for my biological relatives. What if I discover that I was a product of incest or rape or that my birth parents were convicted felons? Even in the best-case scenario, there's a good chance that my birth mother has gotten on with her life and might not welcome a surprise visit from the child she relinquished so many years ago. Even scarier is the prospect that she would be so thrilled to hear from me that she would want to pick up where we left off years ago in the hospital, with her as the mother and me as the baby. I've already got parents, and my daughter doesn't need another grandmother.

"Honestly, I wasn't sure I wanted to know anything about my birth family and I'm still not sure," I say to this woman from Louise Wise.

"Well, I've got some news for you. I hate to dump this on you, but you've got a twin!"

I gasp, but my brain can't begin to absorb the enormity of what I am hearing. Having worked as a reporter for ten years, I automatically pick up a pen and notebook and begin to scribble furiously.

"Who are you?" I ask.

"I'm Katherine Boros, director of postadoption services for Louise Wise Services. I just spoke with your twin sister and she is hoping to meet you. She lives in Paris, but she came to New York to find you."

Right on cue, the drizzle outside my living room window in Brooklyn turns into a heavy downpour. Rain soaks the turn-of-the-century brownstones and the deserted sidewalks of our quiet tree-lined street and fogs the tall windows of our apartment as Katherine's words sink in.

It's as if a slab of cement has landed on my chest, preventing me from inhaling. Now I truly understand what people mean when they say they were "struck speechless." If I was a cartoon character, there would be stars and question marks circling my skull.

Only once in my life have I experienced a similar feeling. On the first day of my sophomore year in college, I stumbled down a flight of stairs in the subway and pounded my head on the cement below. When the EMT workers arrived on the scene with a gurney and asked me how I was feeling, I was unable to form the words to answer and they rushed me to the emergency room.

ELYSE: "I found her! She lives in Brooklyn," says Katherine when she phones me back.

My twin sister has been in New York all along. She's just a borough away. This is happening much more quickly than I could have imagined.

Katherine continues, "I have talked with her. She's watching her two-year-old daughter this morning and is in shock about the news."

"It has taken me a long time to comprehend it myself, so tell her she can take as much time as she needs. I'm returning to Paris in ten days, but I can come back to New York again soon," I tell Katherine.

Now that Katherine has contacted my twin, my mind races with the other big questions. "Why were we separated?" I ask.

"For a study on nature versus nurture," Katherine answers matter-of-factly, as if this were an everyday occurrence.

Of all the scenarios for our separation that I had envisioned, a scientific study had never occurred to me. Was separating twin infants for a study even legal? Stunned, I stifle my desire to ask for more details. I still need Katherine to help me reunite with my twin.

"You are identical," Katherine joyously informs me. Though I had suspected that we were, the news is still startling. There is someone in the world who looks just like me.

"One more thing," I ask Katherine before she hangs up to call back my twin. "Do you have any more information about my birth parents?"

"No, just what was in the letter I sent you."

No letter "to my daughter" or other explanation left in my file. Overjoyed at the prospect of meeting my identical twin, I do not give in to my disappointment.

"They found her!" I exclaim when I call Dad with the news. Amazed that I located her so quickly, Dad sounds as if he wants to leave work right away and catch the first flight out.

"I want to meet her," he says gravely. I feel his love for me emanate.

"You will," I assure him in blind confidence.

PAULA: "What does she do for a living?" I ask Katherine. She has called me back after informing Elyse that she found me. I am still dazed by the news, but I have regained the ability to speak.

"She is a filmmaker and I think she's done some work as a film critic too," Katherine tells me.

"You're kidding me! I studied film and used to be a film critic. This is unreal."

I'm momentarily excited, picturing my twin leading a glamorous life shuttling between European film festivals and carousing with the stars of French cinema. I imagine she is married to a sophisticated jet-setting intellectual with whom she has had several adorable children with names like Stéphane and Eloise. Perhaps our families will spend summers together at their cottage in the south of France. Maybe this whole twin thing won't be so bad after all.

Now that the Pandora's box is open, I want to dig around in it more. My inner reporter will not be satiated until I have all the answers.

"You know, even though I'm still conflicted about this news, there's a very good chance I will meet with this woman," I say, still unable to form the word *sister*. "I couldn't deny her that. I couldn't deny my own curiosity. At this point, I want to hear everything. I want to learn the truth."

"Are you ready to hear her name?" Katherine asks.

"Yes," I say tentatively.

"Your sister's name is Elyse Schein," says Katherine and she gives me Elyse's phone number, which I jot down in my notebook in case I decide to call her.

I've got a twin and her name is Elyse Schein, I think to myself in amazement.

"What's she like?" I ask.

"I'll call her right now and ask her some questions so you can get a better sense of who she is," says Katherine, who promises to get right back to me with some answers.

ELYSE: Katherine calls and interrogates me. Where did I grow up? Am I married? Do I have kids? My twin is asking Katherine about me. I feel like I am auditioning for a role. Have I failed the test by being single and childless? Surely my twin would prefer a married sister with children. My choices in life are being thrown back at me.

"Where did you go to school?"

"SUNY Stony Brook, and then I studied film in Prague."

"Your sister got her master's in cinema studies from NYU."

I wanted to go to NYU, but ended up at a state school. I might have gone for my master's degree had I not gone to Prague. Leaving New York, I had unwittingly created a further separation between us.

"She studied film at NYU!" I tell Joseph, who is entranced by the one-sided conversation.

When I tell Katherine that I have done some writing, she excitedly asks, "About film? Your sister has written about film!"

"She writes about film!" I give Joseph another aside. I wonder what else we'll have in common. The rain is reaching a crescendo. On cue, a burst of thunder accentuates the mood.

PAULA: "You know I talked to your sister just five minutes ago and if I didn't know any better, I wouldn't be able to tell the two of you apart," Katherine tells me when she calls me back.

I begin to sob uncontrollably at the idea that there is someone else in the world who sounds just like me. It wasn't fate that had led me to my parents, as I had always believed. If the agency workers had swapped our adoption forms, my twin might have ended up as "Paula Bernstein." In that one precarious moment, my entire life was orchestrated. My identity was chosen for me.

Paranoia overtakes me. Did my parents know about my twin all along? Does this explain why I was so tiny when I was born? What else have they been keeping from me?

Before learning of the existence of my twin, I was blissfully ignorant. After years of depression and uncertainty about my future, I was finally content. In my twenties, I considered myself permanently single. I had several short-lived relationships with moody indie-filmmaker types, but none of them lasted beyond the three-month mark.

Now I'm married to a loving, supportive man I met six years ago on a blind date. After that first night, during which we talked for hours over glasses of wine at an outdoor café in the East Village, it was clear to both of us that we had found our life partner. Avo and I were engaged one year later and married the following June. We share the same twisted sense of humor, passion for travel, interest in film, and political views. Like most obnoxiously proud parents, Avo and I consider our daughter to be the smartest, cutest, most endearing kid.

Suddenly gripped by fear that my domestic bliss is about to be threatened, I picture my twin as Jennifer Jason Leigh's character, the psychotic who tries to take over her roommate's life in *Single White Female*.

"If you hadn't called the agency years ago, I wouldn't have contacted you now," says Katherine. "But what if you were walking down Fifth Avenue and bumped into yourself?" The disturbing image of running into my doppelgänger on a jammed midtown sidewalk sends me on another crying jag. Katherine may be trained as a social worker, but she knows just the wrong things to say.

"I had to make a decision about what is more morally correct: do I call you and give you information you didn't want or do I not call you with information you want?" says Katherine. "If I made the wrong decision, I apologize. If I did the right thing, I'm very proud."

I can barely breathe. I have to get off the phone.

"Have a nice relaxing day," Katherine says, apparently trying to be funny.

Surely she could have broken the news to me in a more tactful way.

I lay Jesse down to rest in her crib, where she is surrounded by familiar friends, the worn stuffed animals that have helped usher her through her first two years of life. There is one, in particular, she clings to—a teddy bear with a plastic red heart inscribed with the words DO NOT BREAK. My mother gave the bear to me when I first left for college, and at the time, I cringed at the saccharine sentiment. Over the years, however, I grew attached to the soft brown bear, which I slept with until I met Avo.

Watching Jesse slip effortlessly into slumber, I envy her ignorance. "You have no idea that your mother's life has just changed," I whisper. "You will never remember a time when I didn't have a sister."

From now on, my life will forever be marked by "before" and "after" learning I have a twin. For the moment, Avo still exists in the realm of "before." I tiptoe out of Jesse's room and pick up the phone. Hearing Avo's voice reminds me of how dramatically my life has changed since he left for work this morning. Through my tears, I break my bizarre news to him and he sounds excited.

"You have a sister and she's okay. She wants to meet you. This is great news. It's like you've won the lottery!"

"I'm not so sure," I say, annoyed at his enthusiasm. "The whole thing has raised so many questions: Why were we separated in the first place? Have I been living a lie my entire life? I suddenly feel like I don't know who I am."

"It's going to be great," says Avo, reassuringly. "If I were you, I'd be excited."

"It's easy to say that when you've never had someone call you out of the blue and tell you that you have an identical twin! At the moment, I'm not feeling so excited. I'm feeling shocked and confused."

"I know what's going to happen. You're going to meet her and you're going to get along. This will all be an incredible story for you to tell," Avo continues.

"Of course, I'll meet her. How could I not?" I respond. "She's probably just as shocked as I am. And, of course, I'm curious to get to know her. I wonder what she'll be like. Do you think she'll be just like me?"

Chapter | Three

PAULA: The notes from my conversation with Katherine read like a strange, spare poem: *twin, Paris, sister, film, New York, wants to meet me.* Beneath the words are two telephone numbers—Katherine's and my sister's—scrawled in black ink and surrounded by nervous doodles.

On a whim, I dial Katherine's number. I don't know what I'm going to ask her. I just know that I need more answers.

The phone rings and a woman picks up.

"Hello?"

The voice on the other end of the line sounds remarkably like mine played back to me on a tape recorder, an effect that has always made me cringe.

"Elyse?" I say, incredulous that it's not Katherine. I've dialed the wrong number.

Less than two hours have passed since I first learned that I have a twin. Now I am speaking to her on the phone. Any amateur Freudian analyst would say that it hadn't been a mistake at all. Listening to Elyse breathe, I momentarily consider hanging up the phone and pretending that this is all a bizarre dream. Instead, I start talking.

ELYSE: When I pick up the phone and hear a voice that is smooth and sonorous like mine, I instantly I know who it is. Hearing my voice echo back at me, it's as if I'm on a faulty long distance line. An out-of-body feeling overwhelms me.

"I thought I was calling Katherine," she says. Is she going to hang up now that she knows it is me? She bravely breaks the silence, introducing herself. After beginning my search only this morning, I am talking with my twin.

"Where are you?" she asks.

"At a friend's place in the East Village."

"I lived there for years!" Paula says excitedly. "I just recently moved to Brooklyn." Her voice is so soothing and familiar.

"Do you know why we were separated?" she asks me.

"Katherine said something about a twin study, but I didn't get all the details," I say. "All she told me was that a psychiatrist at Louise Wise believed it was better to separate twins. And then a research team decided to study them."

"That's fucked up," she says.

Now that we are in this together, the implications of this information astound me.

PAULA: Were we ever studied? Did my parents know about any of this? I haven't broken the news to them yet, so they too are still lingering in the land of "before."

As if to prove this whole thing isn't some sort of elaborate scam, I ask Elyse what her birthday is.

"October 9, 1968."

"Yep, same as mine," I reply.

Our brothers were born within one week of each other and also adopted through Louise Wise. Had the adoption agency purposely placed both of us in families with older brothers the same age for the purpose of the study?

ELYSE: "My dad is sorry that he didn't have the chance to adopt us both. He wishes I had had a sister. So do I. I always felt that something was missing, but thought it was because my mother died when I was little."

"I'm not sure I've always missed you, but I've always been very dependent on female friendships and have scared men away by clinging to them too much," Paula responds.

"I've had very close friendships, too, though often with men," I concur. "I had a boyfriend in college who I still kind of obsess about. I have a hard time saying good-bye, too." We have a lot of catching up to do.

PAULA: Can I now attribute my feelings of loneliness during college to having lost a twin? At one point, during my freshman year, my best friend temporarily "broke up with me," complaining that I expected her to fill my emptiness. Now I wonder whether I was trying to mold her into my twin.

Throughout my life, I have always felt torn between my dual contradictory natures. I'm the obedient daughter and devoted friend, but also a self-destructive rebel. I thrive on structure and treasure spontaneity. I am smart, but ignorant. Depressed, but optimistic. Confident, but insecure. I have often asked myself which "me" is the true version.

"How can I resolve such seemingly irresolvable contradictions in my character?" I scribbled in my journal a decade ago. "I am an insecure egotist. I am better than the world and not worthy of the world all at once."

It seems the current of duality was running through my life even then. Now on the phone with Elyse, I attempt to weed out which elements of my personality are uniquely mine.

Chapter | Four

ELYSE: *I am on the phone with my twin.* Brainstorming about screenplay ideas, I couldn't have conjured up a more absurd scenario.

"What do you look like?" Paula asks me, "Cute nose, nice boobs, sorta big butt?"

"Yep, that's me."

"People always say I look like Ally Sheedy," Paula says.

"Me, too," I respond, "though in my twenties people often said I looked like Janis Joplin. I guess it's the hair."

"No one has ever told me that," Paula says.

Even if we look identical, I am relieved that our personalities must be different.

"How much do you weigh?"

"About a hundred and twenty-seven pounds," I answer.

"So you're thinner, but I have a baby," Paula retorts.

I cringe. I wouldn't compare having a baby with being thin. This is not a competition. Living on the French regime of cheese, red wine, and baguettes, I had slimmed down. As a teenager, I often binged in secret, but that seems so far away now. Does Paula still feel insecure about her weight? I want so much for us to be in harmony and am so enamored of her voice that I let it slide as we continue to compare notes.

PAULA: "One thing I have to ask you. Have you ever taken any sulfa drugs?" Elyse asks, her tone turning serious.

"Yes, during my junior year in Israel, I took sulfa to treat my acne. My entire body swelled up with a rash and I developed a dangerously high fever. A friend rushed me to the doctor, who told me that if I hadn't gotten to him so quickly, I could have died."

"I nearly died from taking sulfa," Elyse explains. "I took it for my acne when I was fourteen and got a terrible burn. It was so severe that I was in a burn unit for two weeks. I was in a coma and the story made the local papers."

I gasp at the image of a young version of me suffering from third-degree burns, like the burn victims I've shielded my eyes from when they appear on the evening news. I try to put the thought out of my mind.

ELYSE: "Good news! We're good at having babies," Paula declares.

I am not seeing anyone and am not even sure that I want to have children, but I file this information away.

"By the way, you should know that when Avo and I went for genetic testing when I was pregnant with Jesse, I found out that I am a carrier for Gaucher disease, which is common among Ashkenazi Jews," says Paula. "So I guess this means you are too."

It is strange suddenly having someone who could share my genetic background with me. Paula could be saving my theoretical unborn children from a disease that I never knew existed.

"Have you suffered from depression?" Paula asks. "I've had several bouts of depression and have been taking Prozac for over ten years."

"I have suffered from depression, but I've never gone on medication for it. Maybe I should," I say.

She laughs and I join in, though I mean it half seriously. It can't be a coincidence that our birth mother was mentally ill and that we both suffered from depression. How much of mental illness is inherited?

Since Paula hadn't been aware of my existence until minutes ago,

I am not sure how much she knows about our birth mother. I read to her from my letter from the adoption agency: "Your mother's diagnosis was schizophrenia, mixed type, which was successfully treated with medication. She had a history of voluntary hospitalizations for emotional problems."

"Thank goodness we're both okay," I tell Paula.

Since she'll be with her daughter tomorrow and still needs time to absorb the news, Paula and I arrange to meet the day after tomorrow. As soon as I hang up, I call up my friends and relatives to share the good news. "It's a girl!" I joke.

PAULA: On the phone with Elyse, I calmly listened without fully grasping the details of what she was saying about our birth mother. Now that I've hung up, the word *schizophrenia* conjures up an image of a deranged woman bound by a straitjacket and carted off to an insane asylum. Elyse reassured me that it was likely bipolar depression rather than schizophrenia. But no matter what you call it, our birth mother was clearly suffering from a serious mental illness. Hearing her diagnosis reminds me of how perilously close I came to succumbing to insanity myself.

At the age of nineteen, desperately depressed and immersed in a nasty pattern of binging and purging, I contacted Louise Wise hoping to understand what prompted these bouts of self-destruction.

A compulsive overachiever, in high school I had served as editor in chief of the newspaper, class secretary, and photographer for the yearbook. But by my senior year, my good-girl image began to crack and I couldn't maintain the front of normalcy any longer. My acne-ravaged face camouflaged beneath my mop of long, wavy hair, I tried to hide my ballooning figure in ripped jeans and oversized tie-dyed T-shirts. In an attempt to self-medicate my depression, I began to smoke pot. It was also a means of separating my brain from my body, which I despised. In my most demented moments, I fantasized about developing cancer so my body would wither away and I would finally be liberated from my corporeal self.

Away at Wellesley College in Massachusetts, feeling desperately alone, I phoned old friends at all hours of the night hoping they would fill the emptiness I felt. When those fleeting connections didn't satisfy me, I turned to food. During mealtimes, I shoveled oversized scoops of mashed potatoes, bowls of frosted flakes, and plates of French fries in my mouth. To an onlooker, it probably appeared as if I loved food and had an insatiable appetite. Just the opposite was true. I didn't enjoy one bite of the food I forced down my throat, and I binged to the point where I feared my stomach would rupture.

Still, I gorged on anything that would fill me up fast. Ice cream was my food of choice since I knew it came up the easiest, in soft, comforting globs. Then, bloated and nauseated, I snuck out my ground-floor dorm room window and crouched beneath the bushes, where I would stick my fingers down my throat and vomit until I was dizzy.

One fall afternoon during my sophomore year of college after a grueling session of bingeing and purging, I stared intently into my dorm room mirror hoping that if I looked hard enough, I'd understand why I was so hell-bent on hurting myself. "Did my birth mother go through this?" I thought to myself. "Maybe she would understand and could explain what's happening to me."

I immediately sat down at my desk and composed a letter to Louise Wise requesting nonidentifying information about the woman who bore me. I didn't want to know her name or to arrange to meet her, but I needed to know if something was mentally wrong with her. Did she have the same warped body image and obsession with food as I did? I was also curious about whether she weighed five hundred pounds. Even though I was in reality only slightly overweight, I wondered whether I was predestined to be fat.

A week or so later, I anxiously ripped open an official-looking envelope from the adoption agency and pored over the single-spaced typewritten letter inside, hoping it would contain some clues about the disease that was literally eating away at my insides.

"Our records indicate that your birth mother was a twenty-eight-year-old, single Jewish woman . . . of superior intelligence who attended one of the better colleges for a year before dropping out," wrote Barbara Miller, coordinator of postadoption services for Louise Wise. Mrs. Miller noted that because my birth mother came to the agency late in her pregnancy, their records didn't contain much information about her.

According to the letter, my birth mother felt rejected by her parents, who she believed favored her brother. Mrs. Miller suggested that my birth mother dropped out of college to rebel against her family's high standards.

After dropping out of college, according to the letter, my birth mother made a living doing office work. Mrs. Miller had made no mention of any mental illness. Studying each word, I hoped there was some secret code hidden between the letters that would explain why a promising young student dropped out of college and settled for office work. I sensed there was a critical detail omitted from the letter.

I scheduled an appointment with Mrs. Miller. Over winter break from Wellesley, I took the commuter rail in from my parents' home in Westchester and trudged through midtown Manhattan during a blustery snowstorm. Arriving at Louise Wise's headquarters, a tony brownstone on East Ninety-fourth Street, I felt an eerie connection to the building, the only physical link I had to my birth mother. I wondered if she had ever visited these offices.

Mrs. Miller, an elderly woman with thick glasses and an officious manner, interrupted my reverie to welcome me inside her office. "You know that I was at the agency when you were adopted," she told me. "Yes, I remember your case," she said furrowing her brows.

It struck me as odd that she would recall the details of my case out of the many hundreds—if not thousands—that she must have supervised in her three decades at the agency, but I didn't pursue the matter any further. Our conversation didn't add any details to my small pool of knowledge about my birth mother. Perhaps, in retrospect, I was afraid of what I would learn if I pressed for the truth.

In 1983, four years before I contacted Mrs. Miller, New York State enacted a law which required adoption agencies to disclose medical histories to preadoptive parents and adult adoptees. The information required to be disclosed includes "all available information setting forth conditions or diseases believed to be hereditary, any drugs or medication taken during pregnancy by the child's natural mother and any other information, including any psychological information . . . which may be a factor influencing the child's present or future health."

If I had learned of my birth mother's schizophrenia back when I was in college, I might have been relieved to know there was some genetic basis for my emotional problems. More likely, since I believed that schizophrenia was primarily an inherited disease, I would have imagined the worst and feared that I was bound to begin hearing voices and hallucinating. In any case, I—like Michael Juman—was not given the medical information about my mother that by law the agency was required to supply.

Is it too late for me to develop schizophrenia? What about my daughter? Now nearly seventeen years after gazing into my dorm room mirror trying to understand what was making me so miserable, I am confronted with the thought that the letter that had satisfied my curiosity for all these years was essentially a sham. How can I trust the adoption agency that withheld this crucial information from me in the first place?

ELYSE: Due to lawsuits and lack of funding, Louise Wise Services is in the process of closing. If I had begun my search any later, I might not have been able to locate Paula. Had I searched for information about my birth parents in college, as Paula had done, I would have received the same letter that she did, and would have abandoned the search. At that point, unless we had bumped into each other on the street, we never would have reunited.

Sitting at Joseph's computer after getting off the phone with Paula, I frantically type in the Web address that Paula gave me. Posted on her site, I find a cherubic baby beaming back at me. Paula's daughter is blond and blue-eyed, not how I pictured my own offspring.

Rapidly moving from one photo to the next, I feel as if I am glimpsing myself in my former incarnation, when I was eighteen and was still called Stacie. Only Paula is full-grown and looks content. Paula's hair is shorter and a shade redder but is as thick and unruly as mine. Her cheeks are fuller than mine and she is a little heavier than me, but our wide smiles are almost identical. Though I once viewed myself as awkward and embarrassing, I realize that Paula is beautiful.

Clicking onto pictures of Paula when she was pregnant, I wonder what I would look like if I were expecting. In the first picture, her hands, duplicates of my own, grasp her inflated belly. In the background, her face remains in shadow. In one photo, it is spring and Paula is sitting with her husband and infant daughter on a bench in Central Park, nestled under the trees. Wearing the same black V-neck T-shirt and gray cardigan I might wear, Paula smiles contentedly for the camera. If her parents had raised me, would I be sitting there instead of her? Looking at the picture, I wonder if my old friends might have caught a glimpse of her walking through Central Park with her family and thought, "Stacie is happy now."

If Paula had not told me about her struggle with depression and her difficulty in finding the right mate, I might be jealous of her settled home life. Instead, I'm relieved that she is okay. Having spent two months contemplating possible scenarios, I almost surprise myself thinking that, despite the difficulties in my own life, I don't regret the choices I have made.

I wouldn't change places with the girl in the picture if could.

Missing my twin is an impossible contradiction. If we had been raised together, as we should have, I might not have grown up with my brother. I embrace both lives: the life I lead and the one that might have been.

PAULA: "What did you think when you found out that you were a twin?" I ask Elyse on the phone a few hours after our first conversation.

"Of course, I was shocked. And thrilled. I also felt kind of hurt that I wasn't an original. Just from talking to you, I can tell you're very independent and so am I, so it's strange to think of us being so similar," says Elyse.

"I always felt that I was special," I say.

"So did I," she responds.

"But I never felt like I was missing a twin."

"I realize now that yours is the heartbeat that I've always missed," says Elyse.

After sharing a womb for nine months, I wonder if it's possible that for all these years, we each longed for our lost twin without knowing it.

"I wish we had grown up together, because that is the way nature intended it," Elyse adds.

If we had grown up together, our lives would have been entirely different. I'm reluctant to head down the road of what-ifs. It might just be an enormous rationalization, but I have always clung to the notion of fate. Life works out the way it is meant to be, and so I reason that Elyse and I couldn't have grown up together; that's *not* what was meant to be.

Part of my reluctance about having a twin is due to my steadfast belief that I am my own invention, a true original. Whenever people comment that I remind them of someone they know, I grimace. What will it be like to look my genetic replica in the eye? Will I faint from shock? Will I instantly connect with my other half and embrace her?

"I'm nervous about the initial moment that I see you," I confess to Elyse. The truth is that as excited as I am about meeting Elyse, part of me wishes she had never found me.

"We look a lot alike, but we're different enough that you won't feel threatened," Elyse assures me. I know she's seen a picture of me on my website. "We are still very much our own people. You won't feel like you're looking in a mirror."

Because Elyse shares my DNA, I feel the sort of unconditional love toward her that I felt toward Jesse before she was born.

Later that night, too excited to sleep, I write the first of many e-mails to Elyse. "Hello, sister," I type, "I can't wait to meet you."

Chapter Five

PAULA: The day after learning I have a twin, I wake up in a daze, momentarily unsure that I didn't conjure up the whole scenario. I scurry to the bathroom mirror to see if overnight I have metamorphosed into someone new. Will the knowledge that I have a twin be apparent on my face? Is there some secret symbol of twinship that magically appeared overnight? I'm half relieved, half disappointed that I look the same as I did yesterday.

Ever since adolescence, when I suffered from severe cystic acne, I have avoided mirrors. Unlike most women I know, I don't strain to catch a glimpse of myself in store windows to see how my hair has fared through the day. I never catalog wrinkles, scan for visible panty lines, or count my pores. It's not as if I find my appearance repulsive; I just don't relish the opportunity to study it.

While brushing teeth or applying lipstick, when I have no choice but to face my reflection, I try not to focus too closely. I look, but I don't really see. Will it be like looking in a mirror when I see Elyse? I don't know if I'll be more accepting of her looks than I am of mine, or compelled to turn away.

How do I prepare to meet my identical twin for the first time? I compile a list of questions to ask her, as if I'm headed off to interview a celebrity. Was she a fussy eater as a child, like me? Did she write sappy adolescent poetry and listen to corny love songs in the 1970s? Did she invent reasons to be excused from gym class during high school? I am anxious to know what her experience has been living in my body.

I catalog all the characteristics that define my identity. I'm a lightweight drinker and my neck flushes a ruddy pink when I get nervous or excited. I'm an awful liar and a devoted friend. I've never smoked cigarettes and my nose itches around tobacco and perfume. And I've got a definite weakness for chocolate.

Will I feel less unique if Elyse possesses the same traits? Does our identical DNA guarantee that we will get along, or will our similarities cause us to grate on each other?

· | ·

My heart is pounding so loudly I fear I am disturbing passersby as I walk up St. Mark's Place to meet Elyse for the first time, just two days after finding out I have a twin. I've strolled up this block countless times to take Jesse to the playground at Tompkins Square Park or to grab a falafel. But the familiar sights and sounds are jarring to me now, since I am not the person I was the last time I was here.

Every step closer to meeting Elyse feels momentous. A couple of tattooed teenage punks strut beside me, oblivious to the drama unfolding alongside them. I am starring in the movie of my life and the scene has gone slo-mo. The spring sunshine intensifies my excitement. In just a few moments, my life will change forever. I am ready for my close-up.

ELYSE: Café Mogador reminds me of the type of East Village café I frequented in my college heyday, taking the train in from Long Island for my weekly infusion of New York's avant-garde. The warm Middle Eastern–themed interior looks inviting but I opt for a table on the outdoor terrace, so I can chain-smoke until Paula arrives.

Since discovering two months ago that I have a twin, I have scrutinized strangers on the street for signs that they might be related to each other. Creating optical illusions, my overactive imagination has morphed friends and distant relatives into identical twins. Now, as I wait for Paula to arrive, I scan the passersby for someone who could be my own twin.

I've seen photos of Paula online, but my preconceptions of her do not fade easily. Each thought begins like a dictum: "If she's like me, she must . . . have long hair, have been to Prague, Paris, and San Francisco." If she had followed a similar path to mine, I reason, she would have to be just like me. Being so alike, we would experience an instant bond. We would possess a unique understanding of each other, and be able to share things in a way no one else could.

I am relieved about resolving a major mystery of my life, but I am uneasy at the thought of losing my individuality. The fact is that I do not want her to be a carbon copy of myself. I believe that the hardships in my life have forged my character, but I also fear that my twin will be an improved version of me.

PAULA: *Thank God she is not my carbon copy,* I think the moment I spot Elyse sitting at a table outside Café Mogador. Since her hair is darker and longer than mine, it takes me a second to register that I am, in fact, looking at my twin. She is wearing dark sunglasses, so I can't look directly into her eyes.

"You must be Elyse," I say. "Hi, I'm Paula."

No tears. No tender hugs. Instead, we pat each other gingerly. Just two days ago, I had no idea I had a twin and now I'm standing next to her. It is so surreal that I half suspect I'm the butt of a *Candid Camera*–type prank.

"We're definitely twins," I say as we give each other a quick once-over. It's not polite to stare, but I have a strong urge to study every inch of her body.

I scan Elyse's features to see how they compare to mine. Yep, cute pug nose, but hers turns up slightly more. Thinner lips, more angular face. Her complexion is more olive, but her neck flushes red when she gets excited just like mine. She has two deep creases on her brow where her glasses rest. Do I have a matching set? Looking at her, I can see what I might look like in an alternative universe.

ELYSE: The first time I see Paula, it is like seeing another version of me, except she is a little heavier and her hair is shorter with a lighter reddish tint. Her face is bare, except for the hint of berry-colored lipstick, the same color I wear.

She examines me closely, assuming an immediate intimacy. Are my earlobes attached, like hers? She touches them and sees that they are. We are strangers who inhabit the same body.

Looking at her, I can see what I look like from the outside. I feel like Groucho Marx in the movie *Duck Soup,* which I recently watched on TV in Paris. Harpo stands before an empty doorway and pretends to be Groucho's mirror, pantomiming the slightest move he makes. Every gesture I make feels extravagant as I watch it mimicked before me.

When Paula takes out a notebook with questions, I feel self-conscious, as if I am on a very important job interview.

"Where to begin?" Paula asks, slightly raising her eyebrows, like I do.

I recognize my own idiosyncrasies in her. It occurs to me that mannerisms must be inherited.

We study each other like monkeys in a zoo. She gazes back at me with my own big, brown eyes. I now understand what my friends mean when they comment on how beautiful and expressive my deep brown eyes are. I suddenly know what it's like to look into them myself. But Paula's reflect different thoughts.

She doesn't have the same furrowed wrinkle between her brows. Perhaps mine developed because I went without glasses for so long or because of the stress of living abroad. Our other wrinkles are similar. I wonder if we have shared the same worries and fears, or if even the creases on our faces were timed at our conception. As we inspect each other's skin, I am surprised that we don't have the same birthmarks. As adults we are easily distinguishable, yet I imagine that these marks would have helped tell us apart as infants.

It is not surprising that, in the absence of drastically differing environmental circumstances, like excessive sun exposure and smoking, twins age at approximately the same rate. Dr. David Teplica, a plastic surgeon from Chicago, conducted his own informal twin study by photographing more than six thousand pairs of identical twins. Teplica found that almost all secondary skin characteristics are genetically predetermined. In one case, a pair of twins from upstate New York had the exact same three crow's-feet at the corners of their eyes. Another pair he photographed "developed the same skin cancer in exactly the same spot on their left ears within days of each other," said Dr. Teplica in *Psychology Today*. "It's almost beyond comprehension that one egg and sperm could predict that."

According to Teplica, any physical differences between identical twins are due to variances in their environments, including placement in the womb.

I present my war wounds to Paula.

"You can't even notice them!" Paula assures me.

Though I was embarrassed by them in adolescence, I wear my scars proudly now, like tattoos, a testament to the toxic burn that I endured from the sulfa allergy at age fourteen. I insist that they are visible, pointing out the slight keloids on the back of both arms and the IV incision in the crux of my right arm.

Surprisingly, identical twins don't always have the same allergies. While one twin may be allergic to peanuts, the chance that the other will share the allergy is only 65 percent. With asthma, the correlation between twins is a startlingly low 20 percent. And though identical twins may be allergic to the same substances, the intensity of their reactions may differ. This is one of hundreds of new bits of information that Paula and I will begin to acquire about this exclusive club that we have suddenly joined.

PAULA: It's like I'm reuniting with a long-lost friend I never knew. I can trust Elyse with the most intimate details of my life story. Theoretically, my genetic replica should understand me better than anyone else in the world.

We have thirty-five years to catch each other up on, starting with our childhood. How do I begin to fill her in on my adolescence, my career trajectory, my love life? "So what have you been up to since we shared a womb?" I consider asking.

Sitting at Mogador, I think back to the countless key moments I've spent here: with friends from NYU, with Avo on one of our first dates, and with Jesse, for her first meal out when she was just one month old.

"Do you want anything to drink?" asks the waitress.

Since Elyse has been living in Europe for years, and clearly knows a merlot from a Shiraz, I defer to her. Elyse orders a bottle of Marqués de Riscal, a fruity Spanish Rioja.

"To our reunion," we say as we clink glasses.

Listening to Elyse speak, I am struck by how the cadence of her speech, her expressive facial gestures, and her animated hand motions are the same as mine. I never would have guessed that mannerisms are inherited, but meeting Elyse has proven that they are.

ELYSE: "I was the only one who wasn't a vegetarian lesbian!" jokes Paula, recounting her college days living at a feminist co-op.

Back in college, I had often chided my male friends over the slightest sexist implication, but, as the only female in a male clique at Stony Brook, I treasured their attention. Imagining the all-female education that Paula was privy to at Wellesley, I picture snobby girls in uniforms.

"Nearly everyone in my high school went to a four-year college and most kids went to private schools," Paula says. "It was a really competitive environment."

"Neither of my parents graduated from college, but they always expected that I would. They didn't pressure me, though, because they were coping with my brother's schizophrenia and were just glad I was okay," I tell Paula.

I was one of the top students in a small-town high school where the majority of my classmates ended up at the local state university, if they went at all. Paula must have suffered being a bright star among many.

"Regardless of outside pressures, I was driven to succeed," says Paula.

"Me, too," I chime in.

Paula and I marvel at what appears to be our innate ambitiousness. We're not surprised to find later that researchers at the University of Minnesota found that twins reared apart often chose similar jobs as a result of their predisposition for certain skills and personality traits.

In 1986, stopping in for a quick drink at a pub during the annual firemen's convention in Wildwood, New Jersey, thirty-one-year-old Jerry Levey was asked by a stranger, Jim Tedesco, if he had a twin brother. Tedesco worked with another fire captain, Mark Newman, at a firehouse in Paramus, New Jersey, and thought the two men showed a remarkable resemblance. Though both Jerry and Mark knew they were adopted, neither ever suspected that they could have a sibling. When Tedesco arranged for his friend Mark to meet them at Jerry's firehouse, it immediately became clear that the two were identical twins. "Lop off the extra pounds and I was looking in the mirror," Jerry said.

On an IQ test taken at the Minnesota Center for Twin and Adoption Research (MSTRA), Jerry and Mark scored only two points apart. They also discovered they had both been interested in a career in forestry before taking jobs installing electrical equipment. Each had become fire captain of his squad the same year. Both volunteer firemen in New Jersey, Jerry and Mark might never have met if it weren't for their shared occupation.

Even in cases where there is a great disparity in education and home environment, separated identical twins are shown to be more similar in their IQs than fraternal twins and adoptive siblings of the same age.

By comparing identical twins, who share 100 percent of their genes, to fraternal twins, who are no more similar genetically than siblings, researchers can gauge the heritability of various traits. Another method for measuring heritability is to compare identical twins reared apart, who share 100 percent of their genes, but none of their environment, to identical twins reared together, who share both genes and environment.

A heritability of zero percent means that genes play no role in a characteristic. If the heritability is 100 percent, the characteristic is deemed to be influenced entirely by genes.

While clearly genetics play a role in shaping intelligence, environment can't be entirely discounted. An IQ study of 159 pairs of identical twins raised apart revealed a correlation of 75 percent while identical twins reared together had a higher correlation of 86 percent. Unless a child is severely deprived of stimulation and education, environment stimulates what genetics have bestowed upon an individual.

Still, the anecdotal evidence gleaned from stories of twins reared apart is compelling. In the case of separated British identical twin girls, one attended exclusive private schools and the other grew up in a lower-middle-class setting and quit school at sixteen. When the twins were tested at MSTRA as adults, their IQ scores were only a point apart. Robert Plomin, a professor of behavioral genetics at King's College London, found that the IQ scores of identical twins were nearly as alike as the IQ scores of the same person tested twice.

Back in high school, I wanted to go to NYU, but I now applaud my parents for having saved thousands of dollars by sending me to a state college.

PAULA: When I regale Elyse with stories about my liberal activism at Wellesley, she nods approvingly, adding that she became a vegetarian on moral grounds.

We discover that we both consider ourselves liberals and seem to hold the same opinions on hot-button topics such as abortion, school prayer, gay rights, and the death penalty. Compared to our parents, who tend to be more middle of the road, Elyse and I fall somewhere left of center. One would expect that our political views would be entirely shaped by our environment, but research suggests otherwise.

A 2005 article in *The New York Times* revealed the results of a report by political scientists who combed survey data from two ongoing studies of more than eight thousand sets of twins. They found that identical twins' political opinions correlated at a rate of 66 percent, compared with only 46 percent for fraternal twins. Of course, there is no evidence that opinions about specific issues are written into anyone's DNA, but genes do play a role in emotional response to certain topics.

My cell phone rings and I see from caller ID that it's my parents, no doubt checking that I haven't dropped dead from shock. My parents, who retired to Hilton Head, South Carolina, in 1997 after thirty years in the same house in Westchester, live a pathologically wholesome life. My father volunteers to help disabled children learn how to ride horses. Together, he and my mother, who are still best friends after forty-three years of marriage, volunteer at their local hospital and adopted a high-needs dog from their local shelter.

Their spiffy ranch house is so neat and orderly that it could easily be mistaken for a furniture showroom. Last night, when I disturbed their structured, happy lives with the soap-opera-worthy news of my long-lost twin, they were as shocked by the news as I was.

As much as they instilled the belief in me that nurture trumps nature, they seemed to have no trouble accepting the fact that I now have a sister.

"All of the sudden, I'm not sure if I have two kids or three," joked my mom.

"I just hope I don't like her more than you," teased my dad, who has the sense of humor of a Borscht Belt comic.

ELYSE: "We talk almost every day," Paula says as she turns off her cell phone after talking to her parents.

How different our lives are. Since I've lived in Paris for three years, far from relatives, the thought of a daily phone call from my folks seems foreign to me. Though I am close to Jean-Claude and my other friends in Paris, no one calls me regularly to ask what I ate for dinner or which metro I took home. I don't miss it.

Paula and I banter easily about film critics we admire, without having to explain who writes for which publication. I am pleased to be in such accomplished company. She even wrote film reviews for *Interview* magazine, which I read regularly for years, and interned with J. Hoberman from *The Village Voice*. Paula and I laugh picturing me reading an article written by the twin I never knew I had.

I boast about the great film professors I had at college and Paula nods approvingly. I can easily imagine myself venturing down the path Paula has taken and becoming a full-fledged film critic, as I studied film theory at college and wrote some reviews for magazines in Prague. And, like Paula, I was editor of my high school newspaper. Since my parents always assumed that I would end up in journalism, I worry they'll see Paula as proof that I have missed the boat. I am afraid that they will view her as the original and me as the copy. No doubt, they'll be impressed that, as a reporter for *Variety*, Paula has appeared on TV.

PAULA: When Elyse and I rest our hands on the table, I notice that we both have long, lean fingers and delicate wrists. In recent years, I have developed the unseemly habit of nibbling at my cuticles, which, as a result, are perpetually sore. Elyse's cuticles are pristine.

I have always been particularly proud of my narrow wrists since

I viewed them as evidence that I have a petite bone structure, and am therefore destined to be thin. The young psychologist who led my eating disorder support group during my sophomore year in college, asked us each to declare one aspect we liked about our body. I was so disgusted by my appearance that the only positive thing I could think of was my wrists.

Now I see my petite wrists on Elyse's body. Perhaps an outsider wouldn't notice that Elyse is fifteen pounds thinner than I am, but to me the difference is pronounced. Looking at a thinner version of myself is simultaneously unsettling and satisfying. In high school and college, I blamed my birth mother, not for abandoning me, but for passing on her fat thighs and big rear end. Despite my tiny wrists, I had always feared that I was naturally predestined to be fat. Seeing Elyse, I am assured that is not the case.

Obesity is under substantial genetic influence, according to a 1986 study, in which the body weights of identical twins were shown to be closer than those of fraternal twins. Scientists have concluded that approximately 80 percent of the variation in relative body weight among people is due to genetic differences. Not only can genes influence metabolism, but they can also affect behaviors such as eating and exercise.

When scientists compared the body-mass indexes of adoptees with those of their biological families and their adoptive families, they found that the adoptees' body-mass indexes were more similar to the body-mass indexes of their biological familes. Separately, they found there was no correlation between the weight of the adoptees and the weight of their adopted parents. People seem to have a genetic set point for weight that they gravitate to, regardless of environmental influences.

ELYSE: "What would you change about your body?" Paula asks bluntly.

"For the most part, I wouldn't change anything. What about you?"

"My butt," she responds, reminding me of the many misgivings I used to have about my body. My boyfriend in college had lavished me with attention, which made me feel more accepting of my overly round posterior. But after college, when countless visits to the gym made it apparent that I couldn't lose weight exactly where I wanted to most, I took the drastic measure of having liposuction done on my saddlebag thighs when I was twenty-four.

"Why don't you do it?" I urge her.

"Do you think I should?"

Seeing my old butt on Paula as she sashays across the restaurant, I nod empathically. "Yes!"

We both laugh hysterically.

PAULA: "I've always been really proud about the fact that I have such good teeth. I didn't get any cavities until I was an adult and I never needed braces," I brag.

"Me neither," says Elyse. "I assume it was because our biological mother took good care of us while pregnant."

"How funny. I always assumed she didn't take good care of us at all!"

"Why did you think that?" asks Elyse.

"I knew I was tiny when I was born, and not knowing I was a twin, I thought that it was because our birth mother didn't have good prenatal care. I figured that since she didn't want to have a baby, she probably smoked and drank and didn't eat well."

"And I never knew how much I weighed at birth, so I didn't draw any conclusions from that," says Elyse. "I always believed that my strong teeth and bones proved that she took every precaution to have a healthy baby."

Elyse and I compare notes and learn that we've both been dyeing our hair since our late twenties.

"How funny—I thought my hair was prematurely gray because of all of the stress I've had in my life," says Elyse.

"How long have you worn glasses?" I ask.

"I didn't get glasses until I was thirty-three, but I probably should have started wearing them sooner," says Elyse.

"I started wearing glasses when I was in my late twenties, but I rarely wear them now," I say.

When I try on Elyse's dark-framed glasses, I find I cannot see the world through her eyes. Everything turns a foggy blur and my head begins to ache.

ELYSE: "Do you have chubby knees?" Paula asks, glancing below my flowered knee-length skirt.

Before I can respond, she answers her own question, "Not really." She sounds a little disappointed.

Though we have so much in common, we are surprised to find out that, while Paula broke her arm at age eleven, I have never broken any bones. Other pairs of twins, however, have discovered many eerily timed similarities in their lives.

In one case, identical twins Ingrid and Olga, separated at two months of age, first met at age thirty-five and discovered that they had each stopped menstruating around age eighteen. Both sexually active, they each assumed they were pregnant and married their boyfriends. A few months later, they both got their periods.

Separated British twins Barbara and Daphne discovered when they reunited at age forty that they had both fallen down stairs at age fifteen. Known as the Giggle Twins because of their distinctive bursts of laughter, Barbara and Daphne both colored their hair auburn when they were young, had a fear of heights, and drank their coffee cold. Despite their disparate backgrounds, they had followed similar life paths. Though Barbara grew up the daughter of a municipal gardener and Daphne was raised in an upper-middle-class family, they both left school at age fourteen and met their husbands at age sixteen at town hall dances. And both women miscarried in the same month before eventually giving birth to two healthy boys and a girl, in the same order.

When the twins participated in MSTRA, researchers found their

IQ scores were only one point apart, and that they also had the same heart murmurs, allergies, and thyroid problems. When Barbara and Daphne compared their lives, they discovered that they had unknowingly cooked the same meal from the same recipe book on the same day. More and more, I'm starting to believe that such coincidences are the result of predispositions driven by our genes.

PAULA: As we work our way through the bottle of Rioja, Elyse and I compare likes and dislikes, talents and hang-ups. In our frantic rush to get to know each other, we rattle off questions and answer them so quickly that our words often overlap. Occasionally, we finish each other's sentences.

We both disliked vegetables as children, but Elyse has been a vegetarian since she was twenty-one, whereas Avo still has to remind me to eat my greens. We both take pride in our heightened olfactory senses and incredibly fast typing abilities.

"Even when I'm not in front of a keyboard, I find myself mock typing as I speak."

"I do that too!" exclaims Elyse.

"In old class pictures, I was always tilting my head to the right," I tell her. "What about you?"

"I still slightly tilt my head to the left!" she exclaims.

Perhaps we are "mirror-image twins," who account for nearly 25 percent of identical twins. Also known as reversed asymmetrical twins, mirror-image twins occur when the fertilized egg splits later than seven days after conception. In most cases, the reverse asymmetry presents itself in small, obvious ways. One twin may use his or her right hand, while the other twin is a lefty. Sometimes, their hair swirls in opposite directions. Identical twins may also show reversals in dental features, fingerprints, and facial features. In reverse asymmetry's more dramatic form, the internal organs of one twin are reversed, with the heart on the right side of the body.

Scientists have also identified psychological asymmetry in these twins: One twin may be more verbal, while the other is more physical. One may be active and the other more passive. Since twins often make an effort to differentiate their roles, it's not easy to diagnose psychological mirror imaging, especially because there isn't a biological way to test for it. To complicate matters further, differences between identical twins can also be attributed to prenatal trauma and delivery difficulties.

Elyse and I are both right-handed and there are no obvious physical or psychological signs of any asymmetry, so later we conclude that, to the best of our knowledge, we are not mirror-image twins.

ELYSE: "Did you get your period right before you turned thirteen?" Paula asks, taking a sip of wine.

"Yes, when I was visiting my aunt and uncle in New Jersey over the summer."

"From the time I was little, I always rocked myself to sleep," Paula says.

"I still do that! Did you suck any fingers when you were a kid?"

"I sucked my pointer and middle fingers," Paula says.

"I sucked those fingers too!" I exclaim.

In my whole life, I have never encountered anyone else who sucked two fingers or who had the quirky habit of typing out words while thinking them.

We sit in silence as we marvel at our shared peculiarities.

"It's interesting that we both have friends all over the world," says Paula. Like me, she has traveled extensively and is still in touch with friends whom she met in Israel during her junior year abroad.

"You always got a round-trip ticket and I never even thought of buying a return ticket home," I joke.

We discover we both have a penchant for folksy songstresses, though having attended a women's college, Paula is more familiar with Joan Armatrading and Carole King than I am. How can she not be entranced by Rickie Lee Jones, whose deep, soulful voice has resonated with me since college? I used to sing along to the lyrics of one of her songs: "We belong together. We are twinned in a fugitive mind."

The evening chill brings us inside. As the waiter hands us menus, I detect him scrutinizing us. How strange it must be for him to over-hear us comparing our lives.

"Should we get the mussels?" I ask Paula.

Paula responds with a frown. My own tastes must have been in-fluenced by a childhood spent near Long Island Sound, where we'd fetch fresh lobster from the docks after a day out on our boat.

When I get up to go to the bathroom, I am compelled to turn around to look at Paula from another angle. Though the resem-blance between us is uncanny, I wouldn't mistake her for myself. Greeted by my reflection in the ornate gold-framed mirror in the hall, I am relieved to see that I still look like myself. I turn back to look at Paula, who meets my gaze with the same amazement.

PAULA: When Elyse returns to the table, we rattle off a list of art films that made huge impressions on us, nodding our heads in uni-son.

"*The Piano, Breaking the Waves . . .*"

"*Wings of Desire!*" we declare at the same time, and then look at each other in amazement. Who would have guessed that a passion for Wim Wenders films is an inherited trait?

Just months after graduating from Wellesley, I went to see *Wings of Desire* at the then brand-new mecca of independent cinema, the Angelika Film Center, in the fall of 1990. I had moved to Manhat-tan to get my master's in cinema studies at NYU. In addition to tak-ing classes at night, I was working as an assistant at a public relations firm that specialized in independent and foreign films. After a summer of living with my parents in Westchester, I was thrilled to be in the center of the downtown New York film scene.

Between working days and going to school at night, I had little time for a social life. I didn't know many people in the city, and my crazy schedule didn't allow much time to forge new friendships. Movies were my only companions and if I went without sleep, I could sometimes manage to pack in as many as three films a day. On weekends, I'd attend the midnight screenings at the Angelika by myself. I treasured the solitary feeling of sitting in a dark theater, surrounded by a crowd of strangers. I liked to eavesdrop on snippets of their conversations and imagine what sorts of lives they led. During a good movie, I was transported to another world with its own set of rules and expectations. Liberated from my body's limitations, I could temporarily give myself over to the magical images on the screen.

Watching *Wings of Desire,* I was transfixed by its poetic, dreamlike tone. In one scene, a solitary angel sits on a perch above Berlin and provides comfort to mortals in need. Like the angel, the audience can "hear" the mortals' flitting thoughts. "Why am I me and not you? Why am I here and not there?"

ELYSE: During my senior year at Stony Brook, my friends and I often made the one-and-a-half-hour trek from Long Island to Manhattan to watch the eclectic mix of films the Angelika offered. I calculate the times and places my life could have intersected with Paula's. Standing in the ticket line while she was already seated in the theater, we could have crossed paths merely seconds apart.

Perhaps the experience of being separated after spending nine months in the womb together has indelibly imprinted our lives and drawn us to the same films. Maybe such a profound separation causes one to seek out art that expresses longing for another.

Wanting to share the sublime beauty of *Wings of Desire,* which I had already seen alone, I took my first love, Chris, to see it at the New Community Cinema in Huntington. As the black-and-white images danced across his face, I watched carefully for minute changes in his expression, longing to penetrate his thoughts. I yearned to find a way to merge with another but I could never get close enough to Chris.

I even felt this way with strangers. While riding on a bus, I would silently commiserate with the people sitting beside me and what I imagined were their sorrows and joys. I wanted to tell them that I loved the world and living in it, that I empathized with them. When I reached my stop and it was time to go, I would linger, wanting to say good-bye to this stranger with whom I had spent imaginary lifetimes.

It seems that I've always been drawn to an elusive other.

PAULA: Elyse and I have been so immersed in conversation that until now, we haven't noticed that the lunch crowd has long since cleared out and the waiters have begun to put votive candles on the tables.

"Well, there's no doubt you two are twins," Avo says when he stops by on his way home from work. He hugs Elyse warmly. If I never see her again, Avo will serve as my witness that I have a twin in the world.

"He's cute," says Elyse after Avo leaves.

"I guess we've got the same taste in men," I say. "I tend to like them tall and lanky."

"Me too," says Elyse.

"With Avo, it was love at first sight. It was the first time that I really liked someone and my feelings were equally reciprocated."

"I always felt that it would take a special guy to appreciate our beauty," says Elyse.

"What do you mean by that?" I ask, stung by her remark.

"Just that not every guy can appreciate our looks."

"Are we so unusual-looking that most guys wouldn't find us attractive?" I ask.

"No, not at all," says Elyse. "I actually mean it as a compliment. We're not necessarily the kind of women a guy would notice right off. He'd have to be a special guy to give us a second look."

Meeting my twin is bringing the issue of my sensitivity about my appearance to the forefront. I never imagined that I'd be able to discuss my looks with someone who has lived in my body. I can't help but wonder if she is prettier than I am and whether Avo will be attracted to her.

I'm slightly relieved to find out later that, surprisingly, studies of separated twins have found that genes appear to play little role in choosing a mate. "Romantic infatuation, which largely determines who marries whom, is a nearly random event," wrote the late Professor Lykken, who was a key investigator in MSTRA and former director of the Minnesota Twin Family Study.

After questioning more than nine hundred pairs of twins and their spouses about their partners, Lykken concluded that the partners of identical twins are not any more alike than those of fraternal twins. Very few people married to an identical twin said they could have fallen in love with their spouse's co-twin. Clearly, the whims of romantic attraction are more powerful than genes.

ELYSE: When I first looked at Paula's website, I imagined "Avo," because of his unusual name, to be Eastern European. Though he has Eastern European roots, he turns out to be American and Paula tells me that Avo is a nickname for Anthony. A handsome, amiable man with a trim build and gray peppered into his brown hair, he hugs me as soon as he sees me.

Had I met him earlier, I might have fallen for him myself. I wish I could have met someone before discovering Paula. I had resigned myself to being alone. Now I am too immersed in reflection about this new relationship to put energy into finding someone. Why had I forged my life alone and so far forsaken my own chance at a relationship?

PAULA: Like a smitten couple on a first date, Elyse and I are not ready to leave each other. Talking to her, I am completely myself.

I never knew I was missing a sister, not to mention a twin, but now I can't imagine being without her. Once we separate today, I worry that my twin will vanish again. Throughout my life, I have suffered from an abandonment complex; I have irrational fears that people close to me will inexplicably disappear. In fifth grade, I had recurring nightmares that my best friend was moving away. When friends leave a party without saying good-bye, my feelings are wounded. I always attributed this complex to being adopted, but now I wonder if it stems from my early separation from my twin.

The thrill of our reunion is so addictive that I don't want it to end. We head to an East Village bar on First Avenue and East First Street, which I frequented back in my carousing single days.

"ID," a bald bouncer in a black leather vest demands at the door.

Comparing our driver's license pictures, we verify that we in fact were both born on October 9, 1968.

"So what do you want to drink?" I ask Elyse.

Even a simple question prompts us to contemplate the issue of nature vs. nurture. Newly reunited, it seems we want to stay in unison and order the same thing. Even though I tend to favor sweet "girly" drinks like Cosmopolitans, I acquiesce when Elyse suggests scotch. She is clearly more of an experienced drinker than I am, so I hope she doesn't think I'm a Goody Two-shoes.

ELYSE: It's getting late and the time for our parting is inevitable, but I am still wound up, and could use a sedative. Growing up, I used to sip from my grandfather's evening glass of scotch, so it seems like an appropriate drink to have now. It's clear that I'm a more seasoned drinker, though Paula doesn't turn me down when I offer to order another.

Now that we've loosened up a bit, I momentarily forget that I am sitting here with my twin. As we sing hammy renditions of syrupy love songs, it's clear that we both possess a preternatural talent for "Name That Tune." In the crowded and boisterous bar, everyone must be too drunk to notice our loud rendition of "Mandy."

As a child, I would sit listening to Barry Manilow through large cushioned headphones as my family went about their activities. I imagine Paula trying to wrestle a headphone from me. Perhaps we would have sung the song together and driven our family crazy.

It's around midnight when Paula and I begin the stroll back to Joseph's apartment for our inevitable good-bye. What is my relationship to this stranger? Having shared a womb with Paula, she is the first person I ever knew. We hold each other tightly and I am reluctant to let her go. After a taxi shuttles her off, I am left on Avenue A, the streets still slick from last night's rain. After our euphoric communion, I am alone again, a newborn ushered into an unfamiliar world.

PAULA: After a long, giddy day and night together, it is hard to leave Elyse, but I also crave the familiar comfort of my husband and daughter. Elyse and I walk toward her friend Joseph's apartment on Avenue A, just blocks from where I lived until a few months ago.

Dawdling on the sidewalk, we hesitate before saying good-bye.

"It's been quite a day," I say.

My body is so riddled with energy that I can't contain myself. My feet continue to shuffle on the sidewalk even as I do my best to stand still.

"Good-bye," Elyse says mournfully.

We'll see each other again Sunday when she comes to Park Slope with her dad. She'll get to meet Jesse then. We hug each other tightly, until a cab swoops up beside us, beckoning me home.

After slamming the door and sliding across the seat, I turn back to look out the rear window. As the taxi speeds downtown toward the Manhattan Bridge, I watch Elyse's solitary figure disappear in the distance.

Chapter | Six

PAULA: Like a recovering addict overcoming denial, I need to re-peat "I am a twin" in order to accept it. Reveling in the fact that I've got such a juicy story to tell, I grow addicted to people's slack-jawed reactions. After leading a relatively humdrum life, I am suddenly a curiosity, a talk show host's dream guest. "Montel Williams is on the line for you," jokes Barry, the receptionist at Avo's office. I laugh, but also cringe at the sensationalist turn my life has taken. In the pop-culture lexicon, twins, like dwarves, seem to serve as an easy shorthand for "freak."

I think of the mesmerizing Diane Arbus photograph of a pair of sweet, yet demonic identical twin girls dressed in matching outfits. Standing side by side, they stare at the camera knowingly, challeng-ing viewers to detect the subtle differences between them. Arbus's photo became fodder for the spooky twin girls in Stanley Kubrick's *The Shining.* This ominous pair, along with the psychotic twin gyne-cologists in David Cronenberg's *Dead Ringers,* continues to haunt filmgoers. Then there are the sociopathic twins in the 1990 film *The Krays,* which was based on the true story of twin thugs Ronald and Reginald Kray, who terrorized London in the 1950s and 1960s.

Twins are such a curiosity that every year, hundreds of re-searchers descend upon Twinsburg, Ohio, during the annual Twins Days Festival, hoping to study everything from food preferences, to hearing abilities, to the environmental and genetic effects on skin and hair. Last year, the festival, in its thirtieth year, attracted more than two thousand pairs of twins and tens of thousands of onlookers. Dressed in matching ensembles, the identical pairs march through town in the "Double Take" Parade and compete in contests like "Most Alike Females" and "Oldest Twins."

Each summer, Astroland, the famous Brooklyn amusement park on Coney Island, hosts a Twins and Multiples Family Day, highlighted by a talent contest. Harking back to the old days of freak shows, Twins and Multiples Family Day attracts a large crowd, which assembles at the boardwalk to gawk at the hundreds of multiples.

I pity Chang and Eng Bunker, the Chinese brothers born in Siam (now Thailand) who, their bodies joined near the breastbone, traveled with P. T. Barnum's circus in the early 1800s billed as "the Siamese Twins." Siamese, or conjoined, twins result when the zygote (fertilized egg) of identical twins fails to completely separate. Conjoined twins occur in an estimated 1 in 200,000 births and have a survival rate of 5 to 25 percent.

Our country isn't the only place that views twins as unique. Almost all ancient and primitive cultures regarded twins as supernatural beings with awesome powers that could be interpreted as a blessing or a curse. Traditionally, Western societies have worshipped twins. Early Roman and Greek societies revered multiples, awarding twins special treatment. Twins so fascinated the ancient Greeks and Romans that they centered numerous dramas on them. Then, there were Remus and Romulus, the mythical twin founders of Rome. Because of that legend, the Roman public viewed the birth of identical twin boys as a blessing, although identical twin girls were seen as an unlucky burden.

Up until the twentieth century, the Japanese considered twin births bad omens, so families often suppressed the news of a twin birth. To hide the "evidence," they usually gave one twin away. Until modern times, both the Zulu of South Africa and the Yoruba of Nigeria sacrificed twin infants at birth since they believed that twins were an evil portent. The Yoruba have so dramatically shifted their attitudes about twins that nowadays they celebrate the birth of twins. Because they believe that twins have the power to decide their family's fate—either bestowing happiness and prosperity or disease and famine—the contemporary Yoruba treat twins with respect.

Since I have such disturbing associations with twins, I'm dumbfounded by how many people respond to my story with jealousy. "No fair, I want a twin!" declares Avo's cousin, Terry, who was also adopted as a baby.

My reunion with Elyse taps into the common fantasy about having a twin, the romantic notion of twin as soul mate and perpetual best friend. They may be freaks, but pop culture has also deemed twins precious and worthy of special attention. Generations of American children lived vicariously through the Bobbsey Twins and, later, Jessica and Elizabeth Wakefield, the protagonists of the *Sweet Valley Twins* series. Capitalizing on the public's fascination with twins, the fraternal twins Mary-Kate and Ashley Olsen formed a multimillion-dollar production company.

"Congratulations! You're so lucky," friends exclaim, as if I've won the lottery. I have been granted the miraculous but terrifying opportunity to get to know my clone.

I remember Lisa and Michelle Andrews, identical twins who were in my class at school. With their delicate features and glossy black Farrah Fawcett–style flipped hair, they were members of the popular clique, who always had boyfriends and flaunted the right brand of designer jeans. Known as the Andrews, Lisa and Michelle were rarely called by their given names. While I envied the fact that they never seemed to be alone, I pitied them for the inevitable comparisons their twinship invited. Lisa was the petite one, while Michelle was the athlete.

If I had been raised with Elyse, no doubt, we would have been known as the Twins and our appearances and behavior would have been scrutinized for differences. I can't help but feel slightly relieved that I didn't grow up in tandem with Elyse.

"Even though I believe it was wrong that we were separated, I have to believe (simply to make sense of things) that we ended up where we were meant to be," I write Elyse in an e-mail the day after our first meeting. "I know that's a pretty huge rationalization, but I can't imagine having any other life. Then again, I couldn't imagine having an identical twin and now I do!"

·|·

With my new knowledge about my identity, I'm eager to find out all I can about twins. Identical (monozygotic) twins are clones of nature, each descended from the symmetrical splitting of a single fertilized egg into cells that contain the identical sequence of billions of even tinier DNA molecules. Since fertility drugs and in vitro fertilization (IVF) don't cause identical twinning, the rate of identical twins around the world remains constant at 1 in every 250 births. That's about a third as common in America as fraternal (dizygotic) twins, whose numbers are inflated because of the pervasive use of IVF and fertility drugs.

While identical twins share 100 percent of their genes, fraternal twins, who descend from two separately fertilized eggs, share 50 percent of their DNA and are as alike as any other siblings. Fraternal twins may look very similar or may look extremely different from each other. Fraternal twins born to parents of mixed racial origin can vary so considerably in their skin coloration that one appears "black" and the other "white."

As strange as it sounds, if a woman has sexual intercourse with two different men during one menstrual cycle and two separate eggs are fertilized, one by the sperm of one man and the other by sperm from the second man, the resulting twins are only half siblings.

While there are a variety of factors that can result in fraternal twins, nobody is exactly sure what causes an egg to split after conception, producing identical twins. Elyse and I are flukes of nature.

When Elyse and I were growing up, twins like the Andrews were a novelty. Now there is a growing epidemic of twins and multiples—

as evidenced by the abundance of double strollers crowding the sidewalks of New York City. The natural odds for twins is 1 pair per 90 live births. But, as a result of IVF, as well as the rising age of pregnant women, today 1 in about every 35 births in the United States produces twins. The number of twins born in the U.S. from 1980 to 2003 rose 75 percent.

Triplets are also on the rise, but they are still rare. Although the rate has increased 300 percent over the past twenty years, only about 1 in 1,000 babies is a triplet. Since eggs divide more frequently as they age, 17 percent of pregnant women over age forty-five who conceive naturally give birth to multiples. After age fifty, the odds increase to 1 in 9.

For women who undergo successful fertility treatments, the likelihood of producing multiples is about 1 in 3. In wealthier Manhattan neighborhoods, where couples can afford the high price of IVF, New York City's Department of Health found that the twinning rate is as high as 8 percent of all births, compared to the natural rate of 1.1 percent.

Scientists have determined a number of other factors that may contribute to fraternal twinning rates. Fraternal twins seem to run in families through the maternal line, but the father's family may also be involved. Maternal height and weight may also be a factor since studies have shown that mothers of fraternal twins are taller and heavier on average than other mothers. Birth order also may play a role. Fraternal twins are likely to be among the last-born children in the family, which makes sense since fraternal twinning rates increase along with the number of previous children in a family.

Diet can also contribute to fraternal twinning rates. The Yoruba tribe has the highest twinning rate in the world—45.1 per 1,000 births, four times that of the United States. Experts can't agree on the reason, but some attribute this phenomenon to the tribe's consumption of a particular variety of yam that contains an estrogen-like substance. When rural Yoruba women move to the city and change their diets, their twinning rate drops.

In one 2006 study of mothers' diets, Gary Steinman, assistant clinical professor of obstetrics at Albert Einstein College of Medicine in Manhattan, found that mothers who regularly consumed dairy products were up to five times as likely to conceive twins as those who didn't. One theory suggests that cows injected with bovine growth hormone may be responsible for the trend since eating food with these products increased the women's insulinlike growth hormone levels.

Park Slope, a neighborhood populated with driven professionals who spent years establishing their careers before procreating, is a natural breeding ground for twins. Nearly every time I venture outside, I am confronted by tiny duplicates, prompting me to contemplate my bizarre situation. While shopping for toiletries at Rite Aid on Seventh Avenue in Park Slope a couple of days after first meeting Elyse, I stop a haggard-looking woman pushing a double stroller with identical blond girls.

"How old are your twins?" I ask.

"Six months," answers the woman, who clearly hasn't showered in days.

Although twins run rampant in the neighborhood, they still attract enough attention that she is clearly accustomed to answering questions about them.

"I am a twin," I say slowly, practicing the phrase. I grin sheepishly, as if caught lying. It still feels so unreal to me.

· | ·

Although I have blabbed to perfect strangers about Elyse's existence, I am still hesitant about sharing the news with my brother, Steven. Since both of us were adopted and neither of us had met any birth relatives, we have always been on equal footing. But now that I have a biological sibling—a twin, no less—and he doesn't, the equilibrium in our relationship has been thrown off kilter.

Despite our three-year age gap, Steven and I were steady companions throughout childhood. But after his bar mitzvah, when

Steven began to rebel against family life, deciding he'd rather be a rock star than a veterinarian, an unspoken rift developed between us. He no longer confided in me or trusted that I wouldn't tattle on him. When he argued with my parents and stormed out of the house, I was stranded behind to endure their lectures.

"Please don't be like your brother," my parents implored. "We can't handle any more trouble." To compensate for his "bad boy" behavior, it became clear that I would have to be an extra-good girl. In retrospect, I can't help but question whether my brother courted trouble as a way to test my parents' love for him. By acting out, he dared them to reject him and eventually declare that he wasn't really their child.

Steven laughs nervously when I break the news to him over the phone Sunday night. "What is she to me? A second sister? She's my sister's sister, but not mine?"

"I'd love for you to meet Elyse while you're in town doing job interviews," I tell him.

Steven is in the midst of arranging to move back to New York after five years in San Francisco, in part to be close to my family and me. He wants Jesse to see her "Unca," as she calls him, more than once or twice a year.

"Honestly, I don't know if I want to meet her if she looks exactly like you," says Steven, who avoids confrontations whenever possible. "It will be too weird. It doesn't get more surreal than this. God, I hope *I* don't have a twin!"

Like me, my brother has never had any interest in seeking his biological family.

"In an infantile way, I feel jealous. Is she going to be at all family gatherings from now on? It seems strange that she's your sister, but not mine," he continues.

Perhaps he fears that my claiming Elyse as a sister will make him less of a brother.

When people ask if Steven is my "real" brother, I answer yes without hesitation. But Elyse challenges my notion of family. Because we inhabited the same womb for nine months and possess identical DNA, she is literally a part of me and I of her. She is my twin, but not yet my sister. We have no shared memories, just a shared set of tendencies. But, even though we just met, I can't deny that she is family.

"I keep thinking of that *Seinfeld* episode where Jerry dates a woman who is exactly like him," says Steven before we hang up the phone. "At first, Jerry thinks it can't get any better. Then he remembers, 'Oh yeah, I hate myself. Why would I want to be with someone who is just like me?' "

We break into familiar laughter, as if we were kids again sharing a private joke.

ELYSE: Finding Paula has given cause for celebration, and I have been rewarded with my father's presence at a rare family gathering on Long Island. I have urged him to visit me in Paris countless times, tempting him with a trip to the cliffs of Normandy, but it seems we needed an extraordinary event to reunite us. I haven't been in New York since a brief stop in the fall of 2000 on my way to beginning a new life in Paris. Now I am the prodigal daughter returning home after years of wandering.

"Tell us about her!" everyone pleads. The party guests spread out in a backyard in the sleepy town of St. James. It's all happening too fast. Dying of curiosity, my family implored me to invite Paula to tonight's party, but I wanted to have our own family reunion before Paula entered the picture. I want to put Paula on hold while I bask in the warmth of my extended family. Whether through adoption or remarriage, this is my real family.

"You have a sister now!" Aunt Pat proclaims, as if my new family could replace the old one. Since Paula's arrival in my life, I fear my family thinks that I don't need them anymore. Fighting back her tears, Jaime, Pat's daughter, hugs me. Since she lost her one-week-old son Isaak after a pregnancy plagued by twin-to-twin transfusion syndrome (TTTS) six months ago, Jaime has been in mourning.

Twin pregnancies are often fraught with difficulty as the two fetuses compete for space and nutrients. Occasionally, a battle in the womb occurs as one identical twin saps the other of its blood supply. A completely random occurrence, TTTS is an extremely rare condition that attacks roughly 1 in 1,000 sets of identical twins and multiples who share a common placenta. Their shared placenta contains abnormal blood vessels connecting the circulations of the twins, often favoring one over the other. Often TTTS results in the loss of one or more of the fetuses before or shortly after birth.

My reunion with Paula seems to be providing some closure for Jaime. If Paula and I managed to overcome growing up without our twin, maybe Isaak's twin, Gabriel, will be okay. And, unlike us, he will grow up knowing the truth about his beginnings.

We convene in the kitchen, and everyone urges me to make a toast. Since I wasn't sure I would find my twin on this visit, I was too superstitious to bring any champagne with me from Paris. We open one of the many bottles of red wine decorating the marble counter.

"To Paula!" everyone shouts exuberantly.

Looking at their expectant expressions, I turn to my dad. "Here's to you. Though you don't phone me that often"—as the words stream out, I uncontrollably burst into tears—"I never doubted your love." My dad pulls me toward him and the years of estrangement disappear. Hugging my father tightly, I am six years old again and have just lost my mother.

Since finding Paula, I have had the feeling that everyone I have lost will return to me.

· | ·

Dad and I talk most freely when we are in transit. Driving me to the airport after a visit, we both open up and discuss serious matters: where he wants to be buried, who will take care of my nephew, Tyler, and, my brother, Jay, if anything should happen to him.

Driving into Brooklyn the day after the party to meet Paula and her family, I ask Dad a question. "Why did you choose me?" He doesn't know what to say. From his reaction, it's clear that he and my mother didn't choose me because I was an adorable baby, as I had imagined, but because I was the baby they were offered. How random it seems that I ended up with Martin Schein—yet I can't imagine growing up with a different father.

As we stroll down Twelfth Street on the way to Paula's apartment, Dad and I admire the russet-bricked brownstones lining the block. Thrilled at the prospect of buying gifts for a little girl, Dad pops into one of the exclusive children's shops on Seventh Avenue. A moment later he comes out grinning, proudly showing off the soft pink bunny slippers he has found for Jesse.

When Paula opens the door, we kiss each other on each cheek before embracing. The duplex apartment is painted a soothing pale green. Above the mantel, track lights illuminate a framed art-deco lithograph of a woman with her back seductively turned toward us.

Anxiously waiting to hug Paula, Dad checks her out. Seeing the daughter he might have had, my father's face is caught between laughter and tears. Dad recognizes me in Paula's wide smile and deep brown eyes.

"You are definitely her twin!" he exclaims.

I keep hearing that exact phrase. Do Paula and I look that alike? Doesn't anyone notice the differences in our noses and lips? "If you had the same haircuts, I couldn't tell you apart!" Dad remarks. I'm suddenly self-conscious about my own mannerisms, and try to moderate my expressions to make the shock of seeing double less noticeable for my father.

"This is Marty." Paula introduces her daughter to my dad. Jesse, sensing the excitement, smiles. When will Jesse begin to question why Paula and I don't have the same parents?

"And this is Aunt Elyse." Paula presents me to Jesse with a slight gesture of the hand.

"Hi, Aunt Elyse," Jesse says to me as if I had always been living around the corner. It's as easy as that. I have a niece now.

I'm overjoyed to be an aunt again, but I cannot erase the disappointment I feel in my teenage nephew Tyler's behavior. After his recent antics, I fear that he won't live up to my expectations.

I am at least consoled that if I never have a child, my own genes will be perpetuated through Paula's daughter. I feel oddly relieved of the pressure to procreate, though I can also imagine someday expanding the family by producing a cousin for Jesse. Perhaps we would go on family trips together, crowding the kids in the backseat along with camping gear for a high mountain adventure.

PAULA: With his faded jeans, plaid button-down shirt, and cowboy boots, Marty, Elyse's father, looks like a middle-aged cowboy. His unassuming demeanor and warm smile instantly put me at ease.

When Marty breaks out family photos, I am stunned by how indistinguishable Elyse and I were as kids. Same sweet smile, button nose, and thick auburn hair with short bangs, same goofy '70s-style pantsuits. At this point in our lives, we have our own distinctive styles and nobody would confuse us. Is it possible that our different upbringings and environments literally shaped who we are and what we look like?

The answer is yes, according to a recent study conducted by an international team of scientists at the Spanish National Cancer Center in Madrid. The scientists concluded that as identical twins mature, differences in their appearances can be attributed to environmental influences. By studying the DNA of eighty pairs of identical twins between the ages of three and seventy-four, the scientists found that while identical twins are born with the same epigenome (chemical modifications in genetic material), their epigenetic makeup changes as they age. At birth, the young twins had almost identical epigenetic profiles, but as they grew older, their profiles became increasingly different.

Scientists attributed two explanations to the findings. One is that some epigenetic marks are randomly lost as people get older. Another theory is that personal experiences and elements in the environment—including toxic agents like tobacco smoke—change the pattern of these epigenetic marks.

The study showed that twins who were separated longest had the greatest differences in their epigenome, which suggests that life experiences do indeed change your DNA.

In other words, the fact that Elyse smoked cigarettes and became a vegetarian, while I lived in pollution-clogged New York City and gave birth, could have literally altered our DNA so we no longer possess the exact same genetic makeup. My mind reels at the idea that every experience I've had has physically left an imprint on me.

ELYSE: "That could be me!" Paula exclaims, pointing to a photo of me at my grandfather's wedding when I was eleven. I restrain myself from shouting back, "No, that's me!"

Sharing my face with Paula feels eerie. I am possessive of the moments that have made me who I am. It had to be me who lived that life.

"I have a picture just like that taken at my brother's bar mitzvah." Paula scrambles downstairs to hunt for photos to compare with mine.

Back at the kitchen table, we place a photo of Paula and her brother alongside a photo of Jay and me. One could simply pluck me out of one picture and transpose me to another life. Our brothers both possess a similar shock of curly black hair and wear mischievous grins. Jay's blue eyes reassure me that they aren't twins.

I glance over Dad's shoulder at the array of photos he has chosen to show to Paula. There's a horrid one of me preparing for my senior prom, which I would rather forget. In the photo I am at my heaviest. Draped in white silk and lace, I look like a plus-size model for a wedding catalog.

"Don't show her that one," I beg Dad.

"Why not?"

"I look fat."

"No, you don't. You look pretty." My father sees beauty in even my most awkward moments. I ignore him; though I have shared my past struggle with my weight with Paula, I am not prepared for her to see me at my worst.

Suddenly seeking our attention, Jesse takes my hand and places it in her mother's, urging us to form a circle. All three of us slowly spin around and chant, "Ring around the rosie, / Pockets full of posies." So dizzy from joy, I almost fall down.

I get wistful thinking about the early years that Paula and I missed together. Still, I am grateful to meet Jesse while she is young enough to accept me unconditionally.

PAULA: Perhaps because of her uncanny resemblance to me, Jesse has embraced Elyse without question. Since Elyse and I share 100 percent of our genes, Jesse is as related biologically to Elyse as she is to me. If Elyse has a child, that child will not only be Jesse's first cousin, but also her genetic half sibling.

In cases where identical twins marry another set of identical twins, the children of the two pairs are not only double first cousins, but also, in a fluke of genetics, full siblings. They share an average of 50 percent of their genes, just like regular siblings. Believe it or not, this sort of marriage, though rare, does occur—around 250 sets of identical twins married to identical twins have been reported around the world. A number of these quaternary romances began at the annual Twins Day Festival in Twinsburg, Ohio. If you're a set of twins looking to marry another set of twins, what better place to find a love match?

After meeting at the Twins Day Festival in 1998, Craig and Mark Sanders and Diane and Darlene Nettemeier married seven months later in a double wedding. They now live in side-by-side houses with one big shared backyard. They rarely lock their doors, so the twins and their children can freely wander back and forth like one big family.

I can't imagine leading such an entwined life with Elyse, who is in my apartment for the first time. It seems fitting somehow that she should meet Jesse at the same time that I meet her father.

Reading aloud from *The Cat in the Hat*, Marty could easily pass for Jesse's doting grandfather. "He's so sweet with her," says Elyse before she scurries to the kitchen and buries her head in her hands. I follow her into the other room.

"Seeing him with Jesse makes me think, 'What if I never give him a grandchild?' " Elyse cries. I hug Elyse and struggle for the right words to console her.

"You will find love. I know it," I tell her, but I realize that my assurances might not sound so helpful.

At the end of the visit, as he puts on his leather bomber jacket and prepares to leave, Elyse's father turns to say good-bye to me.

"I love you," he says sincerely.

Had circumstances been different, Marty could have been my father, but as it is, he is a stranger to me, albeit a very sweet one. How can he love me when he doesn't even know me? I guess just the fact that I could have been his child—and that I look so much like his child—makes him care about me in the same way that my parents care about Elyse.

"Thanks so much for coming to visit," I tell Marty.

"You won't be getting rid of me so fast. I'll be back again," he says. I know it's impossible, but I am momentarily panicked that he plans to adopt me and make Jesse his granddaughter.

ELYSE: Even though we just met one week ago, Paula has invited me to spend the night at their apartment. Though we are still practically strangers, perhaps because we are twins Paula instinctively trusts me in her home.

Curious to see if we have the same taste in clothing, Paula takes me to a deluxe vintage clothing shop on Fifth Avenue the day of my visit.

"That color looks good on us," Paula comments when I try on a purple blouse.

It still feels strange being part of an "us." When I look at Paula, I refuse to see the similarities. Maybe it's because I prefer the way I look, with my hair, my nose, my lips, my complexion, my style.

"Are you pulling a *Single White Female* on me?" I joke when Paula tries on my suede jacket.

"Do you really feel that way?" Paula asks.

"Well, kind of."

I think of how, when I was growing up, my favorite episodes of *I Dream of Jeannie* and *Bewitched* revolved around their "evil twins," who seemed to appear only to create mischief. Though Samantha's cousin Serena on *Bewitched* had black hair and a funkier style, she had no trouble impersonating fair Samantha while wreaking havoc on her life. Jeannie's dark-haired twin sister went so far as to try to seduce her sister's husband.

When we get back to Paula's, I take off my shoes, as is their custom, and tiptoe on their dark wood floor.

"After you," "But, no, after you!" we say overly politely.

Unlike old friends who raid each other's cupboards, Paula and I are still getting comfortable with each other and I am careful not to overstep any boundaries.

I murmur to attract their cat, Lulu, who skitters away from me.

"I love cats!" I tell Paula.

"And I am more of a dog person," she says, sounding a little perplexed.

As I unpack my overnight bag, Paula notices Pooky, the small teddy bear I bought myself my first day of college. "Oh, is that your bear?" she asks tenderly. She plucks her own small worn brown bear off Jesse's bed.

"When did you stop sleeping with him?" I ask.

"Soon after I got together with Avo."

While sharing a bed with my boyfriend in college and throughout my adult love life, I still indulged my infantile urge without shame. Since Paula has gotten over her habit, I feel a little self-conscious but can tell she understands.

Paula's mother, Marilyn, calls, and asks Paula to put me on the phone so she can welcome me to the family. "You'll have to visit us in Hilton Head!"

Marilyn confers with Paula's dad, Bernie, about their trip to Paris in 2001, when they saw a woman who looked startlingly similar to Paula. "Do you think it could have been you?" Marilyn asks. "At the time I remember we said that everyone has a double somewhere in the world."

I regularly attend events at the Czech Center in St. Germain des Prés, the area where they stayed, and so I shiver imagining being approached by a couple of tourists inquiring about my birthdate.

PAULA: When Elyse gets off the phone, we sip herbal tea in our pajamas. Elyse and I are as giddy as nine-year-olds preparing for their first slumber party.

"Should we stay up all night talking? We can gossip about movie stars we had crushes on when we were growing up!"

"I always had a thing for Robby Benson," Elyse says. "My aunt worked in theater, and I got to meet him backstage after *The Pirates of Penzance*."

"You got to meet Robby Benson! No fair!" We break out in raucous laughter.

As we inflate the air mattress in the living room where Elyse will spend the night, we chat about things we'd like to do together before she returns to Paris.

"We could start looking into how to contact our birth mother," says Elyse casually.

I can barely process this suggestion. "I just found out about you. I don't think I'm ready to even think about finding her right now," I say.

"We don't have to disturb her life. We could always send her a letter."

"I would hate to dredge up the past if she doesn't want it dredged up. And honestly, I'm afraid what we might find out."

"I really believe that the truth will set you free. What are you afraid of?" Elyse asks. "What's the worst possible scenario?"

"I don't even want to imagine the worst possible scenario," I say. I change the subject, but it's hard to rid my mind of our conversation. I can't help but feel that by finding me, Elyse has set in motion a series of events propelling us closer to the truth about our origins.

Chapter | Seven

PAULA: The shock of our reunion hasn't worn off, but since Elyse is in town for only a week, we don't want to wait to begin investigating further the scientific study for which we were apparently separated. With Elyse on Long Island and me in Brooklyn, the telephone is like an umbilical cord keeping us in constant contact. Unsure of exactly what we are hoping to find, Elyse and I are compelled to begin sleuthing.

I input the words *Louise Wise* and *twins* into my computer's search engine, and the headline "The Doctors Knew" pops up. Intrigued, I devour the *Newsday* article from 1997 about Louise Wise triplets who were separated at birth and raised by different families.

"You won't believe this!" I exclaim when I call Elyse.

"I know!" she says. "I just found the story on a website called 'Lab Rat News,' which referred to the triplets as 'A Guinea Pig with 3 Heads.' "

Comparing notes, we piece together the chilling story.

In the fall of 1980, when nineteen-year-old Robert Shafran enrolled in Sullivan County Community College in upstate New York, he couldn't understand why the other students kept calling him Eddy, patting him on the back and asking about his summer break. At first, he thought they were playing a joke on him, but when a fellow student named Michael Dobnitz asked Robert his birthday and whether he had been adopted, he realized it was more than a coincidence.

Like Robert, Dobnitz's best friend Eddy Galland was born on July 12, 1961, at Long Island Jewish Hospital before being adopted through Louise Wise Services. When Dobnitz produced a photograph of Eddy, who had been enrolled at Sullivan Community College the previous semester, Robert saw a young man with the same stocky build and curly black hair. When they called Eddy, Robert took the phone and said, "Eddy, I think you're my twin brother."

Eddy wasn't entirely surprised. He had recently heard from friends that someone on campus was impersonating him. That night Dobnitz and Robert drove to Eddy's house in New Hyde Park, where the twins stared at each other in amazement. They scratched their heads and, in unison, exclaimed, "Oh my God!"

The newly reunited twins spent the next three days comparing their lives. They marveled at how much they had in common: they were both wrestlers who smoked Marlboros and dated older women, they liked the same movies, and they even mimicked the same lines. Although they each had an IQ of 148, they had flunked fifth-grade math and had undergone psychiatric counseling for emotional problems. In both cases, the psychologists had suggested that their problems stemmed from their adoption.

One week after the incredible news of the reunited twins broke in the media, Queens College freshman David Kellman came across a newspaper picture of the reunited twins and was dumbstruck by what he saw. He tracked Eddy down and called him.

"You're not going to believe this . . . but I'm looking in the mirror and at the picture in the paper. I believe I'm the third brother," said Kellman. David, too, had flunked fifth-grade math, received psychiatric counseling, and was a strong wrestler. The triplets found they had the same taste in food, people, and music. "It's all the same! It's all the same!" Eddy kept exclaiming.

When they exchanged information about their sons, the triplets' parents quickly realized that all three boys had been involved in a child development study. As a child, David would tell his parents that he had a brother. "We would all talk about his 'imaginary brother.' We laughed it off," his mother, Claire Kellman, remembers. The triplets' parents then contacted Louise Wise Services, which confirmed that they were triplets. Though the agency initially denied its involvement, faced with the facts, the staff reluctantly acknowledged that the triplets had participated in a twin study.

According to the *Newsday* article, the triplets had been separated on the advice of Dr. Viola Bernard, Louise Wise's psychiatric consultant, who believed that twins and triplets would fare better if they were raised apart. For Bernard, it was a win-win situation: The triplets would be able to better establish their own personalities, and their parents wouldn't have to shoulder the burden of raising three infant boys.

"They were part of the same study!" I exclaim.

"How dare they! What about informed consent?" Elyse rages.

The director of the Child Development Center (CDC) at the time was Dr. Peter Neubauer, a prominent psychiatrist at NYU's Psychoanalytic Institute and a director of the Freud Archives. By all appearances, Dr. Neubauer bought Dr. Bernard's theory. At the very least, he believed that it presented a unique opportunity for important research. If triplets and twins at Louise Wise were going to be separated, he thought their development ought also to be followed. The study, a collaboration between Louise Wise Services and the CDC, was funded in part by the National Institute of Mental Health (NIMH). Horrifying though it is today, to place twins and triplets in separate adoptive homes without full disclosure to the adoptive parents, and study their development thereafter, apparently was not contrary to law at the time. Nevertheless, the magnitude of their loss in being separated for adoption overshadowed the triplets' happy reunion.

"We were robbed of twenty years together," said Kellman.

"How could you do this with little children?" asked his brother Shafran.

From early childhood, the triplets were studied by a team of psychologists who evaluated the boys, using various psychological measures and scales.

"I've thought about it for quite some time," Shafran was quoted in *Newsday*. "I'm sure it all started with some distinguished psychiatrist and a roomful of people, and the brilliant idea arises of a new way of studying nature versus nurture. 'Okay, we'll separate these kids and watch them grow.' This is nightmarish, Nazi shit."

"How could Louise Wise not have told the families that their son was a triplet?" I ask Elyse, incredulous. "And why weren't their parents given the option to raise them together?"

Just like our families, the triplets' families were considered "return customers" at Louise Wise since they had previously adopted a child from the agency.

The triplets' adoptive families were informed that their child was already participating in an intensive child-development study and that agency officials wanted the study to continue. Remaining in the study was not a condition of the adoption, but the families knew how hard it was to come by a healthy, Jewish baby, and they didn't want to hurt their chances.

"We were dealing with Louise Wise Services, which was like dealing with God," Mrs. Kellman told *Twins* author Lawrence Wright. "You knelt down and kissed their feet and said, 'Thank you very much for this baby.' "

Nearly every month for more than twelve years, the families would travel to the CDC on West Fifty-seventh Street in Manhattan where researchers observed and recorded every step of the triplets' development. Some researchers also visited the families, who all lived in the New York metropolitan area, to conduct home studies and interview family members. Researchers filmed samples of their play activity and administered IQ tests.

Reading about the triplets spurs my paranoia. Elyse's dad had no recollection of researchers coming to their home. But could my parents have unwittingly allowed me to participate in the twin study? I phone my parents after hanging up with Elyse.

"No, we were never told that you were in any kind of study, and nobody ever came to the house to study you," my mom reassures me. "We would have remembered that. If they had asked us to participate, I'm sure we would have. We would have done anything they asked us in order to have you and Steven."

ELYSE: Dr. Dorothy Krugman, a former psychological consultant at Louise Wise, was one of the researchers on the twin study. In Stephanie Saul's "triplets" article in *Newsday*, Mrs. Kellman recalled Dorothy Krugman's regular visits to her home to observe her son David. Krugman "gave him square pegs to put into round holes to see his reaction. She took films of him talking, playing. Later on, they would take him on his tricycle, bicycle."

When I call Dr. Krugman, who was involved in the study for about a year and a half, starting from 1958, she says that at the time, she was comfortable with the separation of twins. But Krugman acknowledges that some social workers at Louise Wise didn't agree with Bernard's theory and declined to participate in the CDC study.

In one article about the twin study, Krugman describes the other social workers' reaction: "Separating twins—who ever heard of such a thing! The mystique of twinship is so strong."

After discovering that her son was one of a set of triplets, Mrs. Kellman asked one of the psychologists from the study how she could visit each of the triplets, sometimes on the same day, without revealing the secret.

"As a scientist," the psychologist replied, "how could I resist?"

In addition to the triplets and me and Paula, there were four sets of separated Louise Wise identical twins who were part of the study, a total of thirteen individuals. Were our fates really determined by a couple of psychiatrists? We wonder if there are other twins from the study who don't yet know they are twins.

· | ·

After graduating from college, all three triplets worked at Sammy's Roumanian Steak House on Manhattan's Lower East Side before opening Triplets Roumanian Steak House a few blocks away in the late 1980s. After the restaurant closed, Shafran became an attorney and Kellman stayed in the restaurant business. In 1995, Galland committed suicide and left behind a wife and young daughter.

The study was never published.

The "Lab Rats" story lists Neubauer's telephone number, exposing him to the public. While Jesse's at preschool, I take the train to Brooklyn so that Paula and I can try to reach the illustrious doctor. There are important questions we believe only Dr. Neubauer can answer. Why were Paula and I dropped from the study? How many other twins were involved?

Sitting cross-legged on the floor of Paula's carpeted office, we nervously prepare what we will say to Dr. Neubauer.

"Can you do the talking?" I ask Paula. "I'm not sure I'll be able to keep my cool." Like twelve-year-olds making prank phone calls, our palms sweat as we prepare to dial Neubauer's number.

Instantly reverting to journalist mode, Paula calmly engages the doctor. "Hello. I was adopted from Louise Wise in the late 1960s and I recently found out that I have a twin."

In a distinctive sharp Eastern European accent, Neubauer bellows "I'm busy!" and abruptly hangs up the phone.

"It's like he's the evil scientist and we are the lab rats who have come back to haunt him," I say, and we both crack up laughing.

"I wish we could call him back right now!" exclaims Paula, who is even less patient than I am. Our laughter subsides as we begin to consider our next move.

"He won't even give us the courtesy of responding to our question."

Unable to convey our indignation to Neubauer, Paula and I speculate about how long to wait before trying him again.

"I'm going back to Paris in two days," I say forlornly.

If Paula and I are going to get to the bottom of the study, I should be in New York.

· | ·

As Paula and I say good-bye the day of my departure, tears well up in my eyes as I gush, "I am so happy that you have such a beautiful family. I only hope that I can find the same."

"You're so beautiful that I feel confident you will find the right person," Paula says. "I love you."

"I love you," I whisper back, my tears flowing uncontrollably. As the screen door closes behind Paula, I fall into Aunt Pat's arms sobbing.

"It's okay, baby," she says.

Sitting in Aunt Pat's lap as she cradles me in a wicker rocking chair, I am comforted by her familiar maternal embrace. "You should come home. It's time."

Now that I have met Paula and reconnected with my extended family, I wonder if she's right. But isn't Paris my home? Should I pick up and leave just because my twin lives in New York? Has my life until now been a sham? Have I traveled this long circuitous path just to return to where I started?

Chapter | Eight

PAULA: Of course, I love Elyse. How could I not? We are inextricably linked and love between us is an irrefutable fact.

But, along with love comes an overwhelming sense of responsibility. When we reunited, I instantly became the closest person to Elyse in the world. I worry that she expects me to fill a gap in her life. I am the "heartbeat she always missed" and I am bound to let her down.

Now that Elyse has returned to Paris, I have descended into a depressed fog. No doubt, this cosmic twist of fate has created some intrigue in my life. And yet, intrigue is not what I was looking for at this point.

"I imagine what Elyse and I would have been like as kids had we grown up together and I feel sad for what we lost. Then, a moment later, I feel grateful that things happened as they did," I write in my journal one night after Avo has gone to bed. "My whole life I have pondered the utter aloneness of everyone. Even surrounded by people who love you, ultimately, you are on your own. But I didn't know that there was someone out there just like me."

While Elyse and I are very much our own people, I feel less unique knowing that there is someone else in the world who shares my tics, mannerisms, and tastes. When I make a face, I invariably picture Elyse forming the same expression. When I talk, I hear an echo. Meeting my twin should make me feel whole, but instead I feel terribly alone. As empathetic as Avo is, there is no way he can possibly understand my complex array of emotions.

"Why am I the one on Prozac when she's had a much more difficult life?" I ask Dr. Leingang, my psychiatrist, during my first appointment with him after meeting Elyse.

"Perhaps you were both predisposed toward depression, but Elyse attributed her depression to outside factors, whereas you felt confused because there was no obvious reason for you to be depressed," he suggests.

It's true that I always felt guilty about being depressed when I had such a blessed life. What reason did I have to be blue? Because I had fifteen pounds to lose? Because I didn't have a steady boyfriend? How does that compare to losing your mother to cancer at age six and your brother to schizophrenia as a teenager?

I first visited Dr. Leingang in my mid-twenties when getting out of bed in the morning increasingly became a losing battle. On the days when I managed to make it to work, I would sequester myself in an editor's office so that nobody would notice my unpredictable sobbing. While I had long since overcome the eating disorder that dominated my life in college, I continued to despise my fleshy curves and once again turned to food to soothe my anguish. I decided to seek help.

Shortly after I shuffled into his swank Upper East Side office, Dr. Leingang pronounced me "clinically depressed" and scribbled out a prescription for Prozac. As soon as I began taking the white and green capsules, my hopelessness subsided. The crying spells ceased and the prospect of waking up every day no longer seemed so daunting. Within two weeks, I quit the nine-to-five publicity job I loathed and took a stab at freelance writing. I slowly built a name for myself as a freelancer and eventually landed a staff reporter job at *The Hollywood Reporter* and, later, *Variety*.

I first had an inkling that something was wrong with me when, at around age fifteen, I began keeping an obsessive journal of my calorie intake: "600 calories. Keep up the good work, fatso!" Since I was a generally happy, well-adjusted kid who had never had a weight problem, I couldn't make sense of my sudden preoccupation with dieting.

"Something is wrong with my brain," I told my parents when I begged them to send me to therapy. Sure, I snuck ice cream cake from the freezer in the middle of the night, and some mornings I could barely drag myself out of bed. But as far as they could tell, nothing was wrong with me that couldn't be attributed to the usual adolescent angst. Reluctantly, they sent me to a therapist, who grilled me with questions: "Do you have friends?" "Do you get along with your family?" "Do you do well in school?"

I answered yes to everything. But she didn't believe me.

"If you've got all of these things going for you, what's wrong with you?" she sniped. "Don't come back until you can figure it out."

I left the office in tears with a renewed sense that something really was wrong with my brain. How else could I explain the fact that I felt so awful when everything in my life was so good?

Depression has always felt like an alien intruder that concealed my true optimistic personality. People with negative, depressive personalities often react poorly to antidepressants since the medication makes them feel artificially happy. For me, antidepressants simply allowed me to experience my sanguine nature. The only way to reconcile my optimism with my depression was to attribute it to genetics. After doing some research, I know that it looks as if both depression and happiness are hereditary traits.

Our research has shown us that about 5 percent of the population experiences at least one depressive episode in their lives, but for a close relative of someone with depression the risk is twice as high. Twin studies estimate that genes play about a 30 to 35 percent role in depression, higher for females than for males. Genes alone are not responsible for depression since, as it seems from other studies of heritability, environment accentuates what is already written in our DNA.

By studying fifteen hundred pairs of twins, the late behavioral geneticist Dr. David Lykken concluded that individuals are born with an innate happiness "set point," an equilibrium to which their mood returns, despite life circumstances. In other words, some people have an innate tendency to brood while others will blithely go about their lives.

Like me, Elyse is an optimistic person who has suffered from depression. Like me, she is a sensitive, thoughtful idealist who absorbs other people's suffering and takes it personally when the world lets her down.

"About half of your sense of well-being is determined by your set point, which is from the genetic lottery, and the other half from the sorrows and pleasures of the last hours, days, or weeks," Lykken told *The New York Times* in 1996. Lykken and his coauthor found that there was "little difference in well-being among identical twins raised together, compared with those raised apart."

· | ·

Normally, I would be making the most of the three days a week that Jesse is in preschool by pitching story ideas to magazine editors and brainstorming about ideas for personal essays. But since Elyse returned to Paris, I haven't been able to jump into the swing of my "old" life. Instead, I while away my spare time, drinking tea and ruminating about possible ways Elyse and I can learn more about the "secret study."

Katherine Boros broke the news to me about my twin in the first place, so I feel that she owes me some explanation. Louise Wise officially closed in late February, two months before Elyse found me. As the only employee left in their offices, Katherine is busy wrapping up loose ends.

As I dial Katherine's number, I fiddle with the notebook where

I've been scribbling my recent thoughts and questions. Before she can ask "How are you?" I breathlessly rattle off my list of questions: "Why were Elyse and I separated, but not studied once we were adopted? Did our birth mother consent to the separation? Are there twins from the study who still don't know they are twins? Why wasn't I told that my birth mother was schizophrenic or that I was a twin when I contacted the agency back in 1987 looking for non-identifying information about my biological family?"

"Your parents should have been told you were a twin when you were adopted. You should have been told about your birth mother's mental illness in 1987. But things were handled differently back then," says Katherine.

I'm not surprised that Louise Wise didn't disclose my birth mother's schizophrenia to my adoptive parents. In 1968, such disclosure was not required by law, and the jury was still out about whether or not the disease was inherited. Besides, if my parents had been told of my birth mother's mental problems, they might have held out for another baby. But, more likely, given the general consensus that schizophrenia was caused by the environment—specifically, an emotionally distant mother—they would have adopted me anyway.

Had they been aware of the work of Seymour Kety, my parents might not have been so open to the idea of adopting a baby with a "questionable" history. During the 1960s, while working as a psychiatrist at NIMH, Kety published the results of a series of schizophrenia studies that strongly suggested a genetic component of the disease. Kety discovered that children who are born to schizophrenic mothers and are then adopted develop the disease at the same rate as children raised by their schizophrenic mothers. While the risk of developing schizophrenia in the general population is approximately 1 percent, Kety concluded that the child of one schizophrenic parent has a 10 to 12 percent risk. The child of two schizophrenic parents has a risk of 40 to 50 percent.

Recent studies have shown that identical twins are more likely to develop schizophrenia than the general population, but scientists haven't determined why. If one identical twin is schizophrenic, the chance that his or her identical twin will also be schizophrenic is 40 to 60 percent.

Although schizophrenia has a high rate of heritability from parent to child, the statistics drop considerably—from 12 percent to 5 percent for second-degree relatives like grandchildren. Still, that's 4 percent higher than the 1 percent risk of schizophrenia in the general population. Thinking of Jesse, I console myself with the fact that schizophrenia is not purely genetically transmitted. Rather, geneticists believe that people inherit a predisposition to the disease, which then reacts to environmental factors.

Because of the work of Kety and others in the field, by the late 1970s and early 1980s, psychiatrists generally agreed that schizophrenia, as well as most other mental illnesses, had a genetic element. As a result, in 1983—four years before I contacted Louise Wise—the New York State legislature enacted a law that required adoption agencies to disclose medical histories to preadoptive parents and adult adoptees.

"Whose idea was it to separate twins in the first place?" I ask Katherine.

"Viola Bernard, Louise Wise's chief psychiatric counsel at the time, had a theory that twins would be better off if they were separated," Katherine calmly explains, as if it were the most normal notion in the world. I had read about Bernard's idea in the *Newsday* article, but it sounds like a crackpot theory to me.

"All I can honestly tell you is that there was a study and that twins were separated. Once a year or so, someone would go to their houses and study them," she continues.

"But didn't anyone think it was wrong to separate twins?" I ask.

"In those days, it was legal to separate twins. Ethical, I don't know. When you judge the past, it's always dangerous. Remember, back then things were different. Doctors sometimes wouldn't tell patients they had cancer in order to protect them."

The study now seems obviously immoral, but at the time it was conducted there were no rules requiring the informed consent that would now be mandatory. At Louise Wise, permission was sought from the birth mothers to place multiples in separate adoptive homes. But adoptive families were not generally informed if a child offered them for placement was a multiple. No guidelines governing behavioral studies were in place at the time. In 1979, around the time that the triplets reunited, the U.S. Department of Health, Education, and Welfare published the Belmont Report, which identified ethical principles for all human subject research. Expanding on the Hippocratic maxim "Do no harm," the report demanded that subjects participate in research voluntarily and with adequate information.

At the inception of the twin study, there were no laws prohibiting the separation of twins. Only in 1981 did the state of New York begin to require adoption agencies to keep siblings together. In 1998, the International Society for Twin Studies proclaimed the right of twins and multiples to be reared together.

An image of Elyse and me as newborns creeps into my head and I wonder if we spent time together before we were adopted.

"Yes, you were together in a foster home until you were adopted at five months. But physically the two of you developed at different rates, and allegedly that is why you were not kept in the study," explains Katherine.

"If they wanted to study us in separate environments, why did they give us to the same foster family?"

"The foster mother was advised to keep you separately," says Katherine.

I imagine it would have been fairly difficult to care for two infants separately in the same house. I am skeptical that our foster mother succeeded.

In *Twins,* Lawrence Wright writes that Viola Bernard drew the line at separating twins if and when they had experienced "the twinning reaction." In the early 1960s, psychoanalysts defined "the twinning reaction" as an extreme mutual dependency where one twin becomes more dominant and the other more passive. There is no clear way to measure when it occurs. Dr. Bernard believed that once twins bond, which can happen very quickly, it would be hugely detrimental to separate them.

"How could she be sure we hadn't bonded?" I ask.

"I don't know," Katherine says apologetically.

I ask reasonable questions expecting reasonable answers, but Katherine's answers only prompt more questions.

"Since the letter I received from Louise Wise regarding nonidentifying information back in 1987 was obviously incomplete, can you please send me a corrected version?" I ask. Katherine promises she will.

ELYSE: "Did you know that Viola Bernard was into yoga?" I ask Paula when I call her late at night. "In her obituary it says that she also helped smuggle Jews out of Germany during the war and later fought against nuclear war."

"Well, Katherine said she was a very impressive character!" Paula says.

Born in 1907 to the German-Jewish philanthropist Jacob Wertheim and his second wife, Emma Stern, Viola Bernard had a privileged childhood and was privy to an elite education inaccessible to most women at the time. Bernard met her future husband, the explorer and Tibetan Buddhist scholar Theos Casimir Bernard, while practicing yoga at the Clarkstown Country Club ashram in Nyack, New York. Their marriage lasted for four years; after they divorced, Bernard never married again. In the '30s, Bernard was a staunch supporter of the Communist cause and vocally defended Alger Hiss during his notorious espionage trial. In the early '50s Bernard herself was suspected of un-American activities and investigated by the Federal Security Agency. During World War II, Bernard gave Europeans fleeing Nazism temporary refuge at her mother's large country home in Nyack.

Following graduation from Cornell University Medical School in 1936, Bernard took up psychiatric residencies at the New York Psychoanalytic Institute, where she also trained. Part of the first generation of psychologists after Freud, Bernard believed Freud's psychodynamic theory could offer vital insights into key adoption issues such as infertility and adoptee identity.

As uncompensated chief psychiatric consultant at Louise Wise Services for forty years and a board member for fifty years, Bernard exerted considerable influence at the agency, one of the country's first specialized adoption agencies. The agency was first known as the Free Synagogue Child Adoption Committee and was established by Louise Waterman Wise in 1916, at a time when adoption was still rare among Jews. Wife of the esteemed Rabbi Stephen Wise, a founder of the National Association for the Advancement of Colored People and leader of the liberal American Jewish Congress, Louise Wise felt it was important to find homes for Jewish orphans. Louise Wise's daughter, Judge Justine Polier, assumed control of the agency in 1944 and enlisted the help of her friend Viola Bernard.

In 1996, Bernard, who had consulted for numerous children's welfare organizations, received a Presidential Commendation from the American Psychiatric Association in recognition of her "compassion, creativity, and courageous intervention in human pain." How could such a magnanimous philanthropist, who fought for children's welfare, have been so misguided as to think it was beneficial for twins to be separated?

Looking online for more information about Bernard, I find an online listing of the study's data, titled "The Child Development Center's Study of Twins Reared Apart, 1953–1997." It states that the archives have been donated to Yale University's library and are sealed until 2066. A few particularly sensitive documents will remain restricted after that date.

"How dare we be denied access to records that contain explanations of our past?" I complain to Paula in an e-mail. Paula and I won't be able to examine the records until we are elderly, if we are alive at all. Determined to gain entry before then, we contemplate hiring a lawyer who can help us open them.

Though the primary records of the twin study are at Yale, online I locate a list of Viola Bernard's own vast archives, which are housed at the Columbia University Health Sciences Library. All correspondence with Louise Wise relating to the twin study, as well as meeting minutes, progress reports, financial and fund-raising records, scientific publications and newspaper clippings is also closed to researchers until 2021. Though these files are restricted, there are plenty of other files regarding adoption that are open. Perhaps if Paula and I venture uptown and sort through Bernard's open files, we'll chance upon a reference to the study.

On the library's website, I find a statement by Dr. Bernard, which she wrote in 1963. "[The study] provides a natural laboratory situation for studying certain questions with respect to the nature-nurture issue and of family dynamic interactions in relation to personality development." As in the film *The Truman Show,* our lives have been manipulated without our knowledge. What seemed natural was, in fact, orchestrated by the puppet masters.

Since the study was never published, a book Dr. Neubauer cowrote with his son Alexander in 1990, *Nature's Thumbprint: The New Genetics of Personality,* is the closest we can get to it. Here Dr. Neubauer writes, "It was in this atmosphere many years ago that an opportunity arose to follow the development of identical twins from infancy."

According to Neubauer, Bernard's theory presented him with an ideal opportunity to study the age-old question of nature versus nurture.

"Until then no identical twin study had explored twins reared apart," Neubauer says. "We would be there at birth and continue regular, intensive observations of separated twins and study their relationship with parents and siblings, collecting as much information as possible about behavior and growth."

Reading about Neubauer and his cronies collecting data on their infant subjects as if they were insects or rocks, I am repelled. It's no coincidence that Neubauer's study was the only one of its kind: in the 1960s, separating twins was not common practice. The directors of other adoption agencies said that at the time, they would not have separated twins except in unusual circumstances, such as if one was disabled.

"We would never do it," Jane Edwards, the retired director of Spence-Chapin Services, one of the nation's largest adoption agencies, told *Newsday*.

In the *London Review of Books* in 1998, Neubauer responded to Wendy Doniger's review of Lawrence Wright's book *Twins*. Neubauer challenged her assertions: "Doniger states that neither the twins nor the parents were told that they were being studied. This is not true. It would not have been possible to visit them at regular intervals, to observe and test them, to interview parents without their knowledge."

Playing dumb, Neubauer apparently hoped that readers wouldn't realize that the psychologists had only informed the (adoptive) parents of their child's participation in a child development study without specifying that it was in fact a *twin* study. He would not have been interested in their children otherwise.

PAULA: On May Day, I celebrate the two-week anniversary of meeting my twin by doing a headstand in my yoga class, my first since I was a kid. I've been practicing yoga for months, and I finally manage to keep my feet aloft for ten seconds without toppling over. As the blood rushes to my head, I feel calm for the first time since learning I have a twin.

Still in a Zen state when I arrive home, I work up the courage to call Dr. Neubauer's number. Anticipating his answering machine, I am surprised when he picks up.

"Were you involved in a twin study involving babies who were adopted by different families?" I ask, after reminding him who I am.

He pauses for a moment and I wonder if he's hung up on me again.

Suddenly, he begins talking. When Elyse and I were born, psychologists generally believed that being a twin placed a burden on a child—and on the parents, he says. Although Dr. Neubauer acknowledges that psychologists would never attempt such a study today, he is unapologetic.

"But why didn't you inform the adoptive parents their child was being studied?" I ask, my voice turning shaky.

But they *did* inform the adoptive parents that their child was in a developmental study, insists Neubauer.

"True, but you wouldn't have been interested in studying them if they hadn't been twins and triplets."

Neubauer reluctantly concedes the point. But when I ask more specific questions, such as how many twins were included in this study, Neubauer becomes agitated and refuses to answer.

Nobody set out to do any harm, he assures me.

Maybe not, but I can't help but think that by failing to consider the ramifications of their decision, they behaved irresponsibly.

"Do you still accept the decision to separate twins?" I ask him.

Neubauer growls at me, accusing me of twisting his words.

"There is no reason to raise your voice with me," I say politely. "I am merely trying to understand whether you think this study would be considered ethical today."

Neubauer bellows angry, unintelligible words into the phone before hanging up. Stung by his diatribe, I cling to the phone receiver, half-expecting him to get back on the line and apologize.

"I just spoke to Dr. Neubauer and he conveniently blamed the whole thing on Viola Bernard," I e-mail Elyse. "He said that Dr.

Bernard made the decision to separate twins after reading articles that suggested it was better for twins to be raised apart."

I know that over the years, psychologists have wavered on whether it was better for twins to be in different classes at school so they could better develop their own identities. But I can't imagine that they supported the notion of permanently separating twins.

Elyse and I set out to locate the original research on which Dr. Bernard founded her theory, and we manage to find a handful of articles from 1948 through 1961 that suggested that parenting twins was a burden on both twins and their parents.

Dorothy Burlingame, a lifelong colleague of Anna Freud, asserted in her 1952 book *Twins* that "the twin relationship [is] threatened by negative and aggressive feelings, which manifest themselves in competition, rivalry for the parents' love, jealousy, and the wish to dominate the other."

Although Elyse and I see in black and white the proof that such theories existed, it seems so instinctively wrong—granted, to our modern sensibilities—it's hard to believe that Dr. Bernard could have felt so differently.

We can't possibly know what was in Dr. Bernard's mind, but Elyse and I often find ourselves wondering if she genuinely believed these theories, or if they were a convenient means to an end. We may never know.

Though these controversial theories had fallen out of fashion by the 1980s, in "Disposition and the Environment," published in 1986, Dr. Samuel Abrams writes that "the prevailing scientific literature at the time [the study was conducted] had been discovering features about twins that were bound to attract the attention of any serious practitioner in the mental health field." Discussing the "burden" on twins reared together, Abrams maintains that "the children invariably faced specific developmental hazards that appeared directly attributable to the twinship" and "they also appeared more vulnerable to a wide variety of pathological disturbances." The Abrams article seems to defend the twin study, but it is notable that the article was published in *The Psychoanalytic Study of the Child,* a journal coedited by Dr. Neubauer himself.

Abrams's article goes on to chronicle the case of "Amy" and "Beth," a set of identical twins from the study. After spending their first months together in a foster home, Amy and Beth were adopted into separate Jewish homes in New York State with stay-at-home mothers. Despite the basic similarities of their environments, their family situations were notably different. Amy's family was lower-class, whereas Beth's was more affluent. Amy's mother was overweight and insecure about her appearance, while Beth's mother was slender, self-confident, and dynamic. While Amy's mother was threatened by her daughter's good looks, Beth's mother doted on her. Amy's mother viewed her daughter as a problem child, while Beth's mother viewed her as "the fun child."

Not surprisingly, Amy had serious emotional problems. She was a clingy child who wet her bed until she was four and feared being left alone. A shy, poor student, Amy lacked creativity and was diagnosed with a serious learning disorder. Dr. Neubauer and the psychologists involved in the twin study suggested that if Amy's mother was supportive and affectionate, like Beth's, then Amy would be better adjusted.

Instead, the psychologists were amazed to find that in nearly every respect, Beth's personality resembled Amy's. "Amy and Beth turned out to be remarkably similar at every step in the study," wrote Dr. Abrams. Despite her supportive family, Beth also wet her bed and, like Amy, was afraid of being left alone. She was also a shy, poor student with a learning disorder and limited creativity. Dr. Abrams notes that Beth's "overall mood seemed somewhat more positive than Amy's; however, on psychological tests she voiced an abiding feeling of sadness and a longing for maternal care in terms almost identical to those expressed by her twin."

In *Nature's Thumbprint,* Neubauer writes about a set of male twins separated at birth who were both neat and clean to a compulsive degree. One brother attributed this tendency to the fact that his adoptive mother was so fastidious and the other one blamed it on the fact that his adoptive mother was a slob.

"Although it was once thought that the traits of personality are shaped only by the environment over the course of development, we can now say that much of what becomes personality is intrinsic to the child from the start—in other words, predisposed by natural inclination," writes Neubauer.

Dr. Neubauer recounts another story of identical twin girls who were separated in infancy and raised separately. When the girls were toddlers, the adoptive mothers were asked about their child's eating habits. One adoptive mother complained that her daughter wouldn't eat anything unless it had cinnamon on it. The adoptive mother of the other twin reported that her daughter was a great eater, bragging that as long as she put cinnamon on her food, the girl would eat anything. (My parents might have reacted differently to my picky eating habits had they known that Elyse was also a fussy eater!)

Stories like these seem to suggest that nature is everything and nurture is insignificant. But, over time, the pendulum has shifted back and forth with regard to the influence of nature and nurture. Long before the discovery of the DNA molecule in 1962, poets and philosophers such as Shakespeare and Thomas Hardy referred to the inherent "nature" of literary characters.

As Charles Darwin's theory of evolution spread in the 1800s, so did the idea of genetic determinism. In 1869, Darwin's cousin the British anthropologist Sir Francis Galton noted in his book *Hereditary Genius: An Inquiry into Its Laws and Consequences* that talent in science, the arts, and various professions ran in families. Galton, who conducted the first known study of twins, was convinced of the possibility of creating a more intelligent breed of humans, a theory that became known as eugenics. He was also responsible for coining the phrase "nature vs. nurture."

After the Holocaust, the public deemed genetic determinism racist, and nurture prevailed. In the late 1960s, when Elyse and I were born, the political backdrop had shifted dramatically from the early part of the century. Psychologists and the public believed that humans were blank slates on which life inscribes itself. Given the right opportunities, human potential was limitless. Now most scientists agree that the truth lies somewhere in the middle, and that nature and nurture each play a role in developing personality.

Since 1990, the Human Genome Project has been systematically identifying all the approximately twenty thousand to twenty-five thousand genes in human DNA. It seems that every day there's another news story about how scientists have identified new genes linked to various cancers, Alzheimer's disease, or alcoholism. Behavioral geneticists assert that there is even a genetic basis for predispositions such as homosexuality, affection, aggression, and impulsivity.

A predisposition is not a guarantee that a given disease or personality trait will ever appear. While genes help to determine a person's risk of developing various diseases, recent evidence suggests that environmental factors such as tobacco, diet, exercise, alcohol, drugs, and exposure to radiation play a significant role.

Even Dr. Neubauer acknowledges that although identical twins have identical genes, they will not necessarily express their tendencies in the same way. "What is endowed at birth is not a set of traits but a range of expression," writes Dr. Neubauer in *Nature's Thumbprint.*

No doubt, genes—or one's innate temperament and physical traits—also play a role in shaping one's environment. If Elyse and I were both cute, sociable kids who adapted well to school, then teachers, classmates and parents were likely to treat us in similar ways. Our personalities and interests also prompted us to seek out similar environments—like film school, Paris, and the East Village. Did our genetic makeup predetermine our life's paths?

· | ·

"If your family had raised me and mine had raised you, would I be you and would you be me?" Elyse asked when she called last night from Paris. We paused for a moment to contemplate the mind-boggling question. Does genetics plus environment equal the sum total of our identity?

I figure if anyone can answer this question, it's Dr. Thomas Bouchard, the former director of the MSTRA, which over the course of twenty years has retrospectively studied more than one hundred sets of identical twins and triplets who had been raised separately. I dial Dr. Bouchard's number at the University of Minnesota, where he is a psychology professor. He picks up immediately.

"Bernard and Neubauer put a case forward for the separation of twins that I've never understood or believed," says Bouchard, adding that he is not aware of any psychological literature supporting Dr. Bernard's claim that twins fare better if they are raised separately. Clearly the smattering of articles about the "burden of twinship" did not go down in the annals of history, since even a top twin researcher like Bouchard isn't aware of them.

"My personal opinion is that it should never have been done. I wouldn't testify in court that Dr. Bernard and Dr. Neubauer were evil, but it sure comes close. There are some reunited twin pairs that have not gotten along, but nobody has said they're unhappy that they found each other," says Bouchard.

The twins and triplets in Bouchard's study were subjected to a week of intensive psychological and physiological assessment, including a series of allergy tests and cardiovascular and pulmonary examinations. The twins' heart patterns and brain waves were assessed, as well as their mental agility. Placed in different rooms, the twins completed personality questionnaires with tens of thousands of questions designed to measure "harm avoidance," "social closeness," and "well-being." Separate examiners administered IQ tests and conducted private psychiatric interviews with each twin.

Bouchard and his team have published about 130 papers detailing their findings, which suggested that adult identical twins perform about the same on most physiological and psychological tests, regardless of whether they were raised together or not. "I wanted to find out how the environment works to shape psychological traits," Dr. Bouchard said in Kay Cassill's *Twins: Nature's Amazing Mystery*. "But every conceivable trait we've looked at turns up some genetic influence."

When Bouchard first published his findings in 1986, conventional wisdom lent more credence to nurture than nature. Virtually every theory since Freud had suggested that primarily environment shaped personality. Bouchard found otherwise.

"On multiple measures of personality and temperament, occupational and leisure-time interests, and social attitudes, monozygotic twins reared apart are about as similar as monozygotic twins reared together," wrote Dr. Bouchard and his team in a 1990 article about MSTRA in *Science*.

Surprisingly, Bouchard determined that identical twins reared apart were more alike than fraternal twins reared together, which suggests that growing up together does not necessarily make family members more alike.

Bouchard concluded that for most of the traits measured in MSTRA—including alienation, a sense of well-being, vulnerability, and resistance to stress—more than half of the variation between the twins was due to heredity, which means that less than half was determined by the influence of family, school, and other life experiences. Interestingly, among the traits tested, the need for personal intimacy appeared to be the least determined by heredity.

Bouchard created the MSTRA after hearing the incredible story of "the Jim twins." Separated soon after birth and adopted by different parents, Jim Springer and Jim Lewis met for the first time in 1979. Both sets of adoptive parents were told that their sons had been born twins, but Jim Springer's adoptive parents believed that their son's twin had died at birth. Jim Lewis's parents encouraged him to look for a twin from the time he was young, but he didn't search until he was thirty-nine. After spending a month poring over court records, Lewis discovered that his twin was a records clerk in Dayton, Ohio, less than one hundred miles away.

When they first met, the two Jims shook hands, then hugged, and finally, burst into laughter. Three weeks after meeting, Jim Springer served as best man at his identical twin brother's wedding.

In getting to know each other, the Jim Twins discovered they both drove the same type of Chevrolet, chain-smoked Salem cigarettes, and liked stock car racing, woodworking, and football. They both weighed 180 pounds and they had identical blood pressure. They had each undergone vasectomies and suffered from hemorrhoids, high blood pressure, and migraines. Both had grown up with an adopted brother called Larry and, as children, each Jim had had a dog named Toy. They both married women named Linda and then, after divorcing, married women named Betty. One Jim had a son named James Alan. The other Jim's son was James Allan. Both men gnawed their fingernails and they both had served as sheriff's deputies in nearby Ohio counties. The list of similarities goes on.

"In one test, which measured such personality variables as tolerance, conformity, flexibility, self-control and sociability, [the Jim twins'] scores were so close that they approximated the totals which result when the same person takes the test twice. In intelligence, in mental abilities, in their likes and dislikes and their interests, they were remarkably similar," says Bouchard, who acknowledges that the Jim Twins were more similar than most of the separated twins. "It was just our luck that we started with such an amazingly similar pair since that piqued our interest in the study."

Critics have accused Bouchard of exaggerating the twins' similarities. Some naysayers claimed that the twins had been in contact over the years, or that they purposely tried to act alike in order to attract attention. In fact, on average, the twins in MSTRA were separated at five months. When they were studied by MSTRA, the re-united pairs had, on average, spent two years in contact after a thirty-year separation.

What does Bouchard make of the fact that Elyse and I were both editors of our high school newspapers and that we both studied film theory? "That's clearly more than a coincidence. It's not too surprising since identical twins are variations on a theme. What you have is a configuration of talent and interest that draw you to similar things," Bouchard tells me.

So what about my original question? If Elyse's family had raised me and my family had raised her, would she be me and I be her?

"No," insists Bouchard. "I have always thought that twins were already different at birth and that those differences contributed to differences in adulthood."

-|-

Hoping she'll know how to locate other separated Louise Wise twins, I contact Dr. Nancy Segal, who worked with Dr. Bouchard as assistant director of MSTRA from 1985 to 1991. I reach Dr. Segal at her office at California State University, Fullerton, where she is a professor of developmental psychology and director of the Twin Studies Center. A fraternal twin herself, Dr. Segal has written about twins and often appears on television as a twin expert.

"Do the media know about you?" Nancy Segal asks breathlessly after I tell her about my recent reunion with Elyse.

"No," I answer, befuddled by her question. Were we supposed to have invited news crews to witness our reunion?

Unfortunately, Dr. Segal doesn't know of any other separated Louise Wise twins. In fact, she seems more interested in researching us than in helping us learn more about Dr. Neubauer's study.

"Can I send you a reunited twin questionnaire for you to fill out?" she asks.

"Sure," I say, although I do not intend to complete it. Given the history that Elyse and I have recently discovered, we are not inclined to participate in more studies.

Still, when the fifty-one-page "Twin Relationship Survey" questionnaire arrives the following week, I excitedly rip open the manila envelope and begin to answer the questions even though I don't plan to return it.

"People react differently when they first learn that they are a twin. How did you feel when you FIRST learned that you were a twin?" The instructions ask that I mark an "X" closest to the words that best express my feelings. On one side are positive descriptions like "Happy," "Excited," and "Proud." On the other end of the spectrum are "Unhappy," "Not Excited," and "Embarrassed."

I don't hesitate before marking an "X" next to "Nervous" and "Frightened." And there's no doubt that I feel more "Special" and "Proud" than "Ordinary" and "Embarrassed." Otherwise, my answers skew toward the "Unhappy" and "Insecure" side of the chart.

Asked to rate the closeness and familiarity of my relationship with my twin, I note that we are "as close as best friends," but that she is "less familiar than a best friend, but more familiar than a casual friend." How can I possibly begin to quantify my relationship with Elyse? There is no adequate way to describe what she is to me.

Chapter | Nine

ELYSE: "*Je suis une jumelle,*" I want to tell everyone, but in French you can only say "I have a twin," not "I am a twin." How can I express the sudden shift in my identity? In addition to being the French word for female twins, *jumelles* also means binoculars. Magnifying my view of the world, my newfound twinhood provides a metaphor for everything. Skimming film subtitles in one language while listening to the dialogue in another, I've become accustomed to living a dualistic life, alternating between my French and American identities. Still, having lost a twin can't account for every aspect of my personality.

On my return to Paris, where my future is uncertain, my elation about my reunion with Paula subsides and I sink into depression. I mourn the years that are irrevocably lost to us. Had we been raised together, Paula and I both would have become different people. Though Paula is my twin, she is not the same person I would have known if we had never been separated.

Twin researchers make the claim that twins raised apart are more alike than twins raised together, who make an effort to differentiate themselves from each other. If Paula and I had been raised together, perhaps, wanting to accentuate our differences, only one of us would have studied film. Only one of us could have claimed our true nature. But there is no possibility of testing this hypothesis.

I'm concerned that Paula assumes that I expect her to fill the gaps in my own life and am careful not to pressure her. I understand that

Avo is her partner now. She has settled back into her life and I don't want to burden her with the drama in mine. Preparing for the grueling national teaching exam obliges me to take a leap of faith. I may have already been eliminated after the first exam, in which case my hard work will have been in vain. The irony is that teaching is not my true passion. Though being a government employee would offer me stability, the constraints of the school calendar could also stifle my creativity. The thought of my future being set in stone is daunting. I wouldn't be able to fly off to Tajikistan to work on a film crew at a moment's notice.

Ironically, the only one who could possibly understand what I am going through is Paula. Yet we are experiencing the revelation differently. And, not having grown up together, we haven't developed shorthand communication.

As a teenager, I often so baffled my folks with my quirky neologisms that they dubbed my babble Stacie-talk. Had Paula sat next to me in class, we might have whispered our own private tongue without others even noticing.

It's not uncommon for twins to invent their own language. In 1978 the story of Grace and Virginia Kelly broke in newspapers nationwide. Neglected by their family, who believed they were mentally retarded, Poto and Cabengo, as they called each other, developed a private language that was all they spoke until age eight. Intrigued by the girls, who they believed had invented a new language, linguists, speech therapists, and psychologists conducted intensive tests on them that proved they were of normal intelligence. The tests also revealed that Gracie and Ginny's idiosyncratic language was composed of English and German, which their grandmother spoke, mixed with some neologisms.

Most twins manage to learn their native language, even while speaking their own private tongue. Though twins may have their own private language when they are very young, most eventually grow out of it.

I seek solace in stories of separated twins. Perched on a bench in the Jardin du Luxembourg one afternoon, I peruse one of the rare nonfiction books on the subject, Bard Lindeman's *The Twins Who Found Each Other*. In the book, Lindeman recounts the reunion of separated twins, Tony Milasi and Roger Brooks, at age twenty-four in 1963.

Roger was raised by a family member, but only learned he had a twin when he was fourteen. When he heard the news, Roger's first reaction was, "I knew it . . . I even dreamt it." From that day on, he fantasized about one day reuniting with his twin. Tony's mother told her son that his twin had died. Even so, Tony, like Roger, believed that he would someday be reunited with his twin.

Ten years later, Roger ran into one of Tony's acquaintances at a Pancake House in Florida and the twins were reunited. Though they had grown up in vastly different environments, Tony, in a traditionally Italian Catholic household in Binghamton, New York, and Roger in a less stable Jewish home in Miami, their personality traits and personal tastes were remarkably similar.

They used the same unusual brand of Swedish toothpaste, liked all kinds of music except country and western, smoked Lucky Strikes, parted their hair on the left, and loved sports but were spectators rather than athletes. They had entered separate branches of the military only eight days apart for four-year enlistments and had girlfriends but no thoughts of marrying. Despite the fact that Roger had endured a difficult childhood, shifting between homes, including years at a foster home, both men were naturally optimistic.

Still mulling over the story of these twins, I call my dad to grill him about my childhood. "Does it make sense to you that I was always missing my twin?" I ask.

"No, you were a happy child."

"What about in high school?"

"Uh . . . I forgot about that," my father replies. Dad's faulty memory has reconstructed a more pleasant picture of my high school years than the one I painfully recall. My junior year of high school I had secretly binged, and my weight had ballooned, conveniently concealing my burgeoning sexuality. The pressure to be a perfect daughter had become a strain and I rebelled by shoplifting at the local five and dime. I dabbled in an elaborate game of hiding my imperfections, even as I dared my parents to discover them.

When I returned home late one summer night before my senior year of high school after indulging in my first couple of Bud Lights with friends down the block, my intoxication cast the house in a haze. As I sat on the floor of the living room, bathed in the garish light of a late-night edition of *Entertainment Tonight,* visions of my brother in the mental institution passed before my eyes.

After dropping out of art school, where he was on a scholarship, Jay had been sent to a mental institution where he was diagnosed with paranoid schizophrenia. When he called me imploring me to save him from the nurses who were raping him, my parents said he was just hallucinating. But even though his delusions weren't real, Jay's suffering was. My family had always considered my brother a brilliant but troubled child. After he was institutionalized, the pressure to play the role of the good child had become too much. Now it would be obvious that Dad and Mom had adopted two bad seeds. As an adopted child, I felt the only thing asked of me was to be happy, and I couldn't even do that.

Still sitting in front of the TV, I slowly popped eighty red and white Advil and aspirins into my mouth one by one, as if they were candy. I didn't want to die, but I couldn't help but relish the image of my folks finding me dead the next morning. I see now that my melodramatic gesture was an attempt to get my parents' attention and let them know that beneath my carefully composed surface, all was not perfect.

Several hours later, in a drugged stupor, I lugged myself to bed. My legs temporarily paralyzed, I wormed my way across the carpet, battling the plastic bugs that had woven a web around me. Awakened by my shrieks, my parents assumed I had taken hallucinogenic drugs.

Still in a catatonic state the following day, I overheard my folks discussing plans to ship me off to the same mental hospital as my brother. The fear that they would send me away was enough to rouse myself from silence, though I didn't tell them what I'd done and why I was behaving so strangely. I recall my parents' wounded expression when I confessed to them the following year that I had tried to kill myself.

Now I ask Dad how he could have forgotten Toni and his incessant pleas for me to get help.

"You should just be happy you found each other and get on with your lives," Dad says.

"I am happy now, Dad, believe me, but Paula and I need to know the truth."

· | ·

Sitting in my room in Montparnasse one Sunday afternoon doing research, I reread *The New York Times* article about Michael Juman, whose birth mother's mental illness was concealed from him by Louise Wise. Apparently, Michael was not the only adoptee who discovered that the adoption agency had conveniently rewritten his or her birth mother's story. When another adoptee, "Connie," requested her medical history from Louise Wise in 1988, she was painted a rosy picture of her birth mother as a bright young woman. A chance glimpse of her file proved otherwise. "She was described as an exceptionally intelligent girl," a caseworker wrote in 1962, "though she is not in complete contact with reality at the present time."

Given that Louise Wise had concealed our birth mother's psychosis from Paula, I wonder if there had also been concealed instability in my brother's birth mother.

Despite Dad's advice to leave the past alone, I persist in asking questions.

"What was she like?" I ask Dad from the phone booth across the street from my apartment. Ten years ago, Jay's birth mother tracked him down in Oklahoma and contacted my dad out of the blue.

"Well, she was kind of odd. She didn't know how to drive," Dad says without an ounce of humor.

"Dad! Don't be silly. She probably just grew up in a big city."

After informing her of my brother's schizophrenia, my parents had cautioned her, "If you are going to come into his life, you can't just disappear." Her short visit with Jay apparently satisfied her curiosity, since she never contacted him again.

Though Jay's birth mother was reluctant to speak of her past, Dad was able to glean the basics of her background. Jay's birth father had been a prominent New York rabbi who had had an affair with his birth mother, who was far too young to raise him on her own. Despite her quirkiness, Dad found Jay's birth mother to be of sound mind and body and she reported no history of mental illness. So perhaps Jay's schizophrenia can't be entirely attributed to his genetic makeup.

My brother had displayed erratic behavior since he was a child. Only when, at the age of nineteen, he started climbing the oak tree outside our house at all hours of the night claiming that people were after him, did we become seriously concerned. We rationalized that his hallucinations were caused by the recreational drugs he was taking and took him to a rehab clinic outside Oklahoma City that doubled as a mental hospital. The doctors there determined that he had a biochemical anomaly in his brain, a time bomb that had been lying dormant, waiting to explode.

When my brother was taken away, I was sure that I was next to be carted off. Now I wonder: would my parents have adopted me if they had known about my birth mother's diagnosis?

The sun streams through my window while I read Lisa Belkin's 1999 *New York Times* article about Michael Juman's parents' lawsuit against Louise Wise. I shiver at the choice his family was forced to make. To win such a lawsuit, Belkin points out, Michael's mother would have to swear that she would not have adopted her son had she known his medical history. "I didn't want to have to stand up in any courtroom and say, 'I wouldn't have chosen this child,' Mrs. Juman says. "How do you say that to your son—'I never would have adopted you?' "

Was the depression that plagued Paula and me in college programmed by genetics? Having practically memorized Joseph Conrad's *Lord Jim* for my teaching exam, I recall Marlow's fatalistic response to Jim: "A clean slate, did he say? As if the initial word of each our destiny were not graven in imperishable characters upon the face of a rock."

· | ·

Arriving home from school, I find a photocopy of Paula's updated letter from Louise Wise in my mailbox. In the revised letter Katherine writes, "We inferred from what your mother told us that she may not have been certain of your father's identity."

I am reluctant to let go of my fantasy of our birth parents as a bohemian couple, misunderstood by society. I imagine that our birth mother was simply trying to protect her pot-smoking Catholic boyfriend by not involving him in her decision. Since Paula and I are constrained by law to only nonidentifying information and are not permitted to see our adoption files, we can only go on the agency's story.

"She surrendered you unconditionally without additional comments," the letter reads. According to the agency, our birth mother agreed to our separation. I immediately call Paula and ask, "Why didn't she insist that we be raised together? Was she so anxious to get rid of us that she'd agree to anything?"

"I'm sure she was in no shape to argue with a prestigious agency when she was in such a vulnerable position. She was trying to make the best choice for us," Paula says.

Of course, I want to believe the best of our birth mother, but I still have my doubts. Only she can explain why she abandoned us and allowed us to be separated.

"Are you examining the reasons you are anxious about finding our birth mother?" I write Paula in an e-mail later that evening. "I think we both fear that she is a nut case!" Allaying my own fears as much as Paula's I rationalize, "It may ease her mind to know we are okay and that we have found each other." I ask Paula's permission to register at the International Soundex Reunion Registry.

Paula quickly responds, "I surprise myself by saying that I agree to register. Now I have someone to share the journey. Also, now that we've learned so much, I'm curious to learn more."

"Maybe it's because we are now in solidarity," I respond. "I feel strong enough to face whatever circumstances led to her pregnancy and our adoption and even if she hasn't managed to overcome her mental illness, I know that we have, though it is of course an ongoing struggle to remain balanced. If we were going to go 'over the edge,' we probably would have done so by now! We are good blood!"

Our birth mother didn't register at the New York State Adoption Registry, nor did she leave word with Louise Wise, so I doubt that she's looking for the twins she surrendered. Why would she search, knowing she would be compelled to explain to any daughter who came forward the existence of an identical twin sister and to justify our separation? Even so, I fill out the form, checking in the boxes for plural birth and separated by adoption, and write down Paula's name. Our separate lives are irrevocably bound now. Whatever decisions we make about investigating the study or our birth family must be mutual.

"Let's face it!" I write to Paula when I drop by the Internet café later that night. "We are stuck with each other. I am you and you are me and we are the walrus. Coo coo ca choo!"

Chapter | Ten

PAULA: My father, who thrives on regimens, finds beauty in the manicured landscape of Hilton Head's golf courses and gated communities. Over Memorial Day weekend, I fly down to Hilton Head with Jesse, who is thrilled to be visiting "Gramma and PopPop's house."

"It's so strange for me to think about how different our lives would have been if we had been offered both girls," says my mother once we get settled into their roomy ranch house.

"Why bother talking about what might have been? Things worked out the way they did and it's all for the best," my father huffs before fleeing the room.

"You know your father," my mother tells me as she helps me unpack my weekend bag. "He doesn't like dwelling on the past."

That's an understatement. A relentless optimist, my father is determined to see only the upside in any situation. Rather than feel anger toward Louise Wise for not offering him and my mother twins for adoption, he has opted to focus on the excitement surrounding our reunion. Before my visit, Dad informed me that he had already e-mailed his large circle of acquaintances to announce the new addition to the family, as if he had a new grandchild.

With Jesse napping in the port-a-crib, my mother and I leave Dad in charge and make a quick escape. We go out to run some errands and, more important, sort through our feelings without my father around insisting that we "let go of the past."

"I'm angry that Louise Wise didn't offer me twins, but at the same time, I don't know how I would have responded. I definitely wouldn't have agreed to separate twins. But if I didn't take both of you, I would have ended up with another baby and then I wouldn't have had you," my mom says, fighting back tears.

"I can't imagine not having you for a mother. It seems impossible that another woman gave birth to me," I say as the car winds its way through the flat roads of Hilton Head Plantation, the gated community where my parents live.

"Do you think that you and Elyse will try to find her?" Without waiting for my answer, my mom continues. "Are you prepared for what you might find?"

My parents have always made it clear that they would support me if I wanted to search for my biological relatives. But beneath their assurances I always sensed lurking anxieties. My mom in particular has always expressed concern that I might be disappointed in what I might discover. It's possible there was also an element of self-protection in her apprehension.

"Fear isn't what has stopped me from trying to find her. Honestly, I'm not sure how she would fit into my life. I already have a mother," I say. "I don't need another one." Despite my ambivalence, I have begun to believe that it is inevitable that we will track down our birth mother.

· | ·

Back in Brooklyn I continue to lead a double life. At pickup time outside Jesse's preschool, I arrange play dates and exchange tips about how to get toddlers to eat their greens. I don't dare tell the other moms what is really on my mind. Since reading the *Newsday* story about the triplets, I have become obsessed with the mysterious twin study. I decide to go directly to the source.

At home, I park Jesse in front of a *Dora the Explorer* video and call Stephanie Saul, the Pulitzer Prize–winning reporter who broke the story about the "secret study." She seems excited to be talking to a "real live Louise Wise separated twin." Although it has been years since Saul wrote the article for *Newsday*, it left such an indelible impression on her that she rattles off details as if she had worked on it just last week.

"Do you know what the purpose of the study was?" I ask.

Saul hesitates for a moment. I have the sense that she is thinking carefully—weighing her words. In at least two cases of separated Louise Wise twins, there were signs of mental illness in the family, she finally says. In one case, the twins were born at a mental institution. Although she is too careful a reporter to have announced such a theory in her article (she would have needed more data to support it), I think Saul means to tell me she suspects one possible purpose of the twin study was to determine the heritability of mental illnesses.

"My sister and I both suffered from depression and we recently found out that our birth mother was diagnosed as schizophrenic," I say. Saul responds sympathetically. She does not seem surprised by what I've told her.

The idea that Neubauer and Bernard might have purposely selected twins with a family history of mental illness sickens me. Could reputable psychiatrists really have withheld from adoptive parents what now seem so obviously to be crucial aspects of their children's medical history and then maintained their silence as they waited to see if one or both twins in any given set developed signs of mental illness?

Incensed, I phone Elyse in Paris to run this new idea by her.

"That's impossible," Elyse declares. "It would have been hard enough to find Jewish women who were giving up twins for adoption, but to find mentally ill Jewish women who were giving up twins would have made finding a large enough sample group very difficult. . . . Maybe our birth mother wasn't even schizophrenic."

Elyse makes a good point, but the journalist in me refuses to draw any conclusions before we have more information.

"Ultimately, we just don't know what happened. We can guess all we want, but we just don't know," I say. I am miffed that Elyse seems so confident in her hunches.

"This is why we need to get to the bottom of things," Elyse says. "Maybe we should get a lawyer to open the Yale archives."

ELYSE: I traverse the light Sunday traffic on boulevard Raspail and head for the phone booth across the street, which doubles as my office. "Hi Avo," I say. As I count the units on my phone card, my mind is devoid of small talk. I am relieved when Paula's voice comes on the line.

"Well, I didn't pass the exam. I'm not going on to the orals," I announce.

"You weren't sure about it anyway, so maybe it's a good thing." Paula replies, unable to read my reaction. "Now you're free to move to New York."

Now that a move to New York is plausible, the thought of leaving my microcosm in Paris makes me uneasy. Having successfully maneuvered the maze of French bureaucracy, I feel at home on the side streets of Paris, in its libraries and cinemas. *Pariscope* is my weekly bible, dictating what cultural events I will partake in, or sometimes just letting me dream of all the city has to offer.

My daily life is a carefully devised routine. On Thursday evenings, I take the aboveground metro across town to Trocadéro, where I tutor Monsieur Nathan. Monsieur Nathan is in his seventies and is more interested in recounting tales of his wartime experiences or discussing recent art exhibits than in conjugating verbs.

I spend Sunday afternoons at the historic Hotel Istria on rue Campagne-Première, drinking tea and discussing literature and world events with my friends Jean-Claude and Fabrice. The Montparnasse hotel was once home to Amadeo Modigliani and Marc Chagall. Fabrice holds up its artistic tradition by working on his watercolors while on duty at the front desk.

Even if I should move back to New York, I feel that it's vital that Paula visit me in Paris. I need her to see the environment that has shaped me the last three years, even if it's just a small room off the boulevard.

At my clubhouse in the center of Paris, Forum des Images, I can sip a coffee while perusing their upcoming film calendar, or check my e-mail. Volunteering at the forum's yearly summer film festival, Les Rencontres Internationales, I make professional contacts while discussing the screenings with other cinephiles.

Normally, I rely on the Internet café down the street from me on boulevard Montparnasse to write e-mails but the rambunctious teenagers who hang out there make it difficult for me to concentrate. Now that I am at the forum every day during the festival, it's a luxury to casually drop into their quiet cybercafé to check my e-mail between screenings.

"Volunteering at a film festival is something that I've done too!" Paula writes me.

Having met me just five times, Paula knows me only in comparison to herself. While Paula can picture herself in my shoes, I can't imagine working at *Variety*, as she did, since the focus was on the industry of film rather than the art.

Reviewing the vast backlog of e-mails Paula and I have exchanged, I am surprised by the rapidity with which she referred to me as "sister," just after we had first spoken on the phone. Searching for Paula, I had no idea how our relationship would develop or if she would even accept me.

Sometimes I am elated about her appearance in my life. Other times I feel alienated by this experience, angry at the doctors for separating us, incredibly sad that Paula and I didn't have time together growing up, just for us. And sometimes the separation is unbearable as I etch out my thoughts in letters to Paula so numerous that I can't possibly send them all.

PAULA: I arrive home from a relaxing late July weekend visiting friends in Cape Cod to find a slew of e-mails from Elyse. In one she writes, "How god awfully I've missed you these few days. It's our longest time apart since we met!"

Living on her own in Paris without a full-time job to divert her attention, Elyse has much more time than I do to ponder our new relationship. While I have Avo, Jesse, and my freelance writing life to preoccupy me, I sense that Elyse is looking for a soul mate.

Usually I respond quickly, so when I procrastinate in responding to her e-mails, Elyse calls to check in.

"Your e-mails kind of overwhelmed me," I confess. "You say you wish we had grown up together, but I'm not sure I feel that way. I feel guilty that I don't, but I can't help the way I feel."

"I bet you would feel differently if you were single."

"You're probably right. I already have my soul mate," I say apologetically.

"It's not as if I wish my life had been different, but I feel strongly that we should have been raised together," says Elyse.

"Of course I think it was wrong for us to be separated, but it's impossible for me to imagine what my life might have been like had we been raised together. There is no going back in time. Now I am afraid of disappointing you," I say.

"I'm afraid of disappointing you too," Elyse says.

How can I tell Elyse that I sometimes wish she hadn't found me? Instead, I try to reassure her.

"It's inevitable that we're going to disappoint each other. Sometimes my brother disappoints me, but he's still my brother," I explain.

"Yes, but with us it's different. Since we are so alike in many ways, we both have the sense that we should see things the same way. I have one question for you: Have I asked for too much from you?"

A potent silence settles between us as I weigh my response. All Elyse wants is to get to know me and to forge a friendship. Is that asking too much?

"No," I answer softly.

Sorting through the mail a couple of days later, I find a postcard with a 1920s black-and-white photo featuring two stylish women sitting at an outdoor café. On the back, Elyse has scrawled:

This postcard made me think of us at a café, leisurely watching the hours pass while discussing life and love and everything in between. Though our lives seem so right, I can't help but wish I had known you in the time before we had words (well, we did, but not long enough—just swimming around together in the darkness!). So now my joy in finding you reminds me how much I've missed you and am missing you still.

I can't say that I have missed Elyse since her return to Paris, but she is often in my thoughts. Calculating the time difference between us, I wonder what she is doing at various intervals throughout the day. Is she tutoring her friend Jean-Claude in English right now? Perhaps she is exploring the Rodin Museum, or rushing to catch a matinee at her favorite cinema.

While I'm hesitant to leave Jesse, who has never spent more than a night without me, it is obvious that I need to visit Elyse on her home turf. I am curious to experience the life that Elyse has created for herself in Paris. I imagine that it is the life I might have had if I had been raised by Elyse's parents.

Once I book a ticket to Paris, I begin to picture the two of us lingering over coffee at an outdoor café like the two ladies on the postcard.

ELYSE: Since Paula plans to visit me next month, I begin to see my world through her eyes. Though I want Paula to experience my life the way it really is, I can't picture her sleeping on a mattress on my floor.

My student room on the ground floor of a modern building is like a small chalet, sheltering me from the hustle and bustle of the city. Wooden shutters open up to a view of my neighbor's yard, which evokes a serene country scene. This compact hundred-square-foot box is also an ideal bachelorette pad. While cooking on the hot plate below my desk I can easily swing my chair around to grab a beer from the minifridge. I have everything I need within arm's reach. When my bookshelves fill up, I know it's time to whittle down my collection of worn volumes of English literature by trading one in at the used-book store near Odéon. Between receiving fashionable hand-me-downs from friends and making frequent visits to the library, I rarely have to buy anything.

I feel like the richest poor person in Paris.

Though my room is cramped, I've managed to host as many as three guests at a time. After a night out, one friend squeezes next to me on the twin bed while the other two make a nest on the floor and whisper to each other until we fall asleep. Watching my friends primping in the morning reminds me of a game of Twister. I enjoy sharing such intimacies in my tiny home and can't imagine having my friends stay at a hotel.

Still, I often take advantage of my friends' long French vacations to take my own vacations in their more luxurious apartments, basking in the comfort of their bathtubs and kitchens. Luckily I have coordinated Paula's stay with one of my cat-sitting gigs at a friend's place and will be able to provide her with her own room.

PAULA: I have never suffered from a fear of flying, but two events have changed that: September 11 and becoming a mother. As I pack for my trip to Paris, it is hard not to contemplate the possibility of never returning home. I picture Avo as a stoic widower and single dad regaling Jesse with stories about the mother she lost when she was too young to form lasting memories.

When I say good-bye to Avo, I tell him, "If the worst happens, promise me you'll tell Jesse that I love her."

"I promise," he vows melodramatically.

At the airport, I am greeted by an hour wait to check-in as well as the news that my flight has been delayed four hours. Four fewer hours I get to spend with my twin sister.

"You don't understand. I'm on my way to Paris to meet my identical twin sister I just found out about," I plead with the airline's customer service representative.

"What do you want me to do for you?" she asks without missing a beat.

"Well, if I was in first class at least I could get some rest," I whine before breaking down in tears. The stress of leaving Jesse for the first time and visiting my twin has taken its toll on my nerves. I'm a complete wreck.

"Cheer up," the woman says. "You're going to meet your twin!"

I don't let on that this trip will technically be our second meeting. Clearly, someone at American Airlines takes pity on me or fears that I might create a scene because I wind up in first class sipping a complimentary glass of champagne and nibbling on fresh strawberries.

Of all the cities my long-lost twin could have settled in, it's fortuitous she ended up in Paris rather than, say, Des Moines or Detroit. Since age eleven, when I first saw the movie *A Little Romance,* in which a young American girl falls in love with a French boy while attending school in Paris, I have been a devoted Francophile. In eighth grade, when it came time to choose a language to study, French was the natural choice. I fantasized about spending my junior year in college in France—if not settling there for good. But after three years of high school and one year of college French, I abandoned any hopes of speaking the language fluently. Now, through Elyse, I have the vicarious opportunity to experience my fantasy.

ELYSE: It's the morning Paula is due to arrive and, contrary to the weather forecaster's grim reports, there isn't a cloud in the sky.

Anxiously waiting for Paula at Orly airport, I feel as if I am meeting my twin for the first time. When I spot Paula in a crowd of British tourists, I restrain myself from asking, "What are you doing with my face?"

I'm reminded of the German documentary film about separated identical twins, *Oskar and Jack*. Jack asks that exact question upon seeing his twin for the second time in his life after twenty-five years of being apart.

Soon after Oskar and Jack met in 1979 to take part in MSTRA at age forty-six, their faces were splashed around newspapers everywhere with headlines reading, "Jew and Nazi twins!" Born in Trinidad to a Catholic mother and a Jewish father, they were soon separated as babies by their parents' divorce. While Jack was raised by his father as a Jew in Trinidad, eventually moving to Israel and then America, Oskar was raised a strict Catholic by his grandmother in German-occupied Czechoslovakia where, like all young men, he was obliged to become a member of the Hitler Youth.

Meeting each other again at the airport that day, Oskar and Jack noticed their twin also had a neatly groomed mustache, a similar gait, and many of the same mannerisms. Despite the drastic differences in their upbringings, they each displayed the same idiosyncratic behaviors, such as wrapping rubber bands around their wrists, sneezing in public to get attention, and reading magazines back to front.

"Bonjour!" Paula greets me with a kiss on both cheeks, and I am jolted back into the present.

Paula has donned a French striped boatneck sailor shirt for the occasion. Bubbling with energy, she excitedly recounts the details of her flight. "I drank champagne the whole way here!"

Trying to focus on getting us home, I lead her to the RER commuter train, which will deliver us to our weekend getaway.

· | ·

"Voilà!" I exclaim as we enter the spacious two-bedroom flat, which my friend Juliette shares with her partner and young son. Setting the mood, I turn on the stereo to play the Eric Dolphy CD that I've been listening to incessantly. I crouch down to sit on the low sofa in the living room and hand Paula a glass of Bordeaux.

Even though Paula isn't a fan of cats, she can't refuse poor orphaned Hercules, whose name defies his scrawny frame, when he curls up in her lap.

"I shouldn't really drink because I might be pregnant," Paula says. They have carefully planned their second child and everything seems to be going according to schedule. "Well, since I already had some on the plane, what the hell!" she says, graciously accepting the glass. Relieved that she won't be abstaining, I clink her glass.

"Well, this is it!" I feel like telling her. "This is the life!" We gush about Paris like young travelers meeting up at a youth hostel. Including the four days we spent together in New York, this is our fifth day together. With a mere three nights ahead of us, we are anxious to talk about anything and everything.

"What do you think she's like?" Paula asks, and I realize she's talking about our birth mother.

I blurt out the first scenario that enters my mind. "I like to think she's gotten over her mental illness. Maybe she's on a farm somewhere living in a community of transsexuals or something." Picturing our birth mother as an eccentric old lady living on a commune, we laugh. It's hard to believe that I set out a little more than a year ago to find my birth mother, oblivious, and now I'm sitting with my twin sister giggling about where she might be.

The bellowing sound of French rap music reverberates from across the alley. Looking out the window, Paula and I notice two lanky young Frenchmen in Marlon Brando undershirts peering into the apartment. Having attracted our attention, they shout come-ons to us in French. We smile back at them coyly before pulling the billowing cotton curtains shut.

PAULA: Since I've been to Paris before and have visited most of the popular tourist attractions, I let Elyse guide me through her own personal tour of Paris, the places that matter most to her. Strolling through Elyse's neighborhood, we stop to pay homage to Jean-Paul Sartre and Simone de Beauvoir at their adjoining graves in Montparnasse Cemetery. Elyse cracks me up when, in her best affected British accent, she pretends to be a tour guide to the "Dead and Famous."

Afterward, we stop off at a café where I order a *croque monsieur* and a *citron pressé* in my best high school French. Hearing Elyse speak French fluently makes me regret abandoning my studies.

Looking out at the boulevard, Elyse boasts about her illustrious neighbors.

"I can't believe Jean-Pierre Léaud lives down the block!" I say to Elyse.

"I loved him in *The 400 Blows*." I don't have to ask Elyse if she's seen the classic François Truffaut film since, like me, she is a devoted fan of the French new wave directors. Over cappuccinos, Elyse raves about how much she loves living in such a fashionable neighborhood, but warns me that her apartment is small.

After leaving the café, we stop by Elyse's place, across the street. Nothing could have prepared me for the cubby Elyse calls home. Without a kitchen or a bathroom, her "apartment" is significantly smaller than my old dorm room at Wellesley. The reason she pays so little for the place, she explains, is that it is technically a storage room for the upscale apartment building.

Before I worked at *Variety* and met Avo, I lived a more precarious existence, juggling freelance writing assignments and scrambling to pay my rent. At the time I thought I was living the Bohemian life. Now it is hard for me to fathom how Elyse has managed to live in this tiny room for three years, relying on the bathroom down the hall and warming up her canned dinners on a hot plate.

I restrain my urge to blurt out, "How can you live like this?" and instead say, "It's cute. You've done a lot with the place."

ELYSE: I'm familiar with the surprised look on Paula's face when she sees my room. Many of my friends, though pleased to stay at my pied-à-terre, say that they don't know how I could live in such a small space. I had warned Paula that my room was small, but she apparently expected something more like a New York studio apartment.

"The bathroom is down the hall, but it's really clean and I never have to wait." I give her the pitch. It's really not bad here.

Paula quickly assesses the room and zooms in to my book shelf, where she notices my old Czech metro ID, a memento from my heyday in Prague. In the blurry image, I have a dreamy expression reminiscent of another era.

"That looks like me," she says, picking it up to inspect it more closely. Why must Paula appropriate all the best photos of me?

PAULA: At the Bourdelle Museum, Elyse challenges me to find the sculpture *The Polish Woman,* which her friends think bears an uncanny resemblance to her and therefore, to me. Winding my way around an oversize sculpture of Penelope, the woman who waits for Ulysses, I spot the bronze bust and am instantly disappointed.

"I don't think she looks like me at all. She looks more like you," I tell Elyse as I head outside to the sculpture garden. I sit on a bench and sulk in the hot sun. I am acting like a petulant child, but I can't seem to curb my behavior.

Initially, Elyse and I focused on our similarities, but now we fixate on the differences. Each remark contains the implicit judgment "If I were you, I would . . ." Every decision I make—what to eat, what to wear, what to say—brings us closer together or separates us further. Each of us is so concerned about offending the other, we compulsively apologize and overexplain ourselves.

"But what I really want to say is . . ."

"Sorry I didn't . . ."

"If you don't want to, we don't have to . . ."

Like Tweedledum and Tweedledee, the contrary twins in *Through the Looking-Glass,* Elyse and I argue about the subtlest differences in opinion. If I comment that the weather is nice, she is bound to say, "Well, it's a bit hot" and if she says, "It's too hot," I'm sure to refute her. I can sense I am getting on Elyse's nerves just as she is getting on mine. The more she irritates me, the more irritating I become. Being with my twin seems to bring out the worst in me.

ELYSE: After admiring the picture-postcard view of the Eiffel Tower from the Pont Sully, above Paris Plage, where tourists bask in the sun, Paula and I take seats on the empty terrace at L'Académie de la Bière. So much has changed since I first shared the news with Jean-Claude here six months ago, when Paula existed only in the abstract.

"Maybe we should eat here. I love their mussels," I suggest, watching the late summer sun set in the sky. Paula frowns and I suddenly remember that she doesn't like them. She thinks everything I say that opposes her opinion is a critique. Why do we have to bicker about such insignificant things? Though I have strong opinions, I can easily imagine other ways of living. Seeking the other's approval, we both react defensively.

"Do you think we would be friends if we just met now and weren't twins?" Paula asks.

"I think we both would have been more open if we had met in our twenties," I reply, hinting that perhaps Paula has become more close-minded since settling down.

"None of your friends are married," Paula says, trying to pinpoint the crux of our difference.

"What about Veronika?" Even though my friend Veronika is doing an internship in Brussels, she's still committed to her marriage in France. Paula shrugs.

"We often do things with the kids," Paula says, reasoning how our lives don't fit.

"I love kids! I was so excited about taking Jesse to the Vincennes Zoo when I thought she might come with you to Paris."

"I just don't know. . . . We're so different," Paula says gingerly. "I don't want to hurt you."

"Nothing you say can hurt me. I would just like to be in your life, in whatever capacity you see fit," I tell Paula. But I'm not sure she believes me.

PAULA: Sitting across the table from each other, the distance between Elyse and me feels gaping. If I acknowledge the tension between us, I fear it will only make things worse.

"Things have been so awkward. It is so hard to communicate. Sometimes I start to say something, but then I stop myself for fear I'll hurt your feelings," I say.

"You realize that nothing you say or do could hurt me unless you cut me out of your life entirely," Elyse says.

I guess this isn't the time to confess that the idea of vanishing from Elyse's life has crossed my mind. During our marathon first date at Café Mogador only four months ago, it was love at first sight. Now I feel as if I've committed myself to a long-term relationship with someone I don't even know.

"I'm not sure we would be friends if we met today and weren't twins," I blurt out.

"Why?" she asks, incredulous that her twin could be so cruel.

A moment ago, she assured me that nothing I say could hurt her and already I've proven her wrong. I explain that our lifestyles are dramatically different, but she disagrees.

Of course, I have many single friends, but most of them are leading more conventional lives than Elyse. I try not to be judgmental, but it's hard not to draw conclusions from the fact that Elyse makes ends meet by collecting unemployment. Her future seems so uncertain. Will she ask me and Avo for money at some point? Although she is my twin, she is still a stranger to me, and I can't be certain of her motives.

Other than her handful of tutoring appointments, Elyse has no commitments. Whereas I almost never have a moment to myself, she can often go for days without seeing or even talking to friends. She claims she is living the starving artist's life. But where is her art?

Elyse demands honesty from me, but I don't have the heart or the guts to dole it out.

ELYSE: It's August in Paris and the vendors have handwritten signs, FERMÉ EN AOÛT, in their windows. The late summer silence I usually treasure now numbs me. I mope about the flat where I am cat-sitting while Hercules follows me from room to room as if searching for Paula, who left yesterday. Melancholy washes over me as I remember the awkwardness of her visit.

Every conversation between us led to an exhausting debate. Even a simple outing to the local supermarket around the corner became an ordeal. Deciding which gourmet Dijon mustard to bring home to Avo, Paula, suddenly self-conscious, said, "You must think I'm bourgeois."

"Why do you think I would think that?" I was forced to repeat all weekend. "I go shopping. I am not completely outside of society," I said with an annoyed glare.

At moments like this, Paula seemed to fear my judgment, while more often I sensed her air of superiority. I could almost hear her thoughts. *If I were you, I would have a better apartment, I would* . . . I don't care what other people think of me, but Paula's judgment stings because she is my twin. Does she think she did a better job with our DNA?

Chapter | Eleven

PAULA: I recall a family vacation at a beach resort outside San Juan when I was seven. For what seemed like an eternity, my brother and I amused ourselves by catapulting ourselves into the surf and letting the swells deposit us—giddy and dazed—on the warm beach sand. More than once, a wave caught me off guard and pounded my tiny body underwater. Panicked and struggling for breath, I inhaled mouthfuls of salty foam before eventually righting myself. For that one moment when the wave pinned me to the ocean floor, I had no choice but to succumb to its sheer force.

Now as a wave of melancholy crashes down on me, I feel similarly helpless. I have no choice but to abandon myself to depression. I have never seriously contemplated suicide, but since returning from Paris, I have often wished I could simply cease to exist. Images of Elyse and me in Paris flit through my brain. I replay every scene in my mind, imagining how things might have gone differently if only I hadn't been so judgmental, so withholding, so difficult.

"There was too much pressure to pack so much lost time into a few days," I write in my journal soon after returning from Paris. "I felt tense nearly the entire visit, with a few exceptions—most notably, our last night together when we went to a nice seafood restaurant and stayed up late drinking Russian vodka. For once, we spoke freely without fears of offending or being misunderstood. At moments, I appreciated Elyse's independence, humor, and beauty. Still, despite our similarities, we seem to view the world very differently."

Sitting on a grassy hillside overlooking Park Slope's Third Street Playground, I watch Avo and Jesse cavorting in the sprinklers. The carefree world they inhabit seems so foreign, I might as well be spying on them from a distant planet. I'm punished by self-hating thoughts and contemplate whether they would be better off without me.

Relief washes over me as soon as my eyes pop open the following morning. Instead of wanting to disappear, suddenly I am determined to stick around long enough to watch my daughter grow up. The mystery of my topsy-turvy moods is partially solved when I take a home pregnancy test, which produces two parallel magenta lines. I am pregnant.

ELYSE: Dazed and exhausted after Paula's visit, I am relieved when she calls and apologizes for being so uptight in Paris.

"I would have been the same way," I reassure her. "You were brave to come here. I'm glad you visited."

"So am I," Paula says.

"When I'm in New York, I'm sure there'll be some awkward moments between us, but we'll get through it."

Having surmounted our first dispute, we can now conquer anything.

Since Paula's folks are planning a visit to New York in October, we are hoping to organize a meeting with my family, who will be in town for my cousin Gabriel's first birthday. Paula and I will be able to celebrate our first birthday together after thirty-five years apart.

Back at my flat after weeks of cat-sitting, I meticulously plan the next few months. My unemployment lasts until January. I can leave checks with Jean-Claude to pay my rent each month and if things go awry, there's always my overdraft at the bank.

"I wouldn't feel comfortable couch-surfing for so long," Paula writes in an e-mail when I fill her in on my plans to spend the next three months in America. She doesn't know me well enough to know that I always land on my feet.

"You don't have to feel responsible for me," I respond. But I can still sense Paula's anxiety about my upcoming visit.

By revisiting the places I have lived and spending time with friends and family, I hope to gain insight into my twinship. Almost six months after I reunited with Paula, my brother still doesn't know of her existence. Since Jay doesn't have a telephone or computer, the only chance we have to communicate is when Dad drops by to see Jay and calls me from his cell phone. When I visit my folks in Oklahoma this winter, I'll be able to tell Jay the news in person.

At my parents' house, I'll be able to rifle through the attic for my baby book. The information that Louise Wise has given us doesn't make sense. If, as Katherine recently told Paula, we were placed in our adoptive families at different times because Paula was developing at a faster rate, why was Paula so scrawny when she was adopted at five months, while I was held back?

"I set a date with the lawyer," Paula says, when she calls to discuss plans for my upcoming visit. While we are not litigious people, Paula and I have agreed that if it would help us gain access to the twin study data or to open our records at Louise Wise, we would consider suing.

"Wonder twins activate!" I joke with Paula. "I hope we make it to the New York Public Library. Then there's Viola Bernard's open archives at Columbia. We have so much to do!" I'm energized by the thought of being a more active participant in our sleuthing.

Since I'll be in the States well through winter, I pack up all my belongings, leaving my room in Paris barren.

PAULA: "Sometimes I want to cut myself off from Elyse and then when we talk on the phone or I get an e-mail from her, I get caught up in the excitement and we connect again," I write in my journal one night after hanging up the phone with Elyse.

Since Elyse's upcoming trip to the States will extend for three months, I fear that after wearing out her welcome with friends and family, she'll end up on our couch. Now that I'm experiencing morning sickness, the idea of playing hostess overwhelms me.

I haven't yet shared the news of my pregnancy with Elyse. The prospect of a new niece or nephew might excite her, but it could also accentuate the differences in our lives. Will Elyse view the pregnancy as one more thing that I have and she doesn't? As the day of Elyse's arrival approaches, I'm filled with a sense of impending doom. Perhaps we are taking on too much by trying to meet with a lawyer and researching our birth mother at the New York Public Library. Our relationship is so fresh; we first met less than six months ago. After our tense time together in Paris, maybe we should just focus on getting to know each other.

ELYSE: When I arrive at Paula's, she greets me with a kiss on both cheeks. I lug in my two massive suitcases and a duffel bag full of wine and gifts for friends and family. Paula watches as I rummage excitedly through my bag looking for the French trinkets I've brought for her.

"I'm pregnant," Paula announces bluntly.

I knew Paula and Avo were planning to have another child, but it comes as a shock to hear the news so suddenly. Why didn't she tell me before?

As if reading my mind, Paula says, "I wanted to tell you sooner, but I didn't want to tell you in an e-mail. You are one of the first to know!"

"Congratulations!" I exclaim. Though I am happy for Paula, I can't help but feel that her having another child will create another wedge between us. Our lives are already so different, and soon she will be a mother of two, with even more responsibilities. And now that she's in the throes of morning sickness, I'll have to be even more careful to tiptoe around her. I resent that Paula treats my appearance in her life like an invasion.

PAULA: Admiring the glistening skyline of lower Manhattan from our building's roof deck, Elyse and I deeply inhale the crisp fall night.

"What will you tell the lawyer tomorrow?" asks Elyse, breaking the silence.

Now that our meeting with the lawyer is imminent, I'm having second thoughts. Someone should be held responsible for the twin study, but I don't want my life to be waylaid by an expensive, lengthy, emotionally grueling trial. I refuse to let anger consume me. Maybe my dad is right and I should let go of the past.

"I want to find out whether it was legal for Katherine to notify me that I had a twin considering I never agreed to be contacted by any biological relatives," I blurt out.

"But won't that dilute our argument about how we shouldn't have been separated in the first place?" asks Elyse, sounding dejected.

Bloated and nauseated from morning sickness, I have no patience for diplomacy.

"I'm still angry at the way Katherine told me about you," I explain. "She should have asked me to come in to meet with her before dumping the news on me. Since our birth mother had mental problems, for all Katherine knew I was unstable too. She had no idea how I would react."

"Maybe Katherine wasn't as tactful as she could have been, but I'm grateful she called you or else I might not have found you," says Elyse.

"I still resent the fact that I had no control over being found. I never asked to be separated from you in the first place and I never asked to be found," I say bluntly.

"So you wish I hadn't found you?" asks Elyse. Her neck and cheeks have flushed an angry pink, the way mine do when I'm upset.

I hesitate before answering. "No, but there are moments when I want my old life back. Honestly, I just wish that none of this had happened."

"But it has," says Elyse calmly. "We can't change that."

ELYSE: "Our argument has to be really clear when we talk to the lawyer," I remind Paula the night before our meeting. "We want to petition for our adoption records at the agency to be opened. Maybe he'll know of a way to get into the Yale archives."

"I'm not sure about all of this," Paula says hesitantly.

"The story we got from the agency is inconsistent. The only way to get the story straight is to get the records opened." I project confidence, hoping to sway her opinion.

Paula is still fuming at Katherine Boros for the way she blurted out the news that she had a twin. Six months later, I wish we could just move on. Not only does her complaint undermine the validity of our argument, it also pales in comparison to the wrong the agency did in separating us.

She sounds as if she wishes I'd never found her.

"Though I think it was wrong that we were separated, I still can't say that I wish we were raised together," Paula says solemnly.

Isn't it just a question of semantics?

"Just because I wish we had spent our first thirty-five years together doesn't mean I want to erase the life I've had," I tell her. Paula stares back at me blankly.

It's unfair that I should have to choose between this life and the hypothetical life I might have led had we been raised together.

PAULA: When the elevator stops at the lawyer's floor, Elyse and I pause for last-minute preparations. We give each other a once-over.

"Remember, we don't want to look too happy," I joke.

We simultaneously purse our lips in matching fake frowns.

"But we also don't want to present ourselves as damaged goods or victims," cautions Elyse.

"Just think—if we win a settlement, we can use the money for therapy!" I try to make her laugh.

"It would also finance important bonding camping trips. Think of all of the family vacations we missed out on experiencing together!"

We break out in matching grins. Last night Elyse and I were opposing plaintiffs; now we are in perfect accord.

With his prominent nose and sympathetic smile, David Lansner reminds me of a younger version of my father. In his office near city hall, Lansner listens attentively as Elyse and I take turns recounting the story of our separation as babies and our recent reunion.

"What was done to you was clearly unethical and immoral," Lansner declares, as if offering a verdict. But that doesn't necessarily mean we can sue. Even if the agency had done something illegal, Lansner tells us, New York State's statute of limitations would make this a difficult case.

"But we didn't know until recently that we were separated," I remind him.

"It's a murky area of the law," he says. "What are the injuries for loss of a sibling?"

"There's no way to calculate how much we are owed for what they did to us," says Elyse calmly.

"You'd have to prove damages and the problem is that you've both done so well. The defense attorney would say, 'Paula, you went to Wellesley. Then you went to graduate school at NYU Cinema Studies. Then you worked at *Variety*. You're married and you love your daughter. You love your parents. You've got a great life.' "

A smile breaks out on my face. He's right. While I've weathered my fair share of difficult, lonely times and depression, I am finally happy.

"And Elyse," the lawyer continues, "you went to a good college. You love your family. You live in Paris and get to travel around the world attending film festivals."

The way he presents it, Elyse's life sounds pretty cushy too.

ELYSE: Just because Paula and I are survivors doesn't mean they weren't wrong to separate us.

Mr. Lansner's logic reminds me of the pharmaceutical company's defense when my parents sued them for negligence for my allergic reaction. By the time I was a seventeen-year-old freshman in college, the physical signs of my burn were fading, but the emotional pain endured. The jury was shown gruesome photos of me taken at the burn institute during the worst stage of my reaction, images that I couldn't bear to see. But apparently my composure was more compelling because the verdict they came back with was, "Get on with your life."

We have no photos to present, only the absurdity of our present situation. Besides, who could say if the depression we both suffered might have stemmed from our separation? In any case, had we grown up together, one of us might have been spared a traumatic allergic reaction to sulfa drugs.

"It's my job to play devil's advocate," says Mr. Lansner. "You mentioned that you have both suffered from depression. Were either of you ever institutionalized?"

"No, but I've been on Prozac for over ten years," Paula says.

"And I tried to kill myself when I was a teenager," I offer.

Our suffering does not impress Lansner. He tells us that the case would cost $150,000 in legal work and $10,000 to $15,000 in expert fees alone and there's no guarantee we would win. We will not be pursuing a legal case against Louise Wise. Now we must find another avenue to gain entry into the Yale archives and obtain our files at Louise Wise.

Still, as we leave Lansner's office, we feel triumphant that we presented our case so eloquently. We may never have our day in court, but airing our grievances in front of a lawyer is enough to satisfy us for the moment.

"We made a pretty good team," Paula says to me. I smile back at her warmly.

· | ·

It is October 9. Every year on my birthday, I wonder if my birth mother is thinking of me. I imagine her conjuring up a picture of the woman I have become and asking herself if she made the best decision in giving me up. Perhaps she commemorates the day with a private ceremony that she doesn't tell anyone about.

Celebrating our birthday together for the first time, just six months after our first meeting, I realize that Paula could have been contemplating these same thoughts for all these years.

I meet Paula, Avo and Jesse for a birthday brunch in Park Slope at Cocotte, a casual French restaurant. The autumn weather is temperate enough for us to take seats at an outdoor table. Paula presents me with a birthday card from her parents and a red leather purse-sized photo album. Looking at the cover picture of us in front of the Hotel Istria in Paris, one can only see our bliss at being together, rather than the tension of that visit. Pictures of Paula's family fill the first few pages; Jesse sitting in the sandbox with a pink cap on her head, their trip to Hawaii when Jesse was a baby. Paula has left the last pages in the album empty so that I'll be able to add photos as our experiences together grow. Her gift to me is the future.

Paula's mother made a card for me on the computer. On the front, two auburn-haired identical girls do handstands underwater. I have to turn the card upside down to read what Marilyn has written. "You and Paula would have been so cute together as kids. We probably would have had to stand on our heads to keep up with you both." Like me, Paula's parents can imagine a shared past.

PAULA: Elyse seems anxious to show off *Je Vole le Bonheur,* the short film she directed while studying in Prague. Attempting to create an authentic theater experience, I dim the living room lights and Avo, Elyse, and I settle into the leather couch.

We watch silently as a young woman shoplifts, attempting to obtain the happiness she sees in advertisements. I think back to the short experimental film I wrote and directed during the summer after my graduation from Wellesley. *Images of Julia,* my final project in a filmmaking class I took at SUNY Purchase, followed an obsessive young woman seeking purification in art.

Is it just a coincidence that both of our films revolve around young women with unhealthy addictions who look for happiness outside of themselves?

"So what do you think?" Elyse asks when the film ends.

"I'm impressed," I say honestly. "The photography was beautiful and of course, it was very well directed. It's a hell of a lot more professional than the film I made!"

In Paris I asked myself where Elyse's art was. Now I am proud to see that she has genuine talent.

As the credits roll, Elyse's phone rings.

"But I thought I could stay with you tonight," I hear her say.

"Who was it?" I ask, as Elyse gets up from the kitchen table.

"Joseph . . . Luke has to get up early in the morning, so I can't stay with them tonight," she responds, dejected.

"Well, you can stay here another night, but really . . . If we had a guest room it would be different," I say tentatively.

I join Elyse as she heads out to the stoop to smoke a cigarette. "I don't know how you can live the way you do," I confess. "You even seem proud."

"I am. I've managed to get by. And don't forget that I was preparing for the teacher's exam . . . and then I found you."

"I don't judge my other friends but I can't help but judge you because you are my twin," I admit guiltily. I find it hard not to picture myself in Elyse's shoes and imagine how I might do things differently.

· | ·

I wait until Elyse and I are in our pajamas drinking "tension tamer" tea to broach the subject of our birth mother. We had planned to visit the New York Public Library to begin our search for her, but now that I'm suffering from morning sickness, the idea nauseates me.

"I think we should wait," I say tentatively.

"Why?" Elyse asks. She sounds disappointed.

"There's just too much going on right now. I'm still getting used to the idea of having you in my life. I'm not ready to complicate things even more."

"What are you afraid of? Just because you are married and settled doesn't mean that your life stops evolving," says Elyse. "Aren't you secure enough in your life to realize that nothing we learn will make a difference?"

Caught off guard by her question, I struggle for the right words to explain my apprehension.

"You were searching. I wasn't," is all I can muster before saying good night and heading downstairs to my bedroom where Avo is already sleeping soundly.

The next day, as I ponder Elyse's question, it strikes me that it is precisely because I feel so secure in my life that I don't want to do anything that may jeopardize the status quo. While Elyse is free to make decisions on her own, I must consider my family. I am reluctant to inject an unknown element into our happy existence. As I prepare Jesse's school lunch, one sentence from my *Redbook* essay, "Why I Don't Want to Find My Birth Mother," runs through my head: "Once you find someone, you can't unfind her."

ELYSE: My parents are in town and I had hoped to spend time with them on Long Island. When they decide to go on an outing to downtown Port Jefferson, where we used to dock our boat when I was a kid, they don't invite me. I stomp up to the guest room at Aunt Pat's and brood like a moody teenager.

I have sought Toni's approval ever since she married my dad when I was seven. As much as I tried to please her, I never felt I was the daughter she wanted. Though she cooked my favorite meals and took great care in laying out my clothes for school, we never meshed as mother and daughter. No matter how hard we tried, we were like oil and vinegar. But when Tyler joined our family, Toni at last found the opportunity to be the mother she could never be to me. Perhaps Toni viewed Tyler—who was blond and fair-eyed like her and my father—as the child they never had. Now Tyler has come between us as we argue about how best to deal with his drug-fueled escapades.

Since Toni is the matron of the family and I do love her, I try to keep the peace, if only for my father's sake. I still carry a grain of hope that we will become closer, even though the gap has grown wider since I met Paula. The existence of my identical twin forces my parents to ask themselves uncomfortable questions: If we had sent Elyse to a private school like Paula, would she have found a steady career for herself? Is it our fault that Elyse is still single? Did we really do the best job raising her? I suppose these questions will come to the surface when they meet Paula's folks next week. I cannot comfort them because I have no answers.

My cousin Jaime's son Gabriel curiously dips his fingers into his first birthday cake. Instead of enjoying the occasion, I am plagued by thoughts of Gabriel's lost twin, Isaak. I can't help but picture Paula and me celebrating our first birthday together. Jaime notices that I am tearing up and gives me a hug. "You're okay. You survived without your twin. That gives me hope for Gabriel."

In the kitchen, I overhear Toni in the next room furtively talking on the phone with Tyler in Oklahoma. "What's wrong?" I ask, seeing the grim expression on her face.

"Nothing," Toni responds glibly. "He broke a window to get into the house. Maybe we shouldn't have locked it," she mutters under her breath as she returns to Gabriel's birthday party. I hope that Tyler will really go into rehab this time.

I feel like a foreigner and wonder which family I belong to.

When I get a call from Paula, I head into Jaime's bedroom for privacy.

"Jesse misses you. She asked when Aunt Elyse was coming to visit."

"Tell her I'm coming back soon."

Elyse's parents, Marty and Lynn Schein.

Paula's parents, Bernie and Marilyn Bernstein.

Elyse (left) and Paula, shortly after being adopted.

Elyse with her mom.

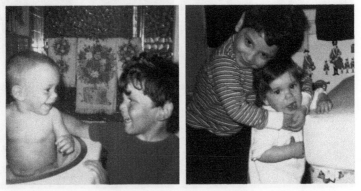

Elyse (left) and Paula with their big brothers, Jay (left) and Steven—also adopted from Louise Wise.

Elyse at age 7.

Paula at age 7.

Elyse at age 11.

Paula at age 10.

Elyse and Jay on vacation in
Ticonderoga, New York.

Paula and Steven on vacation in
San Juan, Puerto Rico.

Marty and Toni's wedding, with Elyse
as flower girl, 1976.

Paula and her family.

Paula (left) and Elyse as teens, both trying to look grown up.

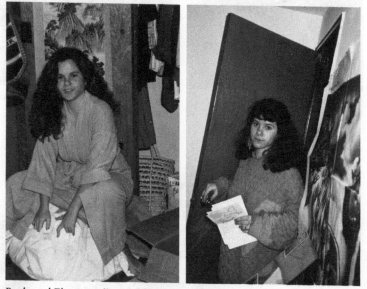

Paula and Elyse at college—difficult years for them both.

Elyse at her film premiere party in Prague, 1995.

Paula in Paris, 1995—unknowingly visiting her twin's stomping grounds.

Paula with Avo and Jesse in the East Village, not long before her world was changed by the phone call from the adoption agency.

Elyse at L'Académie de la bière just after receiving the news from the adoption agency that she had a twin.

Paula and Elyse in Park Slope one week after their reunion.

The sisters in Paris, Summer 2004, just getting acquainted.

Paula on the hunt for their birth mother's name at The New York Public Library (Elyse took the picture).

Elyse and Ruby on the twins' second birthday together.

Tyler.

Paula and Elyse in Park Slope. © 2007 by Elena Seibert

PAULA: A little more than six months after my reunion with Elyse, my parents will finally meet their daughter's twin.

"Since we've talked to her on the phone and have seen her picture, we feel like we've met her already," my mom tells me the day before Elyse is due to arrive with her parents.

In addition to seeing Elyse for the first time, my parents will also meet Elyse's folks. I picture the two couples comparing life stories and regaling one another with anecdotes about what it was like to raise "one of the twins."

In preparation for the big meeting, I prod my mother to recount the tale of how our family was formed.

In January 1960, twenty-four-year-old Bernard Bernstein, a charismatic accountant with a prominent nose and big ears to match, was set up on a blind date with twenty-two-year-old Marilyn Vinikoff. A serious young woman with a slender figure and straight, ink-black hair, Marilyn worked as a medical secretary in Park Slope, Brooklyn.

Bernie's confident, gregarious personality complemented Marilyn's thoughtful nature. Although Bernie had to drive for more than an hour from his home in the Bronx to reach Marilyn's in Brooklyn, he sensed she was worth the effort.

On their second date, Marilyn asked Bernie to accompany her to Queens where her entire family was gathering to welcome the latest addition, a baby girl her cousin had adopted. With his warm demeanor, Bernie blended right in with Marilyn's tight-knit Jewish family.

A mere three months later, on April 20, Marilyn's twenty-third birthday, the couple became engaged. It was a relief to Marilyn, since most of her friends were already married. At twenty-three, she felt she was already on the verge of becoming an old maid. On a rainy Sunday afternoon, the day after tax season ended in 1961, the young couple was married in a small ceremony at Congregation Beth Israel in Brooklyn. Following a week-long honeymoon in Bermuda, the newlyweds moved their belongings out of their respective mothers' homes and settled into a one-bedroom apartment in Brooklyn.

Right on schedule, Marilyn got pregnant a year later, but miscarried only a few months into the pregnancy. Following three grueling years of doctors' visits and invasive fertility tests, Marilyn finally conceived again. But again, she miscarried within the first few months. Marilyn and Bernie knew they could not undergo the disappointment of another miscarriage or the stress of more tests, so they decided to adopt. To prepare for the baby they hoped would arrive soon, the couple moved to a two-bedroom apartment in the middle-class neighborhood of Bayside, Queens.

They visited Louise Wise Services, the premier Jewish adoption agency in New York City. Trying to ascertain whether they would make good adoptive parents, the agency caseworker interviewed them thoroughly. They were asked if they were concerned about the baby's medical background. "We said that there were so many diseases in both of our families and a lot of things we didn't know about," my mom remembers. "If something developed later on, we figured we would deal with it."

After several interviews at the agency, Marilyn and Bernie returned to Louise Wise in May 1966 to meet a smiley six-month-old boy with curly dark locks and big brown eyes who would become my big brother. The following day, the Bernsteins returned to Louise Wise to pick up the baby, whom they decided to name Steven Bruce Bernstein. In the Ashkenazic Jewish tradition, they named him using the same first initial of the name of a relative who had recently died. "Steven" was in memory of Marilyn's late father, Samuel, and "Bruce" was in honor of Bernie's late aunt Betty. It was just a coincidence that Bruce was also the name the baby had been called during his stay in foster care.

At the time, my parents told the agency that they would eventually like to adopt a daughter. The caseworker informed them that the agency recommended a gap of three years between siblings, so they would have to wait.

In March 1969, now settled in a split-level house in idyllic Westchester County, the Bernsteins got a call that their new daughter was ready to go home. They brought three-and-a-half-year-old Steven to pick up his baby sister, a scrawny five-month-old girl. In honor of Bernie's late mother Pauline and his uncle Sam, they decided to name their daughter Paula Sue Bernstein.

ELYSE: "I can't imagine meeting someone who is so much like my sweet daughter Paula," Paula's mother, Marilyn, recently wrote in an e-mail. Paula's parents have been sending me regular updates on their life in Hilton Head, Bernie's favorite horse, Rita, their coon hound, Gracie, and the volunteer work that keeps them both busy. I worry that when they meet me at Paula's today they will congratulate themselves on having gotten "the good twin." Paula's married and settled down, while I'm the bohemian vagabond.

"So Paula's mom grew up in Brooklyn?" Dad asks me. I tell my parents the Bernsteins' story as we drive through East Meadow on Long Island, on our way to meet Paula and her family.

Though Bambi's, Dad's beloved bakery, is no longer in East Meadow, the town hasn't changed much since my parents first met there in 1957. Marty was seventeen and had just moved back from Florida to live with one of his four sisters. In addition to dodging a girl's attempt to snag him as a husband, he was also anxious to get away from the rough crowd he was running with there.

In the up-and-coming Long Island suburb, Marty's customized

baby blue 1949 Ford Coupe drew attention. Marty would boast of how he had fitted the car with a grill from a Mercury Coupe. One day as Marty was polishing the revamped automobile, a neighbor dropped by to compliment him on his handiwork. They talked cars for a while; the man took a liking to Marty and told him about Linda Cohen, a girl just around the corner who had recently broken up with her boyfriend. When Dad met her the following week, it was love at first sight.

Linda, called Lynn or Lindy by her friends and family, was just sixteen, the eldest child of a well-to-do family. Her father had already mapped out her future: an elite college and then marriage to a doctor or dentist. When Marty arrived on the scene with his simple ways and oil-stained hands, Lynn's dad, Milt, the executive director of the Federation of the Handicapped, was incensed. "My daughter is not going out with an uneducated grease monkey."

Marty worked at a local auto shop rebuilding generators and starters, and with the money he earned there, he was soon able to decorate an apartment of his own. Noting the young man's hard work and the couple's adoration of each other, Milt slowly caved in.

Instead of pleading with his boss for a raise, Marty started his own business, an automotive repair shop. Once Lynn had finished dental hygienist school in 1960, the pair wed. Four years later, they felt prepared to start a family. Marty's business was thriving and Lynn enjoyed a position at a dentist's office. They bought a three-bedroom house farther east, in Selden, intending to fill the rooms with a boy and a girl. After months of attempting to conceive, they visited a fertility specialist who gave them the verdict: Marty was infertile. The news was devastating.

Marty and Lynn soon began to consider adoption; one of Marty's older sisters had recently adopted a son, so the idea didn't sound completely foreign to them. Adoption was becoming commonplace. Even their next-door neighbors were going through the administrative process involved in adopting.

Rather than sort through piles of paperwork like their neighbors,

Marty and Lynn called Milt, who stepped in. Through his connection to the United Jewish Appeal (UTA), to which he had been contributing for many years, Milt had heard of a prestigious adoption agency in Manhattan, which connected Jewish families with Jewish babies. Milt made a call to Louise Wise Services and the couple had an appointment the following week.

Though Lynn knew her father had put in a good word for them, the endless scrutiny of the interviews was nerve-racking for her. They were interviewed four times together and once apart to ensure that one of them wasn't concealing any hesitation about adopting. How many times did they have to say that they wanted a child? But among the countless questions they were posed, no one ever asked how they would feel about adopting a child whose parents' medical history was tainted by illness. They never thought about the question of nature versus nurture. They just wanted a family.

Once they were approved, they breathed a sigh of relief, although they would have to wait a little longer. They were told that it was rare to get a newborn because the agency often kept infants for several months to verify that they were in good health.

After a few months, they got the call they had been anxiously awaiting. The next day they drove into the city to the agency, where they picked up their eight-month-old baby boy, whom they named Jay Scott Schein.

All they needed was a little girl to complete the picture. After waiting the three years the agency had suggested, on July 13, 1969, they got a call from Louise Wise that their baby was ready to go home. The adoption of Stacie Elyse Schein was finalized at Suffolk County Courthouse in Hauppauge on November 17, 1970.

PAULA: When Marty and Toni arrive at my apartment, my parents rush to embrace them like long-lost relatives. My mother instantly begins to cry. Later, she tells me that she felt an immediate bond with Elyse's parents because they had had so many of the same experiences.

"Oh my God!" exclaims Toni when she sees me. "You look just like Stacie did when she was in high school. It's incredible."

Although I met Elyse's dad soon after our my reunion with Elyse, I have never met Toni before. She's a perky blonde in her early fifties who I'm guessing was a high school cheerleader.

Even though Elyse has gone by her middle name since after college, her parents insist on calling her Stacie. Occasionally I get confused and refer to her as Stacie myself.

"I hear you're pregnant. Congratulations!" says Toni. "Just think, if we had gotten you instead of Stacie, we would have been grandparents."

I cringe at the notion that Elyse and I are interchangeable. If Marty and Toni had raised me, I might not be pregnant now. I also feel for Elyse, who might be hurt by the comment—as if they wish they had me instead of her.

"There's one question I've been dying to ask you," Toni says. "Did you go to your prom?"

It takes me a moment before I realize that she is asking me about my high school prom, something I didn't even devote much thought to back in 1986.

"No, I didn't go, and I never regretted missing it," I tell her. She seems disappointed.

I think back to my prom night, which I spent with my best friend, Lauren, on my parents' docked sailboat. I remember eating Chinese food out of take-out containers, sipping Bartles & Jaymes wine coolers, and feeding the ducks bread crumbs.

Toni changes the subject. "It's interesting that you both traveled to Europe while you were in high school. That's an amazing coincidence."

"Well, lots of high schoolers go to Europe. I don't think that's so noteworthy," snipes Elyse.

Marty sits silently as his wife interrogates me. Every once in a while, I catch him staring at me. Is he contemplating what his life would have been like if he had adopted both Elyse and me? As genial as Marty and Toni are, I can't imagine having them as parents or spending my formative years in Oklahoma.

The strangest thing about the meeting of the Bernsteins and the Scheins is how utterly mundane it is, considering the extraordinary circumstances. Elyse and I are prone to introspection, overanalysis, and endless debate, but our parents seem to see no reason to rehash the past. Instead of dissecting the absurd situation in which they find themselves, they chat about boating, dogs, and Brooklyn as if they're on a double date.

ELYSE: Embracing me tightly enough to make up for thirty-five years, Marilyn stifles her tears. "You feel like Paula," she says. Her love for Paula envelops me.

Marilyn's short salt-and-pepper hair reveals hints of the ink-black locks I remember from the old photos Paula showed me. Marilyn gazes intently into my eyes. "You look a lot like Paula, but as her mother, I would definitely be able to tell you apart," she says, as if I were trying to pull one over on her.

Bernie's sporty elegance reminds me of an older Groucho Marx. His jovial nature and Marilyn's warmth immediately put me at ease. Even though they don't know me yet, I'm already part of the family. Paula's mom has knitted me a berry-colored poncho and a matching one in blue for Paula.

When we head to a restaurant down the block from Paula's place, we spread out at a family-size table and order brunch. We talk about how the Bernsteins started sailing on Long Island Sound when Paula and I were eleven, anchoring their boat near Port Jefferson. Before we left Long Island, my family had been core members of a group of boaters in Port Jefferson. I wonder if people saluted Paula back then, mistaking her for me.

Dad and Toni are both enthusiastic when the Bernsteins invite them to join them in Hilton Head. The Bernsteins and the Scheins are now one extended family.

Chapter | Thirteen

ELYSE: Now that I'm back in Oklahoma for the holidays, my accent reverts to a southern drawl. Though I spent my formative years here, I only tell people I'm from Oklahoma when it suits me.

We moved to Oklahoma when I was eleven, but I kept my allegiance to the city I yearned for, chanting, "Oklahoma is OK, but I still love New York." While other teenagers bragged of getting drunk at the annual hayride, I longed for the coffeehouse performances and repertory theater that I regularly read about in *The Village Voice*, which I bought at the mall in nearby Texas.

Durant, Oklahoma, pronounced "Doo-rant" by the locals, is just a half hour away from the Red River, where John Wayne defeated the Indians in the film of the same name. There was only one movie theater in town, which everyone went to on Saturday nights, and where the popular kids would make out in the balcony before atoning in church on Sunday morning. In order to be accepted by my classmates, I occasionally took them up on one of their countless offers to visit their congregations. Having a Jewish kid in their midst was so anomalous that instead of mocking me, they concentrated on praying that I would convert.

Baptist churches were plentiful but the closest synagogue was an hour across the border into Texas, in Dallas. Though we were no longer practicing Jews, I still needed the comfort of knowing that a synagogue was nearby, in case I should suddenly turn pious. When

I was seven, my father married my stepmother, and along with her Protestant background came Christmas traditions. Though I rejoiced at the windfall of presents, I was sad to see the menorah relegated to the china cabinet. The only signs that we were Jewish were my father's liberal use of Yiddish expressions and the occasional batch of matzo brei he cooked for us. It was important for me to uphold the Jewish tradition, as it signified the only thing I knew about my birth mother.

When I suggest that we celebrate Chanukah together this year, my parents muster up the necessary excitement and take the menorah out of the cabinet to be dusted. "Do we have the right candles?" I ask worriedly. Though we haven't celebrated in twenty-five years, Dad lights the first candle on the menorah and confidently recites the prayer, "*Baruch atah, Adonai Eloheinu, melech ha'olam . . .*"

When I was in New York recently, Paula proudly showed off her worn pink baby book, which her mother had stuffed with newspaper articles Paula had written and mementos from her childhood. Toni had insisted that my baby book was in the attic, but when we hunted for it, only Jay's turned up.

I must content myself with my own collection of Elyse memorabilia. Since I haven't settled in one place for too long, my boxes of letters and journals are stashed in a secret cabinet in the living room. I plan to move it before Tyler sets fire to the house.

"He's only nineteen." My parents make excuses for him. When I was nineteen, I was going to college and working a part-time job. The fact is, my parents feel too old and too tired to debate with Tyler anymore and easily cave in to his demands rather than put up a fight.

When I confront Tyler about his behavior, he doesn't like that I am on to him, threatening his plush existence. A replica of Jay at the same age, Tyler is just as charismatic as his father. I can't help but soften toward him when I look into his deep blue eyes.

"Finding out about who my mother was from a classmate really

hurt. And then I found out I had a half sister," Tyler says, as if to justify his egotism. Trying to shield Tyler from his birth mother, my
parents had concealed that my brother's troubled ex-girlfriend was
actually his mother.

Hoping we might connect if he knows that my own family story
is equally complicated, I decide this is a good time to confide in him.
"You know, my birth mother was diagnosed as schizophrenic. And
I was separated from my twin," I say. Instead of being drawn into
conversation, he responds vacantly and leaves the room.

I follow him into the living room where I am welcomed by the
din of the whole family cheering along with a football game on the
big-screen TV. Enraptured by the game, they barely notice my entrance.

"Well, there's no doubt I was adopted," I say snidely. Aside from
the occasional match at Wimbledon, I've never been a fan of tele-
vised sports.

Everyone ignores me.

"Who do you want to win?" I ask my brother, figuring he'll have
no opinion and I'll prove that he cares as little for football as I do.

"The winners," he says, as if it were the most obvious answer.

Growing up, Jay was always my idol. Like all the kids in the
neighborhood, I followed him around as if he was the Pied Piper. If
he said camp wasn't cool I would drop out; for that matter, if he told
me to jump off the Brooklyn Bridge, I gladly would jump. He
proudly played the role of big brother, asking me, "Is anyone mess-
ing with you?" and promising to kick anyone's ass who tried.

Now the roles are reversed. Crossing Main Street later that day,
I shield him as if he doesn't know to steer clear of traffic on his own
when I'm not around. "You have to take care of yourself. I want you
to be around until we're old people sitting on the beach together."

"Where, the ocean?" he asks, his eyes widening as if I were inviting him to leave for Long Island immediately. He hasn't been back
to New York since he started displaying signs of mental illness as a
teenager, and it's my dream to help him return for a visit.

I broach the subject of my new twin sister with Jay. I never discussed it with my father, but I'd assumed that they would wait for me to tell him. But I'm wrong.

"You look exactly alike," Jay says. My family must have shown him a photo of Paula and me.

"Imagine what it would have been like having grown up with two little sisters instead of one," I say.

Jay smiles sweetly, and in his eyes I see the reflection of me and Paula as little girls chasing our big brother around the backyard.

When Paula calls me the night before my flight back to Paris, I am careful not to complain. These past three weeks with my family have been emotionally draining but I don't want Paula's pity. My family may be dysfunctional, but they are *my* dysfunctional family and I love them.

PAULA: I wake up with a jolt after an especially vivid dream in which a stranger hands me a photo of my birth mother. I gasp at the monstrous face staring back at me. How could this scary person really be her? But the more I study the picture, the more I see the resemblance.

As I'm wiping the sleep out of my eyes, the phone rings. It's Nancy Segal, the twin expert. The last time we spoke, she was trying to get me to fill out her twin questionnaire. Is she calling because I never sent it back?

No, she wants to see if Elyse and I will appear with her on *Good Morning America*. One of the nation's foremost twin experts, Nancy has made the rounds of various television shows, including appearances on *The Today Show*, *The Oprah Winfrey Show*, and *Dateline*.

"They'll also be featuring a set of female identical twins where one has had a sex change," says Nancy.

"I don't think so," I say before even checking with Elyse. I have no doubt she'd agree with me on this point.

"One more thing," says Nancy casually, "I have been corresponding recently with Lawrence Perlman, a clinical assistant professor in psychiatry at the University of Michigan. He worked on the twin study while he was a twenty-four-year-old clinical psychology student at NYU back in 1968. He has some information about you and your sister."

A flash of anger overcomes me. Knowing that a psychologist I've never heard of possesses details about how Elyse and I spent the first months of our lives—when we know practically nothing—fills me with paranoia. Still, I'm curious to learn what Dr. Perlman recalls about me and Elyse—in particular, whether we had any contact with each other as babies. Perhaps he'll have some insight into the study.

"Please have him send it to me," I ask politely, although I'm raging inside.

One week later, I receive a plain white envelope, and I tear it open. Inside, I find a one-page typed report about our foster mother, titled "Clinical Impression of Mrs. McGowan." On the top right-hand corner of the sheet in capital letters are the names "Marian & Jean," alongside Elyse's and my birth date. I had always known that my name in foster care was Jean, but it will be news to Elyse that she was called Marian.

Apparently, Dr. Perlman had visited us at our foster home when we were twenty-eight days old and noted his detailed observations.

Mrs. McG appeared to be competent in her care of the twins and quite observant. She pointed out some physical differences between them—weight, shape of facial features, birthmarks—which were readily observable upon close scrutiny of the pair. She also noted some differences in behavior—e.g. that Jean tends to be more active than Marian, awakes sooner, cries more lustily and persistently, and is less easily diverted—which were not apparent to me during the course of the visit.... Mrs. McG is very fond of the twins and clearly finds them a joy to care for.... Mrs. McG clearly favors Jean whom she finds the most active and demanding but

seemed to feel somewhat guilty about this, defending her behavior on pragmatic grounds. She tries as much as possible to
provide equal treatment for the twins.

Most people can rely on their parents to tell them about their
first months of life, but all we have to go by is this flimsy sheet of
paper. It is tempting to read too much into every comment. What
does it mean that I cried "more lustily and persistently" and was
"less easily diverted" than Elyse? Were the subtle differences in our
personality obvious even back then? Since Elyse has endured more
losses than I have, I feel irrationally guilty for any extra attention
that Mrs. McGowan showered on me.

I'm relieved to learn that our foster mother seemed to care about
us, although regardless of her true feelings, I assume she would have
put on a good show for a visiting psychologist who was there to observe her behavior. Suddenly, I have a strong desire to locate Mrs.
McGowan, the until-now-nameless woman who cared for us during
the first five months of our lives. Unfortunately, Louise Wise is not
authorized to divulge her full name, and there would have been in-
numerable "Mrs. McGowans" living on Staten Island in the 1960s.

Perhaps when Nancy Segal comes to New York next month,
she'll be able to arrange a meeting with Dr. Perlman. It's unlikely
after all these years he'll be able to remember what Elyse and I were
like as babies, but maybe he'll be able to recall Mrs. McGowan's
first name.

Newborn babies identify their mother by the sound of her voice,
which they are able to hear even in the womb, and by her scent. I
wonder if I was able to recognize Elyse as my twin in the foster
home. Once my parents adopted me, did I scan the nursery looking
for her? Instinctively sensing the magnitude of my loss, did I cry out
for my other half?

ELYSE: Back in Paris, I receive a Klimt card from Paula on which
she has written, "I hope this is not too disturbing for you. I wish I

was there to go over this with you in person." In the envelope, Paula has enclosed a copy of the sole document that Dr. Perlman has retained from the study. The document confirms that Paula and I were placed in the same foster home and were studied for at least the first month of our lives. How surreal being described as Marian, a name our foster mother must have called me. A year ago, I never even knew I spent time in a foster home, and now I wonder what other parts of my past are buried.

In the document, Perlman notes that our foster mother, Mrs. Mc-Gowan, felt guilty about favoring Jean/Paula, whom she considered more active and demanding. Not only was I separated from my birth mother, and later my adoptive mother when she died, but also from my foster mother—and she preferred Paula. I wonder if it's too late for me to experience posttraumatic stress disorder.

"At least now we know that we were together for at least the first month in the same home," Paula says when I call her to talk about the letter.

"That's even worse! Separating us after we had already spent time together. It almost would have been better if they'd separated us immediately at birth."

One thing that Dr. Neubauer has always maintained is that the subjects of his study were never separated for research purposes. "They [Louise Wise Services] decided to do it," Stephanie Saul's *Newsday* article quotes him as saying. " . . . When we learned about the policy, we decided it [gave us] an extraordinary opportunity for research." Even taking this statement, at face value, I am perplexed. If the intention was to study separated twins, why would Paula and I have been kept together in the same foster home?

PAULA: The day after Jesse's third birthday, I brave the harsh February chill to meet Nancy Segal. The moment she strolls into the cavernous bistro in Times Square, I recognize her from her author photo on the back flap of *Entwined Lives: Twins and What They*

Tell Us About Human Behavior. Nancy's youthful enthusiasm and long brown hair belie her age, which I'm guessing is somewhere in the early fifties.

"When are you due?" Nancy asks. Her eyes drift to my visibly pregnant belly, which I've tried my best to camouflage with a black wraparound dress and an oversized shearling coat.

"May eighth," I tell Nancy. "Now that I know I am a twin, everyone keeps asking me if I think I'll give birth to twins. Of course, you and I know that identical twins, unlike fraternal twins, aren't hereditary."

As she nibbles on her salad, Nancy allows me to skim an article that Dr. Perlman has recently written about Neubauer's twin study for *Twin Research and Human Genetics,* the official journal of the Australian-based International Society for Twin Studies.

According to Perlman's article, the Louise Wise families were matched according to parents' ages, socioeconomic status, educational level, religion, and gender/age of older sibling, who was also a Louise Wise adoptee. Including Elyse and me, there were five pairs of twins and one set of triplets, so thirteen individuals were involved.

Perlman doesn't recall any discussion about whether or not it was "inappropriate to conceal the knowledge of the twinship from the families." Although informed consent for research subjects was not yet required, the dictum to respect subjects and not cause psychological harm was firmly accepted at the time. A key premise of the study, according to Perlman, was that the parents and the twins could not know about the twinship because the knowledge could color the results.

Perlman admits in the article that it was strange that none of his fellow researchers ever considered whether the twins had a right to know one another or contemplated whether they might eventually find each other. I'm amazed at how shortsighted they were. Considering that the twins and the triplets were all adopted by middle-class

Jewish families in the New York metropolitan area, they had a reasonable chance of meeting one another at sleepaway camp or school. Hadn't any of Neubauer's colleagues seen *The Parent Trap*?

"Do you think the data from the study should be made available to researchers?" Nancy asks me over cappuccinos.

"I'm conflicted," I say. "I think the twins themselves should have access to the data, but if the study is published, it would send a message to the medical community that it is okay to conduct studies in which the data is unethically obtained."

If Josef Mengele's monstrous "research" could theoretically save a life, should it be used? Mengele's records were never located, so it's a moot point. Comparing Neubauer's "secret study" to Mengele's twin studies is dramatic, but it is still apt. When people hear that Elyse and I were once part of a separated-twin study, most immediately think of Mengele's experimentation.

In an attempt to perfect a master Aryan race, Josef Mengele, the notorious doctor of Auschwitz, conducted gruesome experiments on approximately three thousand identical twins during the Holocaust. As a twin and a Jew, I would have made an ideal subject for him. Mengele came to Auschwitz for the express purpose of studying twins, as a continuation of the work he had done as the assistant to his former professor Count Otmar von Verschuer, at Frankfurt's Institute of Hereditary Biology and Racial Hygiene. To Mengele, Auschwitz, the largest of the Nazi concentration camps, was the key to achieving his mentor's dream. With access to hundreds of thousands of prisoners, Mengele would be able to assemble enough twins for an extensive study.

As early as 1935, Verschuer had written of the necessity of twin research to achieve "complete and reliable determination of what is hereditary in man." It was Verschuer who convinced the German Research Society to financially back Mengele's work. Mengele told one of his colleagues, "It would be a sin, a crime . . . and irresponsible not to utilize the possibilities that Auschwitz had for twin research. There would never be another chance like it."

When new arrivals were unloaded from the early morning trains at the death camp, Mengele made a point of assigning twins, dwarfs, and people with unique physical characteristics to his experimental blocks. Mengele created a replica of an academic research institute as well as a special dissection room. There, the twins were subjected to medical experimentation and surgery, including organ removal, castration, and amputation.

As he saw it, the twins were doomed anyway, so there was no need for Mengele to consider the ethical implications of his work. Mengele's experiments were sadistic: he routinely performed surgeries without anesthesia and some twins were starved, exposed to diseases, or poisoned to track how long they would take to die. Mengele would often kill the twins so he could conduct a postmortem examination. Fewer than two hundred of the approximately three thousand twins survived Mengele's experiments.

"I am inclined to say that nobody should use Dr. Neubauer's research," I tell Nancy. "It sets a dangerous precedent."

Neubauer's data wouldn't be very helpful anyway since the sample group of twins was too small. Also, because the same researchers conducted tests on both twins, they would have been predisposed to find similarities.

"Neubauer does not believe that he did anything wrong," says Nancy, who, along with Dr. Perlman, recently met with Dr. Neubauer at his East Side home. "It may have been Viola Bernard's idea to separate the twins, but it was Neubauer's idea to conduct the research." Nancy adds that Neubauer had tried, without success, to recruit twins from other adoption agencies.

As the check arrives, Nancy proudly presents me with a photograph of her standing alongside Dr. Neubauer, taken during her recent visit with Dr. Perlman. Nancy forces a grin while Dr. Neubauer stares blankly at the camera. With his bushy salt-and-pepper hair, hearty build, and remarkably wrinkle-free complexion, Dr. Neubauer, who is in his early nineties, could easily pass for a sprightly seventy-five. I report back to Elyse about my meeting with Nancy and the picture of Dr. Neubauer. "Maybe the purpose of the twin study was to find the secret to eternal youth!" she says.

ELYSE: I had a very vivid dream last night; doctors were studying me because I was three months pregnant. Empathizing with Paula, who is due to give birth any day, I wonder if I have finally perfected twin telepathy and will receive a sign the exact moment she goes into labor. Though Paula and I often joke about being psychic twins, like everyone else, I will have to wait patiently for news of my niece's arrival.

A mystique has surrounded identical twins since the Middle Ages, when they were both condemned and revered as people possessing special powers, able to psychically communicate. The public is intrigued by the idea of twin ESP, but unfortunately, it doesn't exist. Despite reports of twins feeling each other's pain, finishing each other's sentences, and reading each other's thoughts, scientists haven't found any evidence that extrasensory perception among twins is factual. Aside from identical twins' similar brain waves, it makes perfect sense that two people who share 100 percent of their DNA, as well as many life experiences, can intuit each other's thoughts. Spouses, best friends, and siblings with close bonds often experience the same phenomenon.

Even so, reports of twins' apparent psychic connection continue to baffle scientists and twin researchers alike. Recently, I read about a 1962 case of Bobbie Jean and Betty Jo, thirty-one-year-old identical twin sisters who mysteriously died within minutes of each other. Autopsies performed on the bodies failed to reveal a cause of death. In one newspaper report at the time, a friend of the twins said that the two women were "uncanny in their likeness" all their lives. When one got a toothache, the other did too. When one became ill, the other followed. More eerily, when one sister sang a tune in one part of the house, the other hummed the same song in another room. The sisters were buried side by side. On their death certificate, the cause of death was left blank. Even an FBI investigation failed to find an explanation for their unusual deaths.

A similar unexplained phenomenon occurred in Finland in 1970 when another set of identical twin sisters died within minutes of each other of no apparent reason. The mother of the twenty-three-year-old twins said that there had been an "almost eerie link between the two girls."

PAULA: On bed rest during my ninth month of pregnancy, I dive into Wally Lamb's nine-hundred-page novel *I Know This Much Is True*. The tumultuous tale of a middle-aged divorcé and his self-mutilating schizophrenic twin brother is not exactly light reading, but Lamb's portrayal of the complex relationship between identical twins fascinates me.

"We'd had that telepathy thing off and on our whole lives—had shared each other's life in ways that only twins can. Answering each other's questions, sometimes before the other one even asked," says Lamb's protagonist, Dominick Birdsey.

I lie in bed listening to *Mozart for Mothers-to-be* and let my mind wander to an alternate universe where Elyse and I would have "shared each other's life in ways that only twins can."

Holed up in the apartment, I finally have time to listen to Lawrence Wright's cassette tape of Dr. Viola Bernard. Wright generously agreed to lend me his tape of the interview he conducted with the doctor for his book *Twins: And What They Tell Us About Ourselves*. It is impossible to resurrect Bernard in order to interrogate her, but I have the next best thing.

Bernard was in her late eighties when she spoke with Wright. It is eerie hearing her shaky voice as she tries to justify the decision she made so many years ago. I pretend that it is me, rather than Wright, asking Bernard how she came up with the idea to separate identical twins.

"The existing child psychological literature at the time was of the opinion that the placement of twins who were identical in separate homes had advantages to the children and for the adoptive families," said Bernard.

Maybe so, but no other adoption agencies at the time agreed to separate twins.

"What if the separated twins should meet later in life?" asked Wright.

"There was one situation that by coincidence, there was recognition by a neighbor. One twin knew about it and so I had to tell the other one," Bernard said. She added that she had been in contact with the twins over the years. Later, I learn that after their reunion, Bernard offered the troubled twins free counseling. Considering that she was the one responsible for separating them in the first place, the arrangement doesn't make sense to me.

I begin to ponder how Elyse and I might track down these mystery twins when we don't even know their names.

"I read that since Louise Wise has shut down, their files have been transferred to Spence-Chapin Services," I tell Elyse when I call her in Paris to fill her in on my research. "I called Ronny Diamond at Spence-Chapin and she agreed to send us all the nonidentifying information from our files."

Spence-Chapin is one of the most respected adoption agencies in New York City, and, like Louise Wise, traces its origins to the early 1900s. Ronny, the agency's director of postadoption services, is responsible for meeting with adult adoptees who return to the agency looking for answers. Since Spence-Chapin acquired Louise Wise's records, Ronny's workload has doubled.

"Let her know I give you my permission to get access to my file," says Elyse.

"Maybe she'll know about other reunited Louise Wise twins."

ELYSE: I'm on my way out the door to Monsieur Nathan's for his Thursday night lesson when I get a call from Paula. Shedding my long black wool coat, I make room on my unmade bed to sit down. "I got the Viola Bernard transcript you sent. So, once and for all, we know that they only studied identical twins!" I pronounce. "Can you believe Viola Bernard hauled the twins' placentas in a cab up to Columbia for testing?"

"Back then, I suppose that blood tests were the only way to confirm that they were identical," Paula responds.

Reading the transcript of Lawrence Wright's interview with Dr. Bernard clarifies certain aspects of the study, while others remain as puzzling as ever. If, as Bernard claimed, the separated twins were not placed according to the study criteria, is it simply a coincidence that Paula and I were placed in families with similar socioeconomic backgrounds and older brothers who were the same age? Through minimizing differences in the adoptive families, did the researchers hope to learn to what degree the separated twins would develop the same way, become the same person? Or perhaps, subscribing to Bernard's theory that separation would allow the child to develop a more definite identity, the researchers were convinced that even in similar environments, the separated twins would develop differently. Maybe Bernard was right, and by being reared apart, Paula and I had been better able to develop our separate identities.

"The research was an opportunity, it seemed, to make an additional contribution about child development because they happened to be born that way," said Bernard. By not telling the child that they had a twin, she was "relieving them of their desire to search." How presumptuous of Bernard to assume that by concealing this important truth from me she was doing me a favor.

Perhaps Ronny Diamond at Spence-Chapin can answer some of our questions about our early development. Ronny has located our files, and Paula and I will set up an appointment for us to meet with her when I arrive in New York again next month.

What am I doing in Paris floundering when all the research we need to do is in New York? In addition to being at a distance from new developments in our research, I am anxious to meet my new niece, who is due to arrive soon. I decide it's finally time to come home to New York.

PAULA: "Are you ready to have a baby today?" my midwife asks me after examining me during my thirty-eighth week and finding that I am already four centimeters dilated.

"Yes!" I exclaim. I'm anxious to meet the creature who has been nestled inside my womb for nine months.

At home, I pack my hospital bag and phone friends and family before picking Jesse up from school. Moments after Jesse and I arrive at the apartment, my water breaks, drenching my maternity jeans in amniotic fluid and setting off a flurry of intense contractions.

I phone a neighbor, who has agreed to take Jesse for the night, and call Avo at work and order him home immediately. He jumps in a cab, but by the time he arrives a half hour later, I fear we won't make it to the hospital in time.

Hoping for the best, I climb into the yellow taxi beside Avo. Each time the cab hits a pothole, I groan loudly. When I feel the baby's head begin to crown, I squeeze my legs together and try to hold the baby in.

"Get to the nearest hospital!" I yell. We don't have time to get all the way uptown to the hospital where I had planned to deliver. We're stuck in traffic on the West Side Highway. The cabbie obeys as soon as he can escape the jam.

"Having the baby now?" the security guard asks as I squat in the entry way to St. Vincent's, which happens to be the closest ER, and where nobody is expecting us.

I nod.

Before I know what's happening, a nurse swoops up behind me, helps me into a wheelchair, and rushes me upstairs to the labor and delivery floor. The minute they get me on a bed and the on-call doctor examines me, he confirms what I already knew—this baby is coming *now*.

"You're ten centimeters dilated. Push!" he orders.

Bearing down, I let out a blood-curdling scream and push. Ruby seems to magically appear on my chest. But before I get the chance to embrace her, she is whisked away to the neonatal intensive care unit (NICU) for further examination.

"Her vital signs are good, but due to the precipitous labor, she's in a bit of shock. You realize she was born only eight minutes after you got to the hospital," says the doctor when he returns.

We head down to the NICU, where they make Avo and me don surgical masks and gowns in order to see our baby. Pumped full of postpartum hormones and aching to nurse, I look at Ruby's fragile body, covered with tubes, and sob.

After Avo is ordered home, I lie in my hospital bed, longing to cradle little Ruby in my arms. I can only imagine how alone my birth mother must have felt after giving birth to me and Elyse. I wonder if she was ever given the chance to hold us or even see us. Without any proof she had given birth, after she left the hospital, perhaps she tried to forget that she had ever been pregnant.

· | ·

Later, I read Jan Waldron's memoir, *Giving Away Simone*, in which the author recounts how, as a poor young single woman without any education or family support, she felt she had no choice but to relinquish her baby for adoption.

"When some women have babies, they know the transcendental joy the birth of their children brings and often cannot understand how their own mothers could have walked away from, or never experienced, the euphoria they felt when delivering their own children," writes Waldron, trying to envision how female adoptees think of their birth mothers. "Only a defect, they reason, in the

abandoned child could account for an act of such cold disassocia-
tion during a moment so blessed."

I recall how moments after giving birth to Jesse, the first thought
that crossed my mind was "How could my mother have gone
through this and given me away?"

· | ·

On the morning of May 1, 2006, I scrub my hands with antibacter-
ial soap and put on a surgical gown so I can visit Ruby. As soon as
I enter the NICU, a nurse shares the good news: Ruby is no longer
on IV fluids and her blood sugar is normal. Three days after her
hasty arrival in the world, my baby is coming home.

ELYSE: Frantically checking my e-mail at the Internet café, I am
elated when I receive word that Paula has given birth to a daughter,
Ruby Shaye. I am honored that Paula has chosen the name I preferred. Until I heard the news, I didn't realize how excited I was that
she was having a girl. I imagine Paula's two daughters romping
around together as Paula and I would have, and am ecstatic. At a
going-away party for me held at my friend Fabrice's that night, I
share the good news about Ruby's birth. We sip from a bottle of vintage Bordeaux and listen to Thelonious Monk's *Ruby My Dear* in
honor of my new niece.

My four years in Paris have come to an end. After exchanging
heartfelt good-byes with Fabrice and Jean-Claude last night, I begin
to say au revoir to my neighborhood. I bid farewell to the street ven-
dor who sells me my weekly *Pariscope;* to the *boulangerie* where I
buy my daily baguette; to the plaques on the streets commemorating
the great people who have died here. I am returning home to the
New World.

Chapter | Fourteen

PAULA: I'm home nursing one-month-old Ruby when I get the call. It's Ronny Diamond, the counselor at Spence-Chapin, where our adoption records have been transferred. She is following up on my recent request for updated nonidentifying information from our files.

"At the time of your birth, your birth mother was a voluntary inpatient at a state psychiatric hospital where she had been since her admission on June 24, 1968, after a suicidal gesture," Ronny says sympathetically.

I quickly do the math and my eyes pool with tears as I realize that our birth mother was more than five months pregnant with Elyse and me at the time of her "suicidal gesture." I have to assume her unwanted pregnancy (with twins, no less!) contributed to her desire to end her life. What exactly was her "suicidal gesture"? I wonder. Did she slit her wrists with razor blades or take too many sleeping pills? Either way, if she had succeeded, Elyse and I never would have been born.

I gently set Ruby down in Jesse's old crib, where she nods off to sleep.

"So this was not a onetime problem," I say.

"No, she had a history of several psychiatric hospitalizations since 1959. She had been on Compazine. When you were born she was taking Trilafon because she wasn't displaying overt psychotic symptoms at that point."

I have come to accept the fact that our birth mother was mentally ill, but suddenly I picture her as stark raving mad, the kind of disheveled woman who harasses strangers on the subway and yells unintelligible phrases at nobody in particular.

"Your birth mother was described as a large, obese woman with dark brown hair, brown eyes, bad teeth, and sharp features," Ronny continues.

My irrational hunch during college that my birth mother weighed five hundred pounds might have been accurate after all. Our birth mother must have been significantly overweight for the social worker to describe her as both "large" and "obese" when she was nine months pregnant with twins.

"Since your birth mother's life was so chaotic, she didn't know who the birth father was," says Ronny.

Although the letter from Louise Wise suggested that our birth mother wasn't sure of our birth father's identity, Elyse and I no longer trust the agency's information. Hearing the news from Ronny, who has no reason to obfuscate, hits me hard. I have never thought much about my biological father, but I'm disappointed that now there is little chance I'll ever learn who he was.

Ronny breaks more surprising news: Elyse was adopted at nine months rather than at six months as Louise Wise had mistakenly informed her. I sympathize with Elyse, who was separated from our biological mother, then from her twin, then from our foster mother at nine months, only to lose her adopted mother at age six. Though I consider myself lucky that I was adopted just before the crucial six-months period of child-parent bonding, I realize that there is no scientific way to measure loss.

Sensing that I'm distraught, Ronny tries to console me. "There was no way your mother could have cared for you since she realized that she needed continuing psychiatric help in order to maintain herself," she says.

My composure cracks and I begin to sob.

"She did the right thing in giving us up. I'm crying for her," I mumble through my tears. "Can we still come in and meet with you to talk about all of this?"

"No problem. I know it's a lot to take in."

After hanging up the phone, I am flooded with a mix of emotions. Disappointment that we will likely never know who our birth father is. Relief that Elyse and I turned out relatively normal despite our genetic predisposition.

That night over dinner, I scrutinize Jesse and Ruby.

"How could such perfection be borne out of such sadness?" I ask Avo rhetorically. I wonder if Avo and I should be hypervigilant for any early signs of the disease in Jesse and Ruby.

"Do you think we would have had kids if we had known about my birth mother's mental illness?" I ask Avo that night as we snuggle under our light cotton quilt.

"We would have, but we would have been more nervous about it," he admits.

After Avo dozes off, I lie awake buzzing with thoughts and questions about my birth mother. Did she ever succeed at killing herself? If she's still alive, is she confined to a mental institution? Unable to sleep, I tiptoe to the kitchen table and scribble in my journal. "Learning more about her sad story makes me want to find our birth mother to show her that she did something right in life. She created us and we're okay."

ELYSE: June in New York is scorching. It reminds me of the unbearable French heat wave of 2003, when droves of elderly people, abandoned by their families on summer vacation, were carted into cramped emergency rooms. Drenched in sweat, I wake up on Joseph's couch at his new apartment in Brooklyn. My first morning back, I bolt out of bed before the alarm rings, anxious to get an early start on apartment hunting.

Finding an apartment in New York is more complicated than I

expected. Without a rental history, I might as well be an immigrant fresh off the boat. After several rejections, I wonder if I have an invisible sign on my forehead that says, "I have been living in a tiny box for four years and am completely outside the realm of normality. Don't rent to me." A week later, deflated by so many landlords' refusals, I escape out to my cousin Tracey's house in Northport for a respite. Daydreaming in a lawn chair in her expansive backyard, I am interrupted by the ringing of the phone.

I race inside to pick it up. When I hear Paula's excited tone, I know something is up. "I got my medical information from Spence-Chapin." She tells me everything.

Our birth mother was first institutionalized in 1959, when she was twenty. How dangerously close I came to succumbing to her fate.

At age twenty, I first experimented with drugs. When my friends had long since come down from their highs and were on their way to the diner for breakfast, I continued to lie catatonically in my bed, staring out into space. Unable to reenter the real world, I hopelessly called out "Mommy," unsure if I was invoking Lynn or my birth mother. Ghostly images of my birth mother flashed in my mind. My roommate caressed my brow, trying to console me by telling me that my nightmare would end. For some reason, abandonment was all I could feel at that moment. *Your mother isn't here for you. You are on your own,* I said to myself compulsively. If I had been aware then of my predisposition for mental illness, perhaps I would have steered clear of danger. Or maybe I would have run straight toward it.

Many mothers play Mozart for their unborn children and coo at their bulging bellies. "I keep thinking that when we were in her belly, we must have heard the screams of the other patients at the mental hospital," I say.

"Wow. We've sure come a long way, huh?" says Paula, and we laugh nervously.

Though Paula would not be grappling with this news if I had not found her, I sense her relief at finally knowing the truth. "We're past the age of onset for schizophrenia. We're lucky that we're okay," Paula says.

Did our birth mother really intend to commit suicide, or was her action just an attempt to rid herself of the tiny fetuses inside her? Perhaps we were merely innocent victims of her self-loathing. I think of my friend Jacqueline in Brussels, who, distraught over an unplanned pregnancy at age twenty-one, slit her wrists in a failed attempt to commit suicide. Now, years later, her teenage son struggles with manic depression and Jacqueline is guilt-stricken that she may have passed on her own pain to the child in her womb.

Jacqueline's hypothesis may have been influenced by Françoise Dolto, a French psychoanalyst who theorized that from inside the womb, a fetus is able to sense its mother's emotional state and comprehend it. Because of this belief, Dolto urged parents to talk to the child about everything that could affect it, right from birth.

Paula continues reading the letter to me. " 'She was described as a large, obese woman, with dark brown hair, brown eyes, bad teeth, and sharp features.' " Paula adds, "Like the big bad wolf in a fairy tale." The woman the agency described is unrecognizable to me. Have Paula and I inherited nothing from her but her brown eyes? Picturing an oversized woman in a colorful muumuu, I feel embarrassed. It will be easier for me to tell my family about my birth mother's mental illness, which is somehow less shameful than obesity to me. I wonder if our mother's weight is the root of the eating disorders Paula and I both struggled with. Or perhaps her obesity was due to the medication she was taking.

According to Ronny, our birth mother didn't get prenatal care until two weeks before we were born. Was she so obese that no one at the mental institution noticed her inflated belly? Since her attempt at suicide had failed, she must have simply lived in denial of the growing lives inside her. Our birth mother had been taking Compazine but had switched to Trilafon at the time we were born. I research both medications online, and am relieved that there are no precautions against taking them while pregnant.

"This may surprise you," Paula says, preparing me. My stomach sinks. What else could there be?

"She didn't know who the father was," Paula announces.

"Why did you think I would be surprised?" I ask defensively.

"You said that you thought they might have just been misunderstood lovers. You had a romantic vision of them."

"Well, that's just one picture I imagined. It doesn't mean it was the only one." Still, I'm a bit crushed. I liked to think I was a love child conceived out of a forbidden affair.

"Now we'll never know," I say, dejected. "Unless we meet her one day and she tells us, if she even knows." Trying to lighten the mood, I add, "Well, our birth father must have good teeth!"

Having verified our birth mother's mental state makes me question whether we will continue our search, and I'm apprehensive about what state we may find her in if we do.

"What are we supposed to do if she's in an institution?" Paula wonders, echoing my thoughts. "Will we be obliged to make weekly visits?"

I reassure Paula. "All we owe her is our respect."

According to Ronny's records, at three months I underwent a hernia operation, so the agency kept me in foster care longer to monitor my progress. Paula was placed with her parents at five months, and as a result of the changed variables, the researchers must have dropped us from the study.

So I was left behind. Adopted at nine months, I spent even less time than I thought with my mother, Lynn. I guess Katherine had been confused when she told me I had been adopted at six months.

"Well, at least they were looking out for my best interest and didn't hold me back," Paula says. I scoff at the idea that the agency had our best interest in mind.

Frustrated that I don't have the facts before me, I cannot help but fume that Ronny has sent Paula's medical information but not mine. She didn't explain that I needed to file my own formal request, that Paula's wouldn't suffice.

"I am tempted to call Ronny and give her a piece of my mind," I wail to Paula. Since I have no one to point at, Ronny bears the brunt of my anger. "But I won't," I assure Paula. As upset as I am, I haven't gone off the deep end.

"Don't take this the wrong way, but maybe you should think about therapy," Paula suggests gingerly.

I've analyzed myself for years, and the thought of recounting my epic story from the beginning is dizzying. Still, I cannot help but wonder why Paula is on antidepressants while I am not. Maybe I've been writing off depression as the normal flow of life, an unpredictable cycle I'd long since accepted. Until I met Paula, I never thought I needed therapy. Now I wonder if I have just been pretending to be sane all these years, keeping mental illness at bay.

When I behaved dramatically as a child, my parents would call me Sarah Bernhardt. Is *dramatic* just a code word for *crazy*? In movies, you can always tell that the heroine has gone mad when she starts smearing lipstick across her face. I could go manic right here with all my belongings strewn around the floor. I could lose track of the string of events. Paris. San Francisco. Prague. Paris. How did I end up back in New York, where it all began? If I weren't past the age of onset for schizophrenia, I would fear I might descend into a paranoid spiral.

PAULA: Now that Elyse is in New York, she's able to become a more regular presence in her nieces' life. One afternoon, after we meet for tea at a local café, Elyse accompanies me and Ruby to pick Jesse up from summer camp. Noticing our resemblance, Jesse's preschool teacher says, "I didn't know you had a sister."

"I didn't either," I joke, giving her the abbreviated version of our reunion story.

"When I learn someone is adopted, I know their parents wanted them very badly," Jesse's teacher says sweetly.

"The flip side to being wanted by our adoptive parents is that our birth parents didn't want us," I say to Elyse later as we stroll to the playground with the girls on this balmy summer day. "That hadn't struck me until recently."

"Well, they wanted the best for us and they knew they couldn't provide for us. That doesn't mean they didn't want us," says Elyse.

Growing up, I was proud to be adopted. After all, unlike some kids who were rumored to be the product of an "accident," I was chosen. My parents wanted me. I treasured the lime-green hard-cover book my parents gave me, the touching story of *The Chosen Baby*. It seemed to me the baby in the book was selected from an as-sortment of other babies at the adoption agency because he was so special. He had no biological parents to confuse matters and seemed to emerge fully formed from the adoption agency.

Only now can I see the fallacy of *The Chosen Baby*. Before I could be "chosen" by my adoptive parents (although they did not pick me out of a tot lineup at the adoption agency, as I had imag-ined), I had to be relinquished by my biological parents. In her book *Lost and Found: The Adoption Experience,* published in 1979, adoptee advocate Betty Jean Lifton writes about *The Chosen Baby,* showing how it "focused on how the baby came into the family, not how he came into the world. The word *chosen* was meant to act magically on the child's psyche, dispelling all curiosity about the missing parts of the story."

The romantic tale handily glossed over the truth that while I was eventually chosen, I was, in fact, my parents' second choice since they initially tried to conceive their own biological child. Although my parents were entirely comfortable with the notion of adoption and never shied away from the subject with my brother or me, they no doubt preferred to view us as children without any history. *The Chosen Baby* presents an idealistic vision suggesting that there is one perfect baby waiting to be matched with one perfect couple. My parents didn't choose me in particular. They chose to adopt a baby girl. I was the one selected for them.

Believing that I had been chosen put a huge responsibility on me as a child. If my parents chose me, I reasoned, I'd better behave myself so they wouldn't change their minds and "unchoose" me. Only now do I see that I felt obligated to compensate for the biological children my parents couldn't have. I would have to be better than the phantom biological child whose birthright I felt I had usurped.

I never sensed any regret in my parents about not having their own biological child, but surely they must have fantasized about how a child of their own flesh and blood would have turned out. As a teenager struggling with my weight and severe acne, I thought that if I had been my parents' biological child, I would have been naturally thin, with clear skin. Like them, I probably would have had black hair, olive skin, and blue eyes. And maybe I wouldn't have been depressed.

"You were so lucky to have been adopted by such great parents," friends habitually reminded me when I was growing up. However true that may be, the comment suggested that I should be thankful to have been chosen and rescued from my inevitable fate as an orphan. Later, when my brain was clouded by depression, I felt I had no right to feel so despondent when I was so lucky.

ELYSE: I have no trouble acclimating to my temporary residence, a luxurious three-bedroom apartment with a balcony where I can sit outside to enjoy my morning coffee. After living so far away from each other, Paula and I are now neighbors. The emergency exit at the rear of my building leads directly to the entrance of Paula's brownstone, where I can magically appear to bring over a book or lend a hand with Ruby.

Holding delicate Ruby, who is just six weeks old, feels like the most natural thing. Examining her tiny features and the soft tuft of auburn hair on her head, I can't help but see myself. Jesse treats me like the aunt she always knew, but because I met her when she was two and a half, I was deprived of seeing her first steps. With Ruby, I will be around to cherish each milestone. "Who does she remind you of?" I ask Dad after sending him a photo of Ruby.

"You," responds Dad with an incredulous chuckle.

Though I am proud of my new lineage, I am pleased to confirm that I couldn't possibly love Ruby more than I do Tyler. My love for Tyler is stronger than blood.

Before I moved to New York, my only meetings with Paula were short and intense. Now we have the leisure of meeting regularly for tuna-melt lunches and conversation. Even eating together is a moment of discovery as we compare our tastes. I forget to put ice in Paula's water, the way she likes it, and I have to remind her that I prefer pickles and mustard with my sandwich.

Sometimes while sitting on the balcony reading, I watch Paula and her daughters playing in the courtyard below with a cluster of moms and children. I look up from my book whenever I am interrupted by the gleeful squeals of Jesse running from a miniature sadist with a water hose.

· | ·

Now that I am in New York for the foreseeable future, Paula and I begin to approach our investigation more formally. Until now, we'd just been hoping to glean more information about separated identical twins. But we are beginning to refine our goals. One is to obtain the results of Neubauer's study and learn about his possible conclusions. A second goal is to locate any of the other separated twins from the study. Last, Paula and I hope to find out what became of our birth mother, though we are keeping that one at arm's length for the moment.

Paula drops by the apartment one afternoon so we can draft a letter to the Jewish Board of Family and Children's Services (JBFCS), the not-for-profit mental health and social service agency. The JBFCS continues to operate the illustrious Child Development Center, which was headed by Dr. Neubauer at the time of the twin study. Since the JBFCS has donated the CDC's twin study data to Yale University's archives, which are closed until 2066, we must appeal to them for access.

"As subjects of Dr. Neubauer's study of separated identical twins, we feel that the CDC files would be of invaluable assistance to us," we write in a formal letter. "We would benefit immensely from the insight into the study the files could provide us with."

A week later, Paula races around the corner to my sublet with their response so we can put our heads together and come up with a game plan.

"As you may know, these files are to be held as confidential files for seventy-five years from the date of receipt of the donation. Accordingly, we are not prepared to grant access to these files," reads the letter from Ellen Josem, the JBFCS general counsel.

In my plush air-conditioned living room, Paula and I divvy up the day's detective duties.

"Why don't you call the lawyer from the JBFCS and I'll call the firemen twins?" I delegate to Paula as she settles herself at the kitchen table, taking out her notebook and Pilot Precise pen, the same kind I use.

Though "the firemen twins" Mark Newman and Jerry Levey, were not part of any study, Paula and I figure that as separated twins who reunited twenty years ago at age thirty-one, they might have some insight into our developing relationship.

Mark responds naturally to my inquiry, during a break at the firehouse. Though his parents were unaware that he had a twin, Mark, like me, had the sense that something was missing in his life. He elucidates, "The recurring dreams I used to have about a baby like me being operated on stopped when I met Jerry."

"I was very happy with who I was," Mark volunteers before I can probe any deeper. "When we met, I told Jerry, 'I ain't changing 'cause you're here.' "

When the pair first met, they discovered that they were quite alike. Not only did both bald, six-foot-four-inch brothers enjoy deep-sea fishing and beer drinking, they both held their beers with their pinky finger placed beneath the bottles. Like other separated twins, they were shocked to find that they used the same gestures. "It was spooky," said Jerry, speaking about their reunion. Since they had exactly the same interests, Mark eventually wondered why he would want to spend time with his twin at all. "Why should I hang out with him if he's just like me? If he's doing the same thing?"

"How funny! I can't imagine not wanting to hang out with you just because we have the same taste in film," I say to Paula when I get off the phone.

PAULA: "I am honestly amazed at your lack of empathy," I tell Ms. Josem, the JBFCS lawyer, hoping she'll reconsider her decision.

As Elyse nods approvingly, urging me on, I act as if I'm a lawyer delivering my closing arguments.

"The JBFCS is supposed to look after the welfare of children. We were those children. Whom does it benefit to keep this information from us? Isn't it our right to access information that could give us a clearer idea of what was done?"

Ms. Josem says she is not authorized to comment.

"Who are they protecting? It's a nonprofit organization meant to help Jewish families and children," mutters Elyse as she prepares tuna melts for our lunch.

My own mind drifts from our investigations. Despite the toys strewn across the wood floor, I allow myself to imagine Elyse and me enjoying the bachelorette lifestyle in this oversize loft. If we had grown up together, as young college grads, we might have shared an apartment in the city until we got our careers off the ground.

ELYSE: Hearing about our interest in searching for our birth mother, a friend of a friend recently suggested we get in touch with Nancy Kahn, a fellow Louise Wise adoptee who has become an unofficial search expert.

I spot Nancy at the entrance of a pub a block away from the New York Public Library, where we have arranged to meet her for lunch. Nancy is just a few years older than us, and her olive skin has the healthy glow of long weekends spent in the Hamptons. In a white linen suit and matching leather pumps, she looks like one of the elegant New Yorkers whom ambitious women in the Midwest moon over while perusing the Sunday *Times* Styles section. Nancy welcomes Paula and me with a warm hug, then unobtrusively glances back and forth to compare us in a way we have become accustomed to.

"It took hours to find my birth name." Nancy begins her tale amid the din of Midtown businessmen on their lunch breaks. Since her joyful reunion with her birth mother last year, Nancy has exalted the importance of seeking out one's roots and has taken many adoptees like Paula and me under her wing.

"The library was about to close and then I found her last name—all the way in the W's!" Nancy tracked down her birth mother through classmates.com. When they reunited, Nancy learned that her birth mother had been a promising psychology major and talented dancer when she got pregnant during an affair with a professor. I know both Paula and I are thinking about how our birth mother, plagued by psychotic episodes, probably never returned to college.

"You know, Pam Slaton is a searcher who specializes in Louise Wise adoptions," Nancy offers. "Even if you locate your birth name, it would be hard to track your birth mother down if she got married."

"I don't think she was a candidate for marriage," Paula says ruefully. Given the information we've recently had confirmed by Ronny Diamond, Paula and I are both skeptical that our birth mother will be in any condition to welcome us with open arms. We mainly hope to glean more insight into our birth family.

"She was on medication for schizophrenia," I say bluntly, silencing any further comments Nancy has to make on the subject. I do not confide in her about our birth mother's attempted suicide.

Nancy shows us an eloquent letter that her birth mother had written her, and tears well up in my eyes. In the letter, Nancy's birth mother describes her delight in holding her infant daughter in her arms. Hearing her story makes me wonder if our birth mother ever got a chance to hold us in her arms. Paula, visibly moved by Nancy's depiction of her birth mother's difficulty in surrendering her, begins to cry. She must be thinking the same thing as I am: our story will never have a fairy-tale ending.

Nancy offers us a photocopy of her page from the registry. Next to her birth name, which she has circled in ink, she has penned the name that she has been called all her life. I place the precious page directly in my folder, to help me psychologically prepare for our upcoming visit to the library

"You know, I'll call my friend Bruce's father, Jerry, who is a former president of Louise Wise. Maybe he'll be able to help you. Bruce was also adopted from Louise Wise," Nancy offers after hearing of our quest to get into the Yale archives. As we get up to leave, we notice that besides a few stragglers lingering over a midday scotch, we are the last ones at the pub.

"All of us Louise Wise adoptees are family," Nancy says as she hugs us good-bye.

PAULA: Strolling down East Ninety-fourth Street on my way to Ronny Diamond's office at Spence-Chapin, I am surprised when I spot the tarnished brass plaque for Louise Wise Services. I had no idea that the two prestigious adoption agencies were next door to each other. I imagine eager couples interviewing at Spence-Chapin before popping in to fill out an application next door. Since Louise Wise shuttered its doors last year, the building has been transformed into a luxurious private residence.

I last walked down this sidewalk in 1987, when I came to meet with Barbara Miller to learn about my origins. Here I am again, so many years later, still on a quest for the truth.

Seated in the lobby of Spence-Chapin, I visualize all the prospective adoptive parents who patiently waited here hoping to be granted the gift of parenthood. The walls are lined with photos of beautiful smiling children of every color. It looks like one big Benetton ad.

Once we're ushered into Ronny's office, I begin tentatively. "We wanted to meet with you because we've gotten so many different versions of the facts from Louise Wise and we're not sure what to believe." Elyse perches nervously next to me on the well-worn couch.

"Anytime there's deception, it softens the foundation of trust," says Ronny. Her curly, honey-colored hair and soft features match her maternal demeanor perfectly, and I feel soothed by her voice.

"At the time we were adopted, did Spence-Chapin disclose any information to adoptive parents about the child's family history of mental illness?" I ask.

"God, your smile is exactly the same!" exclaims Ronny before answering my question. "At the time, generally, people believed that adoption was a clean slate and that knowing anything negative in one's medical history would create a self-fulfilling prophecy."

Elyse leaps in. "The truth is I still question our birth mother's diagnosis," she says. "Her psychotic outbursts could have been her shouting 'No Vietnam!' in the streets with peace signs painted on her cheeks."

"Regardless, your birth mother wasn't in any position to raise a child," says Ronny.

"I understand that logically," says Elyse. "But I think in the back of every adoptee's mind is that feeling of abandonment."

Ronny nods sympathetically. Because she is such a good listener, and because Elyse and I feel so comfortable revealing our concerns to her, the meeting ends up feeling more like a therapy session than anything else. Elyse and I hug Ronny, and she escorts us out of the building, where she takes our photo in front of Louise Wise's former headquarters. Wearing pastel sundresses and sandals, Elyse and I grin for the camera as if to say, "This is where it all began."

· | ·

Emerging from the subway tunnel as it barrels over the Manhattan Bridge toward Brooklyn, the train is flooded with afternoon light.

Elyse and I sit side by side, our faces inches apart. It is impossible for us to avoid each other's gaze. Sometimes I wish I could temporarily switch our twinship off. Simply being around Elyse can be exhausting. Every comment of hers prompts me to ask myself, "Do I feel that way?" and every gesture of hers seems like one of mine amplified a thousand times.

"Your facial gestures are so dramatic," Elyse says, as if she had been reading my mind.

"That's funny, because I was just thinking the same thing about yours. They're like mine, only more intense."

"No, I think yours are like mine, but more extreme. Whereas I raise my eyebrows a little bit when I want to make a point, you raise yours a lot. You seem to be overemphasizing everything you say."

"In general, I think you're more theatrical than I am," I say.

"You're right, but I still think your facial gestures are more exaggerated," says Elyse.

"Do you find it irritating?"

"A little," she confesses.

"And I find it irritating to see your gestures, because I wonder if mine are equally dramatic."

I'm hurt to hear that I get on her nerves and I sense that I've bruised Elyse's feelings as well. Suddenly, self-conscious about our expressions, Elyse and I attempt to rid our faces of any shred of personality. We sit in awkward silence for the rest of the ride. I have to assume we'll eventually get used to this.

On my walk home from the subway station, I gaze at my reflection in store windows and car mirrors trying to gauge my own expressions. But it's impossible to behave naturally, and I realize I'll never be able to see myself the way others see me.

Chapter | Fifteen

PAULA: Even when I am "off duty," everything I do seems somehow to link to the research Elyse and I have been conducting. Since so many journalists, twins, and adoptive parents live in Park Slope, it seems that everyone has a tale to tell upon hearing my story. Occasionally, one of these random encounters results in a lead in our investigation.

One balmy summer afternoon at the Third Street Playground, I strike up a conversation with a fellow mom while pushing Jesse and Ruby on the swings. Trading tidbits about our lives, I let it slip that I recently found out that I am a twin.

"You won't believe it, but I know someone else who was also adopted from Louise Wise and found out she had a twin," says the petite brunette. "I think she was in some sort of study." She finds a piece of scrap paper, jots down her friend Sara's phone number on it, and hands it to me. "Give her a call," she says. It's that easy.

That night, when I call Sara, she is flabbergasted to hear from another separated Louise Wise twin. I listen in rapt attention as Sara shares the story of how she discovered she had a twin.

Sara first had an inkling that she had a twin when one afternoon, at age seven, she went to visit her friend Amanda, who lived down the block. Like Sara, Amanda and her brother, Jeffrey, had also been adopted from Louise Wise. "I remember that Amanda and Jeffrey told me they were just at their friends' house and there was a little girl there who looked just like me."

At seven, Sara wasn't savvy enough to connect her friend's comment with the fact that psychologists sometimes visited the house to test her abilities and to film her. But once Sara's parents heard what Amanda and Jeffrey had said, they promptly called Louise Wise to investigate the strange incident.

The agency confessed that Sara had a twin named Jill who also lived with her adoptive family in the New York area. Sara's parents were furious when they learned that the child development study that they had agreed to participate in was, in actuality, a twin study. Once the secret was revealed, Louise Wise called Jill's parents to inform them that their daughter was a twin. The agency implored both families not to tell their daughters the truth. "My parents were told, 'You have to keep them away from each other. It will be devastating if they meet,' " says Sara. "My parents went along with whatever they said because they didn't want to do any further damage. They did what the agency told them was right." Both families promptly dropped out of Neubauer's twin study.

Years later, in 1977, a week before her seventeenth birthday, Sara participated in a swim meet at which another swimmer told her she looked exactly like a girl from her school. The comment resonated with Sara, who had always sensed that her parents were withholding a family secret from her. Soon after the swim meet, Sara met her twin sister, Jill, for the first time. In addition to competitive swimming, they had a lot in common. They each had an older sibling who was also adopted from Louise Wise, and as adults, they both went on to marry Irish men. After Sara's reunion with Jill, her parents confessed that they had known she had a twin since the incident at the neighbors' house when she was seven.

"I felt the earth fall under my feet. I lost all trust in anything. It was very damaging. I was at such an impressionable age," recalls Sara.

Although Sara had initially been excited about the idea of having a twin, the reality was not as easy to accept. Away at college, nineteen-year-old Sara became depressed and dropped out of school. Like Sara, Jill also dropped out of college and never returned. Distraught about their daughter's mental state, Sara's parents contacted Viola Bernard at Louise Wise, the woman responsible for separating Sara from her twin in the first place. Dr. Bernard said she couldn't officially take Sara on as a patient, but that she would meet with her free of charge each week and try to counsel her. She also agreed to provide counseling to Sara's twin.

Sara doesn't recall Dr. Bernard ever apologizing for separating her from her twin or for misleading her family about the twin study. "I can still hear Dr. Bernard's voice in my head saying, 'I wanted to make two families happy.' My parents bought the theory. I bought it too," Sara remembers.

Sara and Jill, soon after their reunion, tracked down their biological mother, who, they learned, suffered from depression. Both sisters, now in their late forties, have been diagnosed with bipolar disorder, also known as manic-depressive illness, for which each has been intermittently hospitalized. Research has shown that there is a strong genetic component in bipolar disorder. If one identical twin has the disease, the other twin has a 70 to 80 percent chance of also suffering from it, in contrast to the 10 to 16 percent chance for fraternal twins.

I recall my conversation with the *Newsday* reporter Stephanie Saul, which first made me consider the possibility that one purpose of the study was to determine the heritability of mental illness. In addition to the depression that has plagued Elyse and me throughout our lives, as children all three of the triplets in the study saw psychologists; one committed suicide as an adult. Now, with the knowledge that Sara and Jill suffer from bipolar disorder, it's getting harder to discount this hypothesis.

"The fact that Sara and Jill also suffered from mental illness, as did their birth mother, makes me wonder. Maybe Dr. Neubauer really was looking into the hereditability of mental illness," I tell

Elyse, who seems to be coming around to the idea that this theory could have been true.

We decide the time has come to try to force the issue of a meeting with Dr. Neubauer in the hope that we can finally get some answers. At home, I phone Dr. Neubauer and do my best to sound as nonconfrontational as possible. After reminding him who I am, I request a meeting.

"You know it was Louise Wise who separated the twins. That wasn't our decision," he insists.

"Yes, we understand that it was Viola Bernard's theory that twins would be better off if they were separated and raised separately," I concede.

Rather than hang up on me again, Dr. Neubauer says, "Call me back another time." There's some hope after all.

ELYSE: At a French café in Prospect Heights, I casually ask the manager if they're hiring. The cozy restaurant, with its warmly painted walls plastered with French posters for pastis, reminds me of the one I worked at in San Francisco. Since Paula's and my research has been all-consuming, I'm relieved at the ease with which I land the part-time waitressing job. Making small talk with customers while I balance plates, I immediately feel at home.

In the heat of midsummer, our investigation is actually starting to build up momentum. On days like this it feels as if Paula and I are twin Nancy Drews, girl detectives living in a story book.

Paula and I recently received a letter from the JBFCS's lawyer, Ellen Josem, denying our request to obtain access to the twin study archives at Yale. As promised, Nancy has set up a meeting for us with a former president of the board of Louise Wise, Jerome Feniger. Paula and I hope that Feniger will be able to convince the board to open the archives of the study, revealing its true purpose. We'll be one step closer to unlocking our past.

Escaping the hustle and bustle of the sweltering streets around

Grand Central Station, Paula and I breeze into the elite Yale Club. With formally attired concierges at our service and a chandelier illuminating our way, we could be in a luxury hotel. Nancy greets us at the door in a sleek little black dress, her skin even more bronzed than when we last met. Nancy introduces us to a friend, Mr. Feniger's son, Bruce, who was also adopted from Louise Wise. It appears we have a quorum for an impromptu meeting of the Louise Wise adoptee club.

Nancy and Bruce lead us into the regal sitting room, where portraits of U.S. presidents who are Yale alumni adorn the ivory white walls. The irony that we are trying to get into the archives at Yale as we sit in their exclusive clubhouse does not escape me. Jerome Feniger, an imposing man in his mid-seventies, sits in a high-backed armchair like a judge. Sitting before him, it's as if we're enlisting the help of the great and powerful Wizard of Oz.

We make our case yet again.

Feniger, having taken time from his busy social schedule to meet us, gets directly to the point. "What do you hope to accomplish?" he asks in a loud drawl.

"We hope to understand a little bit more about what happened," Paula responds.

"Where'd you go to college?" he asks us.

"Wellesley," Paula answers.

"Oh my goodness!" he exclaims. "You know, that's Hillary's school."

As Feniger gravitates toward Paula, I feel invisible.

"Stony Brook," I respond, when he asks me the same question.

"You got no complaints either," Feniger says to me. "Well, you both went to college." Feniger states the obvious. It seems he will begin the same lecture we have heard from our fathers and the lawyer who told us we had no case. Forget about all of this. You have found each other. You turned out fine. Get on with your lives.

It occurs to me that Feniger has the mistaken impression that we are asking him for help in finding our birth family. As an adoptive father, he is defensive. I try another tack.

"Paula and I are both very happy with our families," I reassure him. "In any case, studies have shown there is no correlation between adoptees' satisfaction with their adoptive families and searching for their birth families." I explain what we're really after.

"If the records at Yale were opened up, would you be satisfied?" Feniger asks. "Would that be the end of your trail?"

"That's all we want," Paula assures him.

Feniger reluctantly agrees to help us. "From where you're sitting, we have a certain influence at Yale," he says. With Presidents Ford, Bush (both father and son), and Clinton looming above us, I am inclined to believe him. "Just promise that once I do this for you, I won't ever hear from you again."

Paula and I have to laugh at Feniger's directness.

"We promise!" we respond in unison.

· | ·

Next stop on our investigative trail: the Columbia University Health Sciences Library, to which Dr. Viola Bernard's notes, letters, and files were donated upon her death in 1998. With our summery dresses and backpacks, Paula and I could easily be mistaken for Columbia students. Dr. Bernard's archives are stored in the basement; we are prohibited from entering with more than a pencil. We set our bags aside and take seats across from each other at one of the few wooden tables in the spare room.

Unlike the twin study archives housed at Yale, at Columbia the majority of Bernard's papers are open to the public. Unfortunately, the three boxes that interest us most—the ones related to the Child Development Center twin study—are closed until January 1, 2021. Still, we are hopeful that perhaps Bernard forgot to erase every mention of the twin study, or that we'll be able to read between the lines.

Dr. Bernard was apparently a copious note taker and she seems to have saved every piece of paper that ever crossed her desk. Her archives fill 128.5 cubic feet and amount to 378 boxes, 5 more over-size boxes, and 3 folders. Bernard's records related to Louise Wise alone fill 112 boxes.

Pretending that Dr. Bernard herself is guiding us through our journey, we rely on her scrawled notes to point us in the right direction. We perk up whenever we find anything related to the heritability of mental illness. In Dr. Bernard's affidavit during the Michael Juman lawsuit against Louise Wise in 1996, she suggested that the agency purposely placed children with a genetic history of psychological problems with adoptive parents who weren't concerned about hereditary factors. In their interview with Louise Wise's social worker before they adopted Michael, the Jumans made it clear that they felt that nurture trumped nature. By saying they weren't concerned about hereditary issues, our own parents may have unwittingly asked to be given a child with a family history of mental health problems.

Dr. Bernard asserted during the Juman court case that in 1965, when Michael was adopted, there was no definitive scientific information about the heritability of schizophrenia. But articles in her file prove otherwise. One 1953 study among her papers found a significantly higher incidence of schizophrenia among the relatives of schizophrenics than in the general population. It strikes me and Paula as suspect that so many of the articles that Dr. Bernard saved relate to schizophrenia.

Reading a 1958 letter to Dr. Bernard from the adoption department at Louise Wise, we learn that Louise Wise told adoptive parents about mental illness in a child's biological background only if the child was born in a mental institution. "In other words, we have done it when there has been no other choice. . . . I told the staff that you [Dr. Bernard] . . . felt that where there has been a definitive diagnosis of mental illness, regardless of whether or not the child was actually born in a mental hospital, we have a responsibility in sharing this with the adoptive parents. Everybody on the staff took exception with this."

If Dr. Bernard didn't believe that mental illnesses were heritable, why would she think it was important to inform the adoptive parents of their child's mental health history?

"I think I found something!" Paula exclaims and I hurry to look over her shoulder at the notes from a January 1964 staff meeting of the adoption department at Louise Wise. The agenda of the meeting was to review the practice of sharing information about a child's biological background with prospective adoptive parents. The meeting's secretary summarized Dr. Bernard's comments: "Would we relieve discomfort by sharing information and letting parents decide? Would this stir up anxiety needlessly? . . . Relative to examination of experience is the CDC study of the development of twins in whose background there is a good deal of psychopathology."

Here it is—some sign that one purpose of the study was, in fact, to examine the heritability of mental illness.

Our investigation is progressing more rapidly than we expected so we ignore our grumbling stomachs and decide to postpone lunch. Every article that Dr. Bernard saved and underlined or annotated prompts further questioning. When we are unable to decipher Bernard's scrawl, we wish she were around to explain her annotations. Bernard wrote three exclamation points and circled "Mental Illness" in a 1971 article, "Medical Genetics and Adoption."

"Adoption agencies could offer crucial data for twin studies, if it were possible to place identical twins separately, and keep central (national) records so that they could be followed through life," the article states. A handwritten asterisk highlights the sentence that notes that there is a "high concordance for schizophrenia in identical twins reared apart, which differs little from that for identical twins reared together." It seems even more apparent now that Dr. Bernard was interested in studying twins to examine the relative effects of nature and nurture on the development of schizophrenia.

Our discovery is followed quickly by another. "Aha!" Paula exclaims, interrupting the silence in the library.

"What is it?" I ask, peering over at the open file. The librarian turns toward us, also curious. Paula shows me a letter Dr. Bernard sent to Florence Kreech, then the executive director of Louise Wise, which makes clear that by 1976 Louise Wise was actively trying to conceal the twin study from the public. In the letter, dated March 1976, Dr. Bernard wrote: "We are still being very careful about the research and do not wish to share information about it, especially in these days of informed consent concerns." By 1976, the CDC was no longer recruiting twins for the study, but researchers continued to accumulate data.

Seemingly frightened that a colleague was on to Louise Wise's involvement in the twin study, Kreech reassures Bernard in a separate letter that she has not revealed anything about whether they separated multiple-birth children or not.

Yet we find a letter written in 1965 to Viola Bernard from the agency's executive director at the time, Florence G. Brown, who indicates that Louise Wise Services was trying to "help" other adoption agencies willing to participate in the CDC study. "As long as we are not urging them to separate the twins, I really do not understand why the 'higher ups' should raise so many objections," wrote Ms. Brown.

One article in Dr. Bernard's adoption file particularly piques my attention: "Theoretical Implications of Adoption Research," written by Leon J. Yarrow in 1965. Yarrow writes that children separated from their mother figures during the critical period of relationship development may experience damage affecting their capacity to form deep interpersonal relationships. According to the article, some infants show disturbance following separation from a mother figure as early as three months.

I am deeply saddened when I read Yarrow's conclusion that *all* infants separated from their maternal figure after six months showed psychological disturbance. Having been one of the children placed late, at nine months, I mourn for the abandoned orphan I once was.

Yarrow's theory makes me think about the updated letter I finally received from Ronny Diamond at Spence-Chapin, which chronicled my transition into my adoptive home. The record reveals that I "showed some anxiety in leaving the foster mother," which is not surprising since she had been my sole maternal figure. The letter confirms that I was immediately attracted to my new brother Jay, in whom I must have found a surrogate twin.

Since Bernard has marked "foster care" in the margins of the 1965 Yarrow article, and underlined "critical periods of separation," I begin to suspect that one of Bernard's goals was not only to use twins to understand the causes of mental illness, but also to gauge the impact of maternal separation on a child's development. Even more disturbing is the possibility that Bernard could have been interested in limiting the child's social and sensory stimulation in the foster home in order to study the importance of emotional involvement in infancy. Paula and I are horrified by the idea that one or both of us could have been deprived of care in the foster home. Paranoia strikes me as I imagine our foster home as a living laboratory.

Before the publication of the Yarrow article, the topic of early adoptee placement had already been discussed at Louise Wise. At a staff meeting in 1964, members agreed that it was essential to place infants with well-chosen parents as soon as possible. The only exceptions they made were in what they considered to be problem situations like children of psychotic parents and mixed-race children. But if they suspected that Paula and I might display problematic behavior because of our birth mother's mental illness, why was I the only one to be held back?

Analyzing the dark scribbles Dr. Bernard has made in the margins of Yarrow's article, I realize that the agency may also have been interested in how mothers and children adapt to each other. At one point, Yarrow suggests the intriguing possibility of studying twins placed with different mothers. Surely Louise Wise, which had been collaborating with Neubauer on the twin study since the early '50s, must have considered such a study relevant to its child-placing practice. Neubauer would have been interested in how humans with identical genetic endowments influence their environment.

In a sense, the psychological literature of the '60s could be formulating the hypothesis that the child shapes the parent, rather than the other way around. Since Paula and I shared physical characteristics, we may have elicited similar responses from our families. Our amiable nature would have ensured that our parents would react to us similarly.

Or was the study an attempt to examine the effect of differing parenting techniques on establishing identity? Though our family structures changed with the death of my mother, at the time of our adoptions we joined families with a very similar makeup. Recalling the story of Amy and Beth, whose mothers reacted differently to their capricious tastes, I wonder if the agency deemed one of our mothers to be more indulgent and the other more strict.

With so many questions left unanswered, Paula and I are more determined than ever to gain access to the archives at Yale and to meet with Dr. Neubauer. Every time we get him on the phone, he tells us to call back next week. Is he trying to postpone our meeting indefinitely or wear down our resolve?

PAULA: Taking a brisk walk around Prospect Park on a late August morning, I bounce along to the beat of George Clinton until my cell phone rings.

"We got your fax," says a young woman representing the JBFCS, the gatekeeper for the twin study archives at Yale. We had recently faxed them an appeal, which dropped Jerome Feniger's name. "And we're looking into how we can help you. We are working carefully to see if we can do the right thing—whatever that may be."

I make all the appropriate grateful noises.

"As soon as we have a formal decision, you'll hear from our legal counsel," the woman says.

All praise to the great and powerful Feniger, who seems to have opened up a door that had previously been shut in our face.

Sweaty and out of breath from my speed-walk around the park, I phone Elyse and share the good news.

"It seems we have a shot at getting into the Yale archives after all!"

"That's amazing! It's all happening so fast. And just think, on Monday, we could find out our birth mother's name at the New York Public Library!" says Elyse.

Chapter Sixteen

PAULA: I'm not an especially superstitious person, but I am religious about kissing Avo good-bye before he leaves for his office just in case tragedy strikes and I never see him again. For the same reason, we make a point of resolving any disagreements before going to bed. But on this particular morning, Avo is so preoccupied by the ongoing distribution negotiations for an independent film he has directed, he rushes out the door before I can give him a proper good-bye.

Even though I know it will make him late for work, I call Avo on his cell phone and ask him to come home. Without any questions, he hurries back to me.

"What's up?" he asks.

"I know I'm acting all blasé about going to the library today, but it is a pretty big deal," I say as tears begin to pool in my eyes. Nearly a year and a half after that fateful first phone call, Elyse and I are finally ready to start the process of finding our birth mother.

Avo wraps his arms around me and squeezes me tight.

"By the time I see you tonight, I could know her name," I say.

Focused on the mission ahead, Elyse and I climb the well-worn stone steps of the main branch of the New York Public Library on Fifth Avenue. The imposing lion statues stand guard in front of the Beaux Arts building that contains the secret of our birth.

For most of his career, my father worked in the Lincoln Building, directly across the street from the library, where I visited him countless times. How funny to think that I skirted so close to my "real" name without ever considering obtaining it.

As we pass beneath the grand archway into the genealogy room, Elyse and I glance at each other meaningfully, as if to say, "Well, here we go!" When we ask the clerk for the two oversized books that contain all the New York City birth records for 1968, he gives us a knowing look. The records, which are compiled by the New York City Health Department, are listed alphabetically and divided into two volumes. Most people—who already know their family name—would only request the one covering their section of the alphabet. Our request is a dead giveaway about why we're here.

ELYSE: We lift the large, cumbersome volumes and divide them between us, Paula taking the A–Ks and me beginning with the Ls. Somewhere in these official books there is a record of baby girls born on October 9 in Richmond County, Staten Island.

Paula and I have different search tactics. While I start with the borough column, looking for an "R" for Richmond, Paula scans the birthdate column looking for a "10" to correspond to our October birth. If we find an entry for two babies rather than one, where the county and birthdate match, the last step will be to compare the birth certificate numbers with the numbers on our adoptive certificates. Only then will we learn our original birth names.

I meditate on the letters and numbers, waiting to see what mystical combination they will reveal. Instead of a first name, many of the entries only list the family name alongside "girl" or "boy." I secretly hope that we will find our original first names and that mine will be something beautiful, like Isabelle or Inez.

Five hours go by. I struggle to hold in my bladder. Even though I desperately need to go to the bathroom, I don't get up for fear that Paula will find our family name while I am gone. It is important that we find it together. After focusing on tiny print all day, my eyes are dry and pulsating. Though it's time to go, Paula keeps skimming ahead. I'm afraid that in her perseverance, she will find a name after I have given up.

It feels as if there is an unspoken competition to see who will find the goods first.

PAULA: We are fairly certain that our birth mother was Jewish, so we zip through the Garcias, Hernandezes, and Vittarellis and dive into the Cohens, Steinbergs, and Shapiros. I secretly pray that our last name isn't something awful like "Hyman."

I locate a Lisa, Lila, Judith, Michelle, and Tara Bernstein, but no Paula. According to the birth records, no Paula Bernstein was born on Staten Island on October 9, 1968. I didn't exist before my parents invented Paula Bernstein when they adopted me in March 1969. If they had ended up adopting Elyse or another baby, she would have become Paula Bernstein instead of me.

Nonadoptees can wonder what would have happened had their parents never met or procreated, but adoptees have countless what-if scenarios. Now that I know the unusual circumstances of my adoption, I can imagine exponentially more possible outcomes.

After several hours of mindless, repetitive work, Elyse and I struggle to stay focused. At three months old, Ruby is not even close to sleeping through the night and I am exhausted enough to nod off while reading. The soporific droning of the library's air conditioner soothes me into a stupor. Except for the residual buzz from the morning's café latte, the only thing keeping me awake is the promise of locating our birth mother.

Since I recently watched *Charlie and the Chocolate Factory* with Jesse, I keep waiting for one of us to find a "golden ticket." I picture Elyse and me triumphantly leaping onto one of the long wooden tables and breaking into song.

I locate several old classmates from elementary school who had been born in New York City. There's Lauren, Jennifer, Melissa, and Amy, listed alongside their family names and their father's given names. For some reason, no mothers' names are listed. I'm jealous that if they wanted to, my old friends could locate their birth record so simply—they don't have to go to the Herculean effort of scanning through thousands of names. They have the luxury of taking their lineage for granted.

It's unusual to find two consecutive matching birth dates so I naturally pause at every twin pair. Maxwell and Maxine. Jenny and Penny. Helen and Helaine. I wonder why they were all given such precious names. If Elyse and I were raised as twins, would we, too, have alliterative or rhyming names? Would our parents have dressed us in matching outfits?

After five hours poring over thousands of birth records, we've only made it to F and R, respectively.

"I guess we'll have to come back next week to finish up," Elyse says despondently.

"Just one more page," I say. "I keep thinking our names will pop out at us. I am not ready to admit defeat."

It's as if I'm a high roller in Atlantic City, picking numbers at a roulette table, hoping to win big. I jump ahead to sections with particularly Jewish names. But it's not our lucky day. Elyse and I vow to come back soon to finish.

ELYSE: After two months of living out of suitcases, I've finally left my sublet and have settled into an apartment in Clinton Hill near where Joseph and his boyfriend recently moved. Though I enjoyed the summer in Park Slope, I naturally gravitated to a more diverse neighborhood filled with young singles. I also realized that Paula and I both needed our own space. I would leave her Park Slope and claim Clinton Hill as my own.

My tiny apartment in Paris could fit into one room of my spacious one-bedroom in this postwar co-op. I am ready to create a home for myself in Brooklyn. I unpack the glass Magritte coasters I earned drinking Grimbergen beer at a bar in Brussels and have started measuring my prized film posters for framing. I have been gradually assembling my decor by collecting discarded furniture advertised on the Internet. Each piece I have acquired is unique and has its own story. A middle-aged woman was sad to see her beloved vanity go. She had been saving it for her own daughter, who at sixteen had no interest in inheriting her mother's signature piece. It seemed that I was the sole heir to a number of underappreciated gems. All I claimed from my family's own legacy was some tarnished silverware that had been handed down from my stepmother's grandmother.

Transporting these items home has become a burden. A sympathetic taxi driver helped me lug a handsome wooden bookshelf to the curb, but after that it was up to me to get it home. I thought that living near Joseph and my extended family in New York, I would have a constant support system, but life's continual dramas have kept everyone busy. I realize that, like most people who move to a new city, I will have to rely on paid help. After dealing with two disappointing furniture movers, I call a third number. His "Man with a Van" ad on craigslist.com ended, "Have a nice day. Wells." What kind of name is Wells for a mover? I call him to organize a Sunday move for the beloved vanity and a big-screen TV. He is easy to talk to, and sounds like an English major chatting with a fellow student.

On the day before Labor Day, I greet Wells outside my building's security booth. We both smile warmly as we climb into his pine green Toyota truck to pick up the furniture. Buddy Holly tunes stream from the radio. Conversation flows freely as we discuss music and compare notes on living in Brooklyn. Though he just moved here from North Carolina nine months ago, he speaks about New York as authoritatively as a native.

"Where did you move from?" he asks me.

"Paris."

"Ah, bon. J'ai vécu trois mois à Annecy," Wells replies with a decent French accent.

I've met a fellow countryman.

He's got hair as blond as a towheaded child and creamy white skin. His bright green eyes radiate intelligence. He studied in Germany and volunteered in Senegal. He moonlights as a mover while holding down a full-time job at a media corporation. For someone in his twenties, he's certainly had a lot of life experience. Wells is essentially my hired help, but spending time with him feels so familiar that I almost forget to pay him. When we're done, I offer him a Coke so we can prolong our conversation.

He notices a book on my table on the heritability of schizophrenia. Though I have been guarded about our research, I feel comfortable enough to tell him that my birth mother was diagnosed with schizophrenia.

"My great-grandmother spent many years in a mental institution," Wells responds as if it were the most commonplace thing in the world. He hands me his phone number in case I need his services again, but I sense that he's looking for a way to ask me out. After a giddy good-bye, I tightly grasp the small paper with his phone number, unable to let go.

I call him right away and ask if he'd like to get together sometime.

"Yeah!" he answers enthusiastically. We make plans for that night.

If my family had helped me move, I never would have met my boyfriend.

· | ·

One week later, we're back in the genealogy room where Paula and I resume the tedious process of scanning through names and dates. Immersed in the T's, I hear Paula's book close. Having perfected her search method, Paula has already finished looking at her half of the registry, negating the possibility that our last name begins with the letters A–K. We've both skipped ahead and looked up Schein and Bernstein, picturing the irony of possessing the same name as our adoptive parents. I motion to Paula to sit beside me, leaving her responsible for the left-hand pages of the book. Sitting side by side like Siamese twins, we turn each page in synch.

Though we've been proceeding carefully down the list of names, I wonder if we've made an error since we've been stopping to whisper. As Paula points out entries for people she went to school with, I've been remembering things to tell her about Wells.

"I feel so comfortable with him. He tells me how beautiful I am."

"That's a compliment for me, too," Paula responds. I grimace, claiming the compliment for myself.

"Shh," mutters a haggard-looking middle-aged woman sitting at the end of the long table.

"Sorry," we say in unison as we roll our eyes and struggle to suppress laughter. Suddenly, Paula and I are naughty little girls being scolded by the teacher. Despite the solemnity of these lengthy proceedings, we are finding the occasion to be more lighthearted than we had expected.

PAULA: I've already completed my book and Elyse has just twenty-two pages to go in hers, but I have to relieve the babysitter in one hour. Will we go home empty-handed yet again?

"What if"—Elyse voices desperately—"we've overlooked it? Then we'll have to start again from page one."

"Don't worry, we'll find it," I say, mustering some encouragement as much for me as for Elyse.

Looking over Elyse's shoulder, I gasp when I spot "10/9" in Richmond County and "Jean" listed as the first name. There's a space after the entry, so it takes me a moment before I see "Marian." I point to the name and Elyse's face lights up.

ELYSE: Only when I glance down and see the name "Marian" beneath "Jean" does it sink in that after 1,054 pages, and with only 22 pages left in the book, our search is complete. We now know our birth name is Witt. Marian and Jean were the names we were called at the foster home. Since they are listed here in the birth registry, we realize it was our birth mother who gave them to us, not our foster mother, as we had imagined.

The space for our birth father's name is blank.

Perhaps our birth mother will choose to reveal his identity if we meet her. In any case, learning our birth mother's surname has brought us one step closer to finding her.

PAULA: I wonder why our birth mother picked the names Jean and Marian. Perhaps she named us in memory of relatives she had lost. I stare at the name "Jean Witt," waiting for it to reveal more to me. How strange to think that this name, which a civil servant typed into a book thirty-six years ago, refers to me. It doesn't sound very Jewish, but it's got a certain ring to it. "Jean Witt" conjures up the image of a glamorous 1940s film star or a nightclub chanteuse.

For the first five months of my life, I was Jean Witt and then, after my parents adopted me, I morphed into Paula Bernstein. Then, at age thirty-one, when I married Avo and legally took his name, I became Paula Orkin. So now I'm a Bernstein, an Orkin, and a Witt. Though each name refers to the same person, they represent different incarnations of "me." Paula Bernstein marks my childhood as my parent's daughter. Paula Orkin represents my adult life as Avo's wife and Jesse and Ruby's mother.

Jean Witt is my phantom identity, the life I never led.

ELYSE: Sitting in the library, my eyes fill with tears. When I began the search for my birth mother two years ago, I never imagined I would be accompanied on my quest. I want to hug Paula for helping me get here, for all that we have already shared, yet she seems to be internalizing the experience. Even though we have grown closer, I don't dare penetrate her shell.

"Jean doesn't sound very Jewish," Paula says. Knowing that our foster mother was Irish and presumably Catholic, we had assumed she chose these Christian names for us.

I could have been Marian Witt. The name itself exudes a swanky residence on the Upper East Side and a private-school education.

That night when I look up the origin of the names *Marian* and *Jean* on the Internet, I am pleased to learn that Marian is a French name dating back to the Middle Ages. And Jean, in fact, has Hebrew origins.

"Witt," I keep saying to myself, getting used to the ring of it. The name is devoid of any connotation. Is *Witt* one of those Ellis Island truncations of a name such as Witowski? Is it a Polish or a Russian name? I used to imagine that my Polish boyfriend in college, Artur, and I were linked by our ancestors, neighboring Jewish and Catholic families, who managed to live together peaceably in Warsaw.

"We are descendants of the Witt family," I announce to myself, as proudly as a princess claiming her rightful heritage.

PAULA: The rush of all this sleuthing is so addictive that I continue the search for our biological mother after I arrive home. As I prepare mac and cheese for the kids, I fiddle with the Internet. Since we know from the nonidentifying information Louise Wise gave us that our birth mother's older brother and father were attorneys, I search online for male lawyers with the last name "Witt."

I come up with an attorney named Max Witt, whose son is also an attorney. According to our adoption files, our biological grandfather was in his mid-sixties when we were born. Max Witt, who was born in 1903, fits that bill. I located other attorneys with the last name of Witt born around that time, but none of them were lawyers with sons in the same profession. It seems like too much of a coincidence. But in Max Witt's obituary, there is no mention of a surviving daughter. Perhaps the family disowned her or was too ashamed to include a reference to their troubled daughter. Or maybe she's dead.

His son, David Witt, who was born in 1936, three years before our birth mother, is listed as Max Witt's sole survivor. Could he be the older brother that the agency mentioned?

When I see him described online as a Communist leader, I'm excited at the prospect of having Max Witt as a grandfather. Born to Russian immigrant parents and raised on the Lower East Side of Manhattan, Max Witt attended New York University and worked his way through Harvard Law School driving a cab. In college, I flirted with the revolutionary Communist Youth Brigade and started a leftist alternative newspaper. During my sophomore year, I spent a night in a shanty I helped build in protest of the college's investments in South Africa. My parents joked at the time, "Every Jew has to go through a Communist phase." Elyse told me that while she was living in Prague, she was a strong supporter of the proletariat and pored over Emma Goldman's autobiography. Maybe we have inherited our liberal leanings and sense of justice from our grandfather.

"So we've got a schizophrenic birth mother, but maybe at least we'll have some cool uncle or grandfather!" says Elyse when I tell her about Max Witt.

· | ·

Already familiar with the search process, on our third visit to the genealogy room of the public library Elyse and I easily locate the 1939 registry. Confidently opening the musty volume, we are certain that our birth mother's name will reveal itself. Since Elyse and I were born in New York City, we naively assume that our birth mother was born here as well.

Our birth mother was about to turn twenty-nine when we were born in October 1968, so she must have been born in late 1939. Helen, Margaret, and Maxine Witt were all born in autumn of 1939, but on the basis of their names alone, it is impossible to determine who the most likely candidate is. We suddenly realize that we don't even know which borough our birth mother was born in or if she was, in fact, born in New York City.

Craving some sort of catharsis, I look up "Marilyn Vinikoff" in the records for 1937 and feel oddly comforted when I find my adoptive mother's name. Regardless of whether I ever locate my birth mother's name, I have a mother and she is supporting me in my search for my origins. Seeing my mother's name in fine print on the page in this dusty old book reassures me that I exist even if there is no evidence that "Paula Bernstein" was born on October 9, 1968.

· | ·

Waiting outside Beansprouts to pick Jesse up from school one crisp autumn afternoon, I answer my cell phone. Expecting it to be Avo with tonight's dinner plans, I answer with a peppy "hi!"

"Hello," the deep voice says. It takes me a moment to register that it's Dr. Neubauer calling. Elyse and I had left him yet another a message, but we didn't expect him to call back. While the other mothers arrange play dates, I speak in hushed tones to this venerable psychiatrist, who finally tells me he's able to see us.

We arrange for Elyse and me to meet with him at his apartment in December, which is still a couple of months away. I hope he doesn't change his mind or die before then. Since Dr. Neubauer is already in his nineties, it is not out of the question.

ELYSE: "Return again," the rabbi chants. Along with the Jewish New Year, autumn and the start of the school year has always symbolized beginnings for me. At a Reform synagogue in Park Slope, I watch proudly as Jesse rushes to the stage to join in the Rosh Hashanah children's service. I hold Ruby in my arms, content to be Paula's unofficial mother's-helper for the day. The congregation sings, "Return to who you are. Return to what you are. Return to where you were born. Return to the land of your soul."

Chapter Seventeen

ELYSE: Lingering in bed after Wells leaves for work, I get the call. "I need you to be strong," my cousin, Jaime, begins, and I resist the urge to hang up the phone immediately.

Be strong? Something must have happened to Dad. Otherwise, he would be calling me from the road. He's driving Tyler to Wilmington, North Carolina, where Tyler will move in with drug-free friends and, at age twenty, make a fresh start in a new town.

"No, I can't," I tell her, imagining my dad lying dead on the side of the highway.

"It's Tyler," she says. "He's in the emergency room. He OD'd." Expecting the worst does not shield me from the sharp rush of pain that juts through me. I shut down and go on automatic pilot. Call Paula. Call Wells.

"I don't know if he's going to make it," I say numbly to Paula.

"He'll be okay," Paula responds, trying to reassure me. But I sense that this time is different. Tyler tempted fate one too many times.

For so many years I have blamed my parents for Tyler's downward spiral into drugs. They shouldn't have spoiled him. They shouldn't have sent him to military school. They should have sent him to live with me in San Francisco, where I would have taken him under my wing. They should have told him sooner who his birth mother was. Now that the worst has finally happened, the blame fades away as I rush to be by their side. It was my family's decision to adopt him and we will face this nightmare together.

I book a flight and roam around my apartment, throwing essentials into my suitcase. I toss in a black skirt in case there is a funeral.

This isn't supposed to be happening. He is like my brother and my son and I can't help but feel that there was something else I could have said or done to prevent this nightmare. Are we to blame for wanting him to be part of our lives? Would Tyler have been better off having been adopted and raised by strangers, never knowing us? Never knowing his birth parents' story?

I down a double scotch at the airport bar in Raleigh-Durham, preparing to face Toni, who has flown in from Dallas. When I arrive at the gate for Wilmington, Toni, hunched down in her seat, looks up at me expectantly.

"The nurse said that there's no brain activity," I say calmly as if reciting the evening news. Before boarding my flight from New York, I had gotten the most recent report from the hospital. Toni shields her face with her hands. On the connecting flight to Wilmington, a small two-engine jet, we clutch our hands together and cry. It's taken this tragedy to bring me and Toni closer.

In front of the entrance to the cardiac ICU, my parents stand in a hazy fluorescent white halo clutching each other as they sob uncontrollably. Feeling isolated and alone, I take baby steps toward them.

When we first adopted Tyler, when I was sixteen, I told my friends that he taught me how to love. I would cut my arm off for him, I declared proudly, to demonstrate the infinity of my love for him. But something inside him made Tyler feel he was never loved enough and now I realize that I was powerless to help him.

Tyler's chest rises steadily with tubes inflating him with air. It looks as if he is merely dreaming. The nurses have been waiting for our arrival before taking out the tubes.

My parents couldn't bear to see Tyler as an empty shell but I needed to see him one last time. I was there when he was born. Now, as he leaves this world, I will him to go in peace.

The following day, after arranging to have the body shipped back to Oklahoma, my parents and I drive all night like fugitives. We arrive in Durant shortly after dawn and race to the funeral home in town to make sure Tyler's obituary makes it into tomorrow's paper. Which picture of him should we use? Which coffin should we choose? Should Tyler be buried or cremated? My world is suddenly reduced to these horrifying questions.

Despite all the twin studies, which point to genetics, I realize how my environment has required me to develop a shell of resilience. Circumstances have spared Paula from death, and I can't imagine her confronting this tragedy. As similar as we are, some differences are so great that they cannot be measured in statistics or percentages.

Ever since I called Paula with the news, she has been leaving me warm consolatory messages on my voicemail, but I don't have the energy to respond. Insulated by pain, I have not regained my full voice. After the funeral, back at my parents' house, which is packed with friends offering their condolences, I seek a quiet corner where I can finally talk to Paula. Struggling to produce a sound, I slowly recount the day's events to her. I tell her what it's been like seeing Tyler at the viewing; greeting guests at the funeral with a dutiful smile; consoling my brother, who has lost his only son, and my parents who have lost their only grandchild.

I can actually hear Paula listening attentively as I mutter beneath my breath. Her sympathy is palpable. "I wish I could be there to give you a hug," she says. Then for the first time since shortly after we met, Paula says, "I love you," and I believe she means it.

"I wish you could have met him," I respond.

"Me, too."

PAULA: Is it possible to mourn someone I never knew? After hearing so much about Tyler from Elyse, I had hoped we would eventually meet, but now that opportunity is lost forever.

"If Elyse and I hadn't reunited, I fear what her life would be like right now," I tell Avo when I break the sad news to him. While my family can't begin to compensate for Tyler, maybe we can help ease her pain.

Elyse has undergone so many losses. Now that Tyler is gone, how does she will herself to get out of bed in the morning? Rather than pity her, I respect Elyse for being a survivor. In fact, I feel guilty that she is the twin fated to endure this painful experience. If it were possible, I would gladly alleviate her burden of suffering. Tyler's death has put our petty bickering in perspective. She is my sister and I love her.

I contemplated flying to Tyler's funeral so I could be by Elyse's side, but decided against it. I worry that my presence in Oklahoma might exhaust Elyse. She might feel responsible for introducing me to her friends and family. I certainly wouldn't want our "reunited twin story" to overshadow Tyler's funeral.

· | ·

While it's difficult to focus on anything else knowing that Elyse is in mourning, I am determined to continue the research we have begun. I decide to track down Barbara Miller, the former director of post-adoption services at Louise Wise, whom I met with back in 1987. I'm curious to see if she recalls our meeting and if she can shed any light on the twin study.

There are eleven Barbara Millers in the Manhattan phone book. I'm not even sure she's alive or where she lives. After three failed attempts to find her, I am nearly ready to abandon my search. I make one last-ditch effort, which pays off. Bingo. I've found her.

"I was adopted from Louise Wise and it was a happy story," I say, wanting to reassure Mrs. Miller that I'm not calling to hassle her. "When I was in college, I requested nonidentifying information and I met with you. You didn't tell me that my birth mother was mentally ill or that I had a twin."

Mrs. Miller has no recollection of our meeting.

"Why didn't you tell me my birth mother was diagnosed as schizophrenic?" I ask.

According to Mrs. Miller, attorneys for Louise Wise Services neglected to inform the social workers at the agency that a 1983 law obligated them to disclose all medical information about adoptees' biological families.

"I was just an employee. I wasn't responsible for making the policy," says Mrs. Miller. I don't buy it. As a social worker at one of the top adoption agencies in Manhattan, how could she have remained ignorant of a crucial law that affected her job?

"I thought I was doing the right thing," says Mrs. Miller wistfully.

"I am not judging the decision you made or accusing you of anything. I am just curious. How did it feel to sit across from a young girl looking for answers and to not reveal that she was a twin and that her birth mother was mentally ill?"

Mrs. Miller is momentarily silent as she ponders my question.

"When parents adopted a child at Louise Wise," Mrs. Miller explains, "they were routinely asked if they were concerned about mental illness in a child's background. If they said they weren't, then they were considered for children with 'questionable' backgrounds."

"So you're basically saying that it was my parents' fault? Assuming they were asked about their feelings regarding mental illness, which I'm not sure they were, they had no idea they were being screened specifically to see if they could raise a child who might become mentally ill. They thought the question was theoretical."

Mrs. Miller explains that the agency told adoptive parents that adoption is characterized by unknowns. "It takes a particular type of parent to love a child that isn't their own. It sounds like your parents did an excellent job," she says.

"They did," I assure her. When I hear Ruby wail from upstairs, I realize that I need to go do my own job—I am late to relieve our babysitter. I thank Mrs. Miller and hang up the phone.

Later that night, I call my parents. They have no recollection of anybody at the agency asking them how they would feel about adopting a child with a family history of mental illness.

"I remember that someone asked if we would adopt a disabled child and we said we didn't think we could handle it," my mother recalls. "They asked, 'What if a child became disabled or sick later on?' and I said, 'That would be different because they were already our child.' "

My parents had no idea that their response to that particular question could result in their taking home a baby with "an uncertain history."

ELYSE: After the last mourners have left my parents' home, an aura of death lingers. "We need you to decide what you want us to do if something happens to you," my parents tell me. Paula used to say that she felt responsible for me since I was on my own. With Tyler gone and my parents in middle age, I now realize that when I make a living will, Paula's the one I will ask to pull the plug.

Leaving Oklahoma and saying good-bye to my family is agonizing, but I am consoled that I have a family to return to in New York.

Chapter Eighteen

PAULA: The first snowfall of the season has left the sidewalks of Brooklyn a slushy mess. Jesse is excited to puddle-jump, but first we need to buy winter boots. I'm at a children's shoe store on Prospect Park West when I get the call from Hillel Hirschbein at the JBFCS. "It's not a good time to talk. Can I call you back?" I say, but he proceeds to tell me the bad news. Because the CDC dropped Elyse and me from the study before we were adopted, the JBFCS has decided that the archives at Yale do not pertain to us. Therefore, they are once again denying us access to them.

We revise our game plan. If we can team up with the other separated twins and triplets, the JBFCS won't be able to use that argument. The other subjects are also anxious to determine the true purpose of the study. After sending out an updated request for access to the JBFCS signed by some of these twins and triplets, Elyse and I are finally going to meet with Dr. Neubauer this week.

"Even though we're angry, we should be cordial," I remind Elyse when we meet up on the subway platform the morning of our meeting. "And let's try not to share personal information with him. I don't want him to get the satisfaction of 'studying' us now."

"I'll try to keep my cool. I'd love to yell at him, but I promise to behave myself!" says Elyse.

"We know he's got a temper, so let's do our best not to set him off. Maybe he's luring us to his apartment so he can kidnap us and brainwash us!" I say, trying to keep things light.

"I told Wells where I'll be today in case I don't return!" Elyse says and we both giggle.

When Elyse and I are greeted by three doormen in full regalia, I half-expect them to salute us. Instead, they escort us into the well-appointed lobby of Dr. Neubauer's Upper East Side apartment building. Standing outside the doctor's door, we inhale deeply and mentally prepare to face our nemesis. The door opens and Dr. Neubauer smiles at us warmly and beckons us inside.

When he hears that Elyse recently moved to New York from Paris, Dr. Neubauer begins to converse with her in French. He coos as she tells him that she lived in the chic neighborhood of Montparnasse. From his curt responses on the phone, we had expected Dr. Neubauer to be gruff and downright nasty to us. Instead, he is so cordial that I feel as if he could be our long-lost great-uncle who has invited us to afternoon tea.

Dr. Neubauer's dark apartment is so cavernous, I imagine we could easily get lost in it. He leads us through a salon decorated with fine drawings of birds toward a sitting room that is presumably used for his psychoanalytic consultations. Surrounded by books on poetry, psychology, and literature, Elyse and I take seats opposite him. Dr. Neubauer, dressed in tan corduroys and a black cardigan, sits in a worn armchair and removes his wire-rimmed glasses, prompting us to begin our inquisition.

Before we can get in the first question, Dr. Neubauer takes out a notebook and starts to jot down notes. The tables are turned, and he, it seems, plans to interview us. When he asks why we came to see him, I launch into our now oft-repeated story.

"I never wanted to meet any biological family, but things changed once I found out I had an identical twin. There's no denying that we're family," I say.

"When I asked Louise Wise why we were separated, I was told it was for a study," adds Elyse. "Do you know why we were dropped from the study?"

Dr. Neubauer concedes that at some point the CDC, which administered the study, had contact with us, but says they dropped us because of the differences in our weight. Since I was adopted four months before Elyse, the study's results would be skewed. At nine months, the influence of the foster family on Elyse would have been too great to compare her with me, Dr. Neubauer tells us.

Whenever Elyse or I ask Dr. Neubauer what exactly he and the other researchers were hoping to learn through the study, he takes off his glasses and looks uneasily at us. Reluctantly, he acknowledges that the goal of the study was to examine what makes a person who they are. Which has greater influence: nature or nurture?

Viola Bernard, Dr. Neubauer explains, felt strongly that twins do not get enough attention from their parents. Since Louise Wise separated siblings, why not separate twins?

With obvious pride, Dr. Neubauer says that the CDC study was the only study that followed separated twins from birth. He continues to insist that twins were not separated for the purpose of being studied.

"How was the study conducted?" I ask.

Researchers went into each twin's house every two months early on, and later, every four months. During those visits, the twins and triplets were tested, photographed, and filmed.

Why was the study never published? Dr. Neubauer says it would be harmful for the twins to read it, since many of them did not know they were twins. How ironic that he is now claiming to be protecting the subjects.

"What about the people who already know, like us?" I ask. "If you'd help us gain access, we would be willing to sign a legal document saying that we won't share any confidential information."

Dr. Neubauer reiterates that seeing the data could be harmful.

"To whom?" I ask, but he refuses to answer. Dr. Neubauer won't give us an entirely straight answer, but he suggests that the researchers were looking into how to better match an adoptive mother with a child. Also, they wanted to track the development of the twins in order to see how being adopted was a burden.

"So you were studying the effects of different mothering techniques?" Elyse asks and Dr. Neubauer nods approvingly.

"I'm dying to know what your conclusions are," I say.

"I'm sure you are," he says with a devilish laugh.

I ignore his comment. "So was Viola Bernard right about her theory that separating twins is beneficial?"

He acknowledges that today she would never suggest such an idea.

"But did you agree with her theory?"

Dr. Neubauer refuses to answer, except to once again remind us that he had nothing to do with her decision to separate the twins.

"Certainly, you had your own hunch about whether her theory made sense," I say, prodding him to answer.

Dr. Neubauer tells us that if he thought she was doing something wrong, he wouldn't have been involved.

ELYSE: "Do you know what Louise Wise's policy was regarding separating twins? Certainly no other agencies supported the separation of twins," I say.

There was no effort to keep siblings together, Dr. Neubauer says. So why should it be any different for twins?

"But twins have a special bond," I say. "I'm not sure I would have met with a sibling, especially if it was a half sibling, but it was impossible to deny the significance of an identical twin."

Dr. Neubauer recounts the story of a visit he made to a Catholic adoption agency to see if they would be willing to place twins separately. The nun refused, saying, "What God has joined together let no man put asunder." Dr. Neubauer asked her whether the bond between mother and child is any less holy.

Paula and I balk at the comparison. Adoption agencies don't purposely separate mothers from their children; they are separated by circumstances. Regardless, it seems to us that Dr. Neubauer has just acknowledged that on at least one occasion he was actively trying to recruit twins for the study, not just passively studying twins who were being separated anyway, as he had claimed.

"Since we never tested you, why do you care what we did?" Dr. Neubauer asks.

"Because you played God with my life, and changed it in uncountable ways." I say.

"What difference would it make to know if you first smiled at five months or six months?" asks Dr. Neubauer.

"It would help to know if I was well cared for. If I was loved," I say softly. Dr. Neubauer remains silent.

"We've found in our research that in most of the cases of the separated twins, there was some history of mental illness in the family," Paula says. "And both Paula and I have experienced depression. So you were studying the hereditability of mental illness," I add confidently, as a statement rather than a question.

I detect a smirk on Dr. Neubauer's face as he tells me he can't discuss the study further. It almost seems as if he's gloating.

Dr. Neubauer turns the tables and starts to question us. What was the age of onset of our depression? He seems excited by the notion that we could have each experienced depression at the same time.

"It must have been very hard to find identical twins who were given up for adoption, who were Jewish, and who had at least one parent who was mentally ill," Paula says, trying to trick Dr. Neubauer into answering.

"Indeed, it was," he says. Bingo. Dr. Neubauer has tacitly acknowledged that our hunch was right. While the overarching goal of the study was to examine the relative importance of nature versus nurture, clearly, the psychologists were also interested in the heritability of mental illness.

"Was one purpose of the study also to examine the response to separation on infants?" I ask.

"Yes," says Neubauer. He explains that part of what they were studying was the child's response to separation and new attachment. If I put a face to his abstract twin subject, perhaps he will realize the damage he has caused.

"Could depression be the result of my multiple separations? First losing my birth mother, then my identical twin, then the foster mother?" I ask.

Dr. Neubauer acknowledges that this is one of the questions that he and his colleagues at the CDC were trying to answer: the question of what imprint the earliest periods of time leave on a person.

As if offering us an explanation, Dr. Neubauer mentions the name of the renowned child psychoanalyst Melanie Klein, who based her work on Sigmund Freud's theories. While Freud's psychoanalytic theories about children came from his work with adults, Klein sought to interpret children at play for use in therapy.

Curious which school of psychoanalysis Dr. Neubauer belongs to, I casually inquire where he studied. In Vienna and then in Switzerland, under the famed psychoanalyst Eugen Bleuler, who invented schizophrenia, Neubauer tells us. In actuality, Bleuler, a contemporary of Freud and Jung, only introduced the term. By joining the Greek words *schizo,* "split," and *phrene,* "mind," Bleuler created a less stigmatizing term for the mental illness formerly known as dementia praecox. Bleuler opposed the prevailing view that irreversible brain damage caused schizophrenia.

By raising the topic of schizophrenia, perhaps Dr. Neubauer is speaking to us in code. Should we read this as confirmation that his pet project was to determine the heritability of schizophrenia?

It is surprising that unlike Freud, Dr. Neubauer, who served as executive director of the Sigmund Freud Archives, appears to attribute little importance to the mark of psychic trauma in childhood on later development.

"Do you feel satisfied with the study even though it was never published?" Paula asks.

Dr. Neubauer seems wistful as he tells us that he wishes he could publish the study.

"Don't you want to take this opportunity to tell the public the truth and straighten out any misconceptions?" I ask.

The media have been hounding him since 1980, when the triplets

story broke, so Dr. Neubauer is wary of the negative public attention that could result if the study is published.

He seems anxious for us to stay and chat, but we don't want to
reveal anything else and it's clear he won't divulge any more information. As he escorts us to the door, Dr. Neubauer pauses to examine
Paula and me as if seeing us for the first time. He mentions that
though our bone structure is very similar, Paula's complexion is
slightly lighter than mine. For a moment, as he studies us silently,
turning from me to Paula, I think he might hug us. Instead, he helps
us on with our winter coats and says that he is sorry he didn't offer
us any Viennese cake. "Maybe next time!" I say as the door shuts behind us.

On the F train back to Brooklyn, Paula and I try to take it all in. Although Dr. Neubauer didn't give much away, we feel rather triumphant. We have done something incredibly important, which is to
confirm our theories about the purpose of the study. What these researchers did angers us—but worse, how galling that these strangers
knew more about our own early childhoods than we did. That they im-
periously, peremptorily kept this knowledge to themselves.

We have faced the monster in the closet—this figure who took on
an almost mythically dark force in our lives. Despite the fact that
Neubauer ceded no ground, we feel empowered. It feels like a huge
victory—as if we've taken back a piece of our lives that had been
toyed with and locked away forever. Paula and I are beginning to
think that with a few more answers, we may soon find resolution.

Chapter | Nineteen

ELYSE: Paula and I have been on the lookout for other twins from the study since we first met. In addition to Sara and Jill and the triplets, there are still three sets of twins whose whereabouts we don't know and who may not even be aware that they have a twin in the world.

Paula and I recently learned of one of these remaining sets—Doug and Howie, who reunited in 1999 at age thirty-six. When I call Doug in Massachusetts and explain that I have a similar story, he affably recounts the tale of how he first found out he had a twin. Coincidentally, he and his twin both contacted Louise Wise for non-identifying information around the same time in 1997. While Doug procrastinated and didn't return the signed form to the agency, Howard sent it in immediately and was informed by Katherine Boros that he had a twin.

After two long years of waiting for Doug to recontact the agency, Howard, impatient to meet his twin, beseeched Katherine to contact him on his behalf. When he heard the news from Katherine, Doug practically drove his truck off the road. "I was thrilled," he recalls.

When the twins talked on the phone, they discovered some remarkable similarities. "Our experiences in college, everything was the same. Listening to Howard talk, I would be nodding, 'I know.' " It turns out that the two men met their wives the same year, married the same year, and had children at the same time. They both grew up in the New York area; they were raised in families of the same socio-economic level; and they had sisters who were three years older.

Still, the men discovered some notable differences between them. Though genetic factors may explain 90 percent of individual differences in height in twins, Doug is six foot two while Howie is only five foot ten. Doug weighs 195, while Howard weighs only 165. This might be explained by the fact that twins' average weight differences increase after age thirty-eight and genetic influence on weight becomes less important as one ages.

"My parents were told, 'You have to participate in the child development study. It's part of the adoption process,' " Doug recalls. His family was upset when they found out that they had unknowingly taken part in Neubauer's twin study and were never given the option of adopting both boys. Doug vaguely remembers being visited at his home by psychologists who would film him playing.

When Doug asks me if I want to find my birth mother, I give him my usual pat response. "We don't want to interfere with her life, but we definitely want answers. How about you?"

"She left a letter at the agency for us so we only have to register for identifying information to get in contact with her, but I have mixed feelings about finding her." Though he's happy to have reunited with Howie, Doug isn't certain that he would like to meet the rest of his birth family.

"It's hard to get upset, because I'm happy with my life, but I still feel robbed of something," Doug replies when I ask him if he feels he was always missing his twin. Doug was the twin who was found but, unlike Paula, he doesn't seem to have any qualms about being found.

PAULA: "Doug was found by his twin brother and he didn't have a problem with it. He accepted Howie right away," says Elyse when she calls me to report about her conversation.

"Everyone reacts differently. You can't predict how you would have felt if I was the one who had found you," I tell Elyse defensively. I feel she's annoyed that I didn't respond more like Doug.

"I know that if the tables were turned and I found out I had a twin, I would have looked for you," I concede. "But I can't help the way I felt."

It has taken two years for me to be able to confess to Elyse my early feelings of doubt about our relationship. Now that we've grown closer, I feel compelled to clear the air between us.

"Remember when we were in Paris and you told me that the only thing that would hurt you is if I didn't want to have contact with you at all? Well, I didn't tell you at the time since I didn't want to hurt you, but my first reaction was 'Oh shit.' "

"Really?" asks Elyse softly. "Why?"

"We were having such a hard time communicating and I wasn't sure I wanted you in my life," I say tentatively. "I was thinking maybe we would see each other once a year and exchange e-mails every once in a while."

"I'm in shock," says Elyse. "I wasn't sure of where our relationship would lead, but I wouldn't have considered cutting you out of my life. I can't believe that after four months of e-mails and phone calls, you felt that way."

"My life was finally settled. I wasn't looking for anything else," I say. "I admit that sometimes I was really excited about the whole thing, but other times I just wanted my old life back."

From the beginning, Elyse has taken it for granted that because we are twins, we will have an intimate relationship, but for me, that isn't a given. Even though we have the same DNA, when I visited Elyse in Paris, she was still a stranger. The idea of being bound to her for the rest of our lives overwhelmed me, while I sensed that it comforted her.

"I don't feel this way anymore," I assure Elyse. "Now I'm glad that you're a part of my life. Now I think you're a terrific person, a really special person. Since you've moved to New York, I have come to understand you more and to respect you. I think I can honestly say that I love you now."

Still, as much as I try to explain, Elyse will never fully understand how I ever could have contemplated cutting off contact with my twin. If I were her, I would feel baffled and hurt too.

ELYSE: I knew that Paula was ambivalent about being found, but I am still shocked. Her feelings may have been conflicted, but her actions expressed an interest in a relationship. Sending me photos of her daughter and introducing me to her family felt like an invitation. Soon after we first met, she wrote me enthusiastically, reassuring me that nothing I said could scare her off. In e-mails, Paula referred to looking at pictures of me as "getting a dose of Elyse" and signed off her notes "Missing you" or "All my love."

I had no preconception of what my relationship with my twin would be. If Paula had not reciprocated, I would not have pursued a relationship with her. Led on by promises of a shared future, I am now the jilted lover.

Still reeling at Paula's confession, I soften when she adds that she no longer feels this way and that she now loves and accepts me. Initially I had asked Paula to be completely honest with me, and now I'm glad our relationship has evolved enough for her to open up.

PAULA: Since we first learned that Dr. Perlman, the graduate student who worked on Neubauer's twin study, visited us in our foster home, Elyse and I have been compiling a list of questions to ask him. Dr. Perlman, now a clinical assistant professor at the University of Michigan, has agreed to meet with us while he is in New York during his summer break.

When he arrives at our prearranged meeting place, a friend's loft apartment in Chelsea, we politely kiss him on the cheek as we would a relative we haven't seen in years.

"So have we changed much since you saw us last?" I joke and

Perlman laughs nervously. It's been thirty-seven years since he last laid eyes on us and he's not sure what to expect. Perhaps he fears we have brought him here to ambush him with accusations.

Dr. Perlman, now in his early sixties with a gray beard and lean physique, takes a seat in an armchair across from me and Elyse. His gentle demeanor immediately puts us at ease.

"What were we like when you visited us at twenty-eight days old? Were we exceptionally bright and attractive?" I ask with a smile before launching into more serious questions.

"Do you remember anything about our foster mother?"

Unfortunately, after so much time has passed, Dr. Perlman can't recall Mrs. McGowan's first name. He has no idea whether Elyse and I interacted at the foster home or what the conditions were like there. To jolt his memory, we present him with the one-page report he composed after observing us as infants, but he draws a blank.

Because I was so malnourished at the time of my adoption and Elyse was kept in the foster home for so long, we both wondered whether researchers purposely deprived us of food or affection to see how we would react. Was that the case?

"There wasn't any notion of depriving one youngster to see what happened. They weren't that Machiavellian," says Perlman.

"Well, that's a relief to hear!" I exclaim.

"I don't think anybody would even think of doing something like this now—separating twins and not letting the parents know," says Perlman.

"So what was the study about?" Elyse asks. "Were you interested in the question of mental illness?"

"They wouldn't have wanted that because they were looking for normal development," explains Dr. Perlman, who, in addition to teaching, also is a practicing therapist. "What they wanted to see were variations in normal development based on things like differences in parenting styles or the parents' personalities."

As a graduate student, Dr. Perlman may not have been clued in to Dr. Bernard and Dr. Neubauer's interest in the heritability of mental illness. I'm more inclined to trust Dr. Neubauer's revelations and our findings in Dr. Bernard's archives.

"Going from home to home, what were your conclusions? Were all the twins very alike?" Elyse asks.

"I went into this thing pretty strongly believing that people are molded by their environment and I was really struck by the similarities in these youngsters," Perlman explains. "During that year, I became sold on how much of your personality is biologically programmed."

· | ·

After saying good-bye to Dr. Perlman, Elyse and I roam the streets of Chelsea and digest our conversation with him.

"Again and again, we keep hearing that personality is programmed from birth. But surely our different upbringings accounted for something, don't you think?" I ask Elyse.

"Of course, our families, friends, and life experiences have influenced us. How could they not? And as we keep saying, if nurture made no difference, we might have turned out exactly the same," Elyse responds.

"It's true. Even identical twins who grow up together turn out different."

As Elyse and I wind our way toward the Hudson River, I can almost feel the anger we've been harboring toward Dr. Bernard and Dr. Neubauer fade away.

"We are who we are," says Elyse.

There's still one big question looming: who was our birth mother?

Chapter | Twenty

PAULA: "I realize more and more how much I want to hear the story of our birth from our birth mother's perspective," says Elyse. We're strolling through Prospect Park on the sort of bright summer day when the entire human race seems to be in a good mood.

I look up at the clear blue sky and stare directly at the sun until my eyes begin to tear.

"I want to learn the circumstances of our birth, but to be honest . . . I know it sounds awful, but I secretly hope that our birth mother is dead. It would make it a lot easier in a lot of ways," I say guiltily.

Elyse looks at me blankly, so I try to explain.

"Well, if she was dead, we wouldn't have to worry about disrupting her life or about finding a place for her in our lives. The story could all be in the past," I say.

Deep in my bones, I still don't fully accept that our birth mother exists. Even though I understand intellectually that Marilyn Bernstein didn't give birth to me, I continue to harbor the irrational notion that I grew in her womb.

In my Intro to Psychology class in college, the concept of cognitive dissonance, the awareness of incompatibility between one's beliefs and one's behavior, fascinated me. Now I must reconcile the fact that, although I have steadfastly insisted that I have no interest in searching for any biological relatives, I am doing just that. My body rebels against me as I struggle to resolve this irreconcilable contradiction. Lately, my stomach troubles have been flaring up more aggressively than usual. Itchy patches of eczema have sprung up on my fingers, and after years of enjoying a clear complexion, I find my acne once again flourishing. A large cyst has set up camp next to my nose and is threatening to take control of my face. The symptoms are as easy to read as subtitles—I fear what Elyse and I will discover when we find our birth mother.

Over the past few days, Elyse and I have agreed to call David Witt, who we have good reason to believe may be our birth mother's brother. As we prepare for this last step of our journey into the past, anxiety bubbles just below the surface, ready to emerge at the slightest provocation.

This morning as Avo is getting ready for work, I snap at him over something as trivial as what he fed Jesse for breakfast.

"What's the big deal?" he asks.

I stand by helplessly, watching myself pick a fight. Why can't I control my emotions? What's wrong with me?

I decide to walk Avo to the subway so I'll have time to explain my behavior. But before I can apologize, Avo confesses, "You've been acting a little psycho lately. One minute you're down in the dumps and the next moment you're really upbeat. It's pretty unnerving."

I hear him, but just barely. As people stroll by on their way to work, I am immobilized on the sidewalk. Avo's voice fades into the distance as fear crystallizes in my warped brain. A panicked spiral sends me reeling. I begin to sob uncontrollably and fear that I will never stop.

Psycho. Just like my birth mother. Gasping for air, it's as if I am breathing water. I am so crazy that Avo will leave me. Jesse and Ruby will be saddled with a lunatic for a mother. I picture them smiling politely during their obligatory visits to me in the mental hospital. Choking back tears, I grab Avo like a drowning woman clinging desperately to a life preserver. I don't want to pull him into the abyss with me, but I need something to keep me afloat. Squeezing me as tight as a straitjacket, Avo urges me to breathe until my body finally relaxes and my panic subsides. I can breathe again. I am going to live.

Once the crisis passes, Avo continues to the subway, leaving me with one clear option. I call my shrink and have him increase my dosage of Prozac. For good measure, he prescribes Ativan, an anti-anxiety medication. If that was a panic attack, I don't ever want to have another one.

ELYSE: Paula tells me, "I think you should be the one to call since I'm a mess these days. I don't trust myself to talk." We sit side by side at her kitchen table, clutching our phones.

"I'm feeling pretty shaky myself, but I think I can manage it," I say. I dial David Witt's number at the prestigious law firm where he works.

"Are you calling on professional business or are you a solicitor?" a secretary asks.

"I'm not a solicitor. Actually, I'm doing genealogical research and believe that we might be related."

I hear an abrupt click. The secretary puts me through to Mr. Witt. A gruff voice asks bluntly, "What is this about?"

"My name is Elyse Schein and I think we might be related," I say in a professional tone. "I was adopted and I recently learned that my birth name was Witt. I'm trying to find out some information about my birth family without intruding on them. I'm looking for a family that was composed of a successful attorney who had an older son who was also an attorney and a younger sister, who was born in 1939. Do you have a sister?"

"I have no information for you," Mr. Witt says curtly before hanging up.

· | ·

What are we to make of Mr. Witt's cryptic response? Perhaps he is simply a suspicious lawyer, understandably reluctant to share any personal information over the phone with a total stranger. But if that's the case, why didn't he simply say "You've got the wrong family"? Is his refusal to admit or deny our relation an admission that we are on the mark? It's possible that he doesn't even know we exist—and if he does know, he might not want to be reminded of the twin girls his schizophrenic sister got rid of so many years ago.

Now it's clear we have no way to locate our birth mother except to hire a private investigator. "I guess we'll be calling Pam Slaton," Paula says.

PAULA: Of all of the reunions that Pamela Slaton has facilitated, her own was by far the worst. When she finally tracked down her biological mother, the woman denied the documented fact that she had given birth to Pam. She then proceeded to tell Pam that she never thought of her over the years and didn't care about her at all. Pam's personal disappointment didn't prevent her from becoming a professional search specialist, hired to help other adoptees locate their birth families. According to Pam, she has solved over twenty-five hundred cases, with the majority of them resulting in happy reunions.

Recently, Elyse and I saw Pam on the VH1 documentary special, *DMC: My Adoption Journey*, in which hip-hop legend Darryl McDaniels, the DMC of Run-DMC, learns he's adopted and searches for his biological mother. In the special, Pam helps Darryl navigate the bureaucracy of the search and successfully reunites him with his birth mother, who appears happy to be found.

When I call Pam to enquire about hiring her, she senses my hesitation.

"Are you sure you want to find her?" she asks me in a thick Long Island accent.

"Honestly, I don't know if I want to meet her. I just want to find out what happened to her."

"Only she can tell you that. I can tell you if her life has been stable—if she's had forty-seven addresses in twenty years, or has been in the same house, if she's been married, or if she has any other children."

There is no turning back. Elyse and I are determined to get some answers. I tell Pam everything we know about our birth family, which amounts to quite a lot. In addition to her last name, we know the month and year our birth mother was born, as well as the fact that her brother and father were lawyers.

Pam is confident she can locate her within days. Since Avo, the girls, and I are heading to Hilton Head tomorrow, I ask Pam to hold off on sharing any news until we return to town after the Fourth of July weekend. I don't plan to tell my parents anything about our search until we have a name—and perhaps a story—to share. I want to spend one carefree week with my family before learning the ultimate truth about my origins.

ELYSE: Since Wells and I mesh so well, I sometimes wonder if he also shared his mother's womb with a twin. One night recently when he stayed over, Wells gently teased me about still sleeping with my bear, Pooky. "Didn't you say Paula stopped sleeping with her bear soon after she got together with Avo?" Wells asked as he tucked the stuffed animal between us. I was single for so long that I am surprised by how quickly I have fallen into a natural rhythm with Wells.

Over dinner at my place the night before he's set to visit his folks in North Carolina for the long Fourth of July weekend, Wells tells me that he might not make it back before our meeting with Pam Slaton.

I surprise myself by letting out a guttural cry.

Now that finding out our birth mother's name is imminent, I revert to the original questions I have been asking myself since before meeting Paula. What if she's mentally ill? What if she's dead? What if she's alive?

When Wells offers to change his flight, pride compels me to reassure him that I'll be okay, even though I'm not sure.

"You'll be with Paula," Wells says, trying to comfort me. But how can I express my innermost fears to her when she says that she'll be relieved if our birth mother is dead? I cannot share my secret hope that our birth mother is alive and has surmounted her bouts with mental illness. I fantasize that my faith will be vindicated when we find her and I'm able to say, "I always believed in you."

PAULA: We return from Hilton Head the evening of July fourth, in time to watch the fireworks explode over lower Manhattan from our neighbor's rooftop deck. When I awake the next morning, the sky, as if anticipating the impending drama, suddenly grows dark and the clouds release a torrent of rain.

While I prepare Jesse's lunch for camp, she lounges on the couch watching a DVD of *Annie*. Mouthing the words to "Maybe," Jesse is oblivious to the significance of the song, which served as my childhood anthem to my birth mother. I expect that today, my fantasy will disintegrate.

A neighbor knocks on the door to bring me the mail she collected while we were out of town. I immediately spot an envelope from the Jewish Board of Family and Children's Services. When I rip it open, I find a letter from Alan Siskind, the executive vice president and CEO of the JBFCS.

The JBFCS is denying me, Elyse, and the other separated twins and triplets' request for access to the Yale archives. "These papers contain highly confidential information concerning numerous individuals, including the twins, their siblings, and their parents. . . . Those individuals are entitled to have their privacy respected and the confidentiality of this information maintained," writes Mr. Siskind. This time, the JBFCS is rejecting requests from twins and triplets who were studied for years. So their previous claim that Elyse and I don't warrant access because we were dropped from the study doesn't hold up. The archives will remain closed until 2066—when Elyse and I are ninety-eight years old.

When I am ready to leave for our meeting with Pam Slaton, I stand under our stoop awning, taking cover from the rain as I wait for the car service to pick me up. I dial Elyse as I wait.

"The car is on the way and we should be there to get you in a few minutes. I don't know if now is the right time to tell you," I say.

"Well, now you *have* to tell me!"

"It's just that we heard from the JBFCS. They turned down our request again. They said they're concerned about the subjects' privacy and confidentiality."

"You know what—I suddenly don't care as much about the Yale archives," Elyse says. "In fact, I don't give a shit!"

I smile broadly at Elyse's feistiness.

"It's funny you should say that, because I'm starting to feel the same way!"

"What are we going to find anyway—films of the triplets on tricycles?" Elyse asks. "A lot of psychological mumbo jumbo and charts about things that were done a long time ago?"

"What would it really tell us about ourselves? In a way, we've managed to conduct our own twin study," I add.

"It's more important that we found each other and have forged a relationship," says Elyse.

Elyse is right. Maybe we won't get access to the files until we are little old ladies, but today we will learn the truth of our origins. After we have devoted so much time and energy to opening up the archives, we laugh at the idea that suddenly our mission has faded into insignificance.

ELYSE: I feel surprisingly tranquil. No matter what we discover, the eternal questions will be quieted. Even though we will only get a sketch of our birth mother's life and her contact info, I have the odd impression that I will meet her today.

Since Paula and I are both dressed in somber colors, riding in the backseat of a black Town Car, I tell her that it's like we're on our way to a funeral. I'm trying to be light, but it sounds more ominous than I intended. I add, "Wells decided to come back from his trip early, so he'll be with me tonight. I told him that I would be all right on my own, but he insisted."

"You could have come to our place," Paula says. I am touched by her offer, but can't imagine breaking down in front of Avo and the girls.

Once we arrive at the restaurant, we head up the narrow staircase to the second floor for our meeting with Pam. Paula flushes red.

"No matter what happens, we're going home to our nice lives," I reassure her.

With her frosted bottle-blond hair, mesmerizing blue eyes, and voluptuous figure, Pam reminds me of a femme fatale.

"So what do you think I'm going to tell you?" Pam asks, after we take a seat opposite her.

"I just have a feeling that she's deceased," Paula says, "that she's no longer with us." Pam nods without giving anything away.

"I don't know if it's my hope speaking or if it's a gut feeling," I pronounce, "but I do know that if she did survive her bouts with mental illness and if she's alive today, she's got to be an amazing person, a very wise and strong woman."

The look of pity in Pam's eyes throws me off balance.

PAULA: "Unfortunately, you are the one who is correct," Pam says solemnly, nodding in my direction. "Your birth mother did pass away."

A bittersweet mix of relief and sadness sweeps over me. There will be no emotional reunion, no pressure to find a place for our birth mother in my life. I turn to Elyse and hug her tightly, waiting for her tears to flow, but they don't. She is surprisingly calm.

ELYSE: She is dead. I hear the words, but cannot react. Instead of sadness, I am numb. Overcome by a surprising sense of relief, I realize that Paula and I have finally come to the end of our search.

"Her name was Leda Witt," says Pam.

Ironically, in Greek mythology, Leda was the mother of twins. After being seduced by Zeus in the form of a swan, Leda gave birth to Castor and Pollux, who lend their names to the star cluster Gemini, the Twins.

Pam tells us that Leda died in 1978, when Paula and I were only nine years old. Leda lived in Manhattan, so when I made regular trips to visit my grandparents in the city I might have passed her on the street in Greenwich Village. Leda died so long ago, when I was too young to even think of looking for answers. In some way, it takes away a burden: if she had died just a few years ago, I would be kicking myself that I hadn't searched sooner. It's clear that there is no way she could have raised us, so there is no question about why she gave us up, no feeling of rejection.

PAULA: Although Pam couldn't learn the cause of Leda's death, she suggested that "mental illness puts a major strain on a person."

"Giving us up must have exacerbated her already vulnerable mental state," says Elyse when we settle in and order some wine at the restaurant after Pam has left.

Leda already had a history of attempted suicide, so Elyse and I both suspect that she eventually succeeded. Or perhaps she accidentally overdosed on her prescription medications. Since Elyse and I share a vivid imagination, a flair for melodrama, and a taste for black humor, we trade worst-case scenarios.

"Maybe she was hit by a car," suggests Elyse.

"Or maybe she was living on the streets and was murdered," I say.

I'm sure to any eavesdropper we'd sound a bit nuts. But who is to say how anyone should react when they find out the mother they never knew is dead?

ELYSE: "I'm sad that our birth mother never learned that she did the right thing in giving us up, and that we're okay and that we found each other," Paula says.

As we clink our wineglasses and toast Leda, we laugh at the notion that we're commemorating our mother's death—twenty-eight years after the fact. Doing the math, we figure out that Leda would have been thirty-eight when she died, the same age we'll be on our next birthday. It feels like so much has come full circle, and it all has a strange sort of symmetry.

I had half expected to go home after our meeting with Pam and curl up under the covers until Wells returned from vacation. But instead of feeling mournful, I am giddy, almost gleeful. A great mystery of my life has been resolved. We are Leda's daughters and we are celebrating the woman who gave us life.

PAULA: Now that I know that Leda is dead, I can no longer examine women of a certain age wondering if they might be my birth mother. I think back to myself at age nine, when I was ignorant of the fact that my twin had recently lost her adoptive mother and that our birth mother had just died. Was Leda thinking of us when she died? She was certainly the last thing on my mind in 1978. That year, I was the teacher's pet in my fourth-grade class. I had a crush on David Epstein, liked jumping rope, and went on a family vacation to Puerto Rico.

When I was blaming my birth mother for my acne and fat thighs, she was dead. When I wrote about how I didn't want to find her, she was dead. When I got married, she was dead. From the time I was little, each birthday I wondered whether she was thinking of me. Now I know she wasn't even alive for most of them.

"My mother died," I practice saying to myself, but the words taste bitter on my tongue. My mother is alive and well and living in Hilton Head.

I am in the unusual position of mourning the loss of someone I never knew and never wanted to know.

"I'm proud of you and Elyse for doing all this research," says my dad after I tell him the news about Leda. "And I'm sad that your birth mother had such a hard life."

My parents must feel some sense of relief that the trail ends here. There won't be an awkward meeting with my biological mother, or questions about whether to invite Leda to family functions. They are the only parents I will ever have.

I once described myself as "the poster girl for adoption," but I wouldn't claim that title anymore. Of course, I still love my parents as much as any biological child does, and I have no doubt they love me as much as they would a child who carried their own DNA. But now it is impossible to deny that as comfortable as we are in our relationship, our gain resulted from others' losses. No doubt, my parents must have mourned the child they never were able to conceive, just as Leda must have mourned the children she was not able to keep. And while I denied it for years, perhaps the fact that I was relinquished for adoption shaped my identity more than I was willing to acknowledge.

ELYSE: Paula and I are not sure how to refer to Leda. Up until now, we have been careful to use the qualifying terms *biological* and *birth* before *mother*. When I read Ann Fessler's book *The Girls Who Went Away*, I am struck by the birth mother's point of view, which the book presents.

Fessler herself is an adoptee who located her birth mother, but waited fourteen years before contacting her. In researching her book, she gathered the stories of one hundred birth mothers from the end of World War II in 1945 until the *Roe v. Wade* verdict legalized abortion nationally in 1973. As adoption became more commonplace, the demand for healthy infants increased. The number of nonfamily adoptions increased from eight thousand in 1937 to seventy thousand in 1965. At the time these adoptions took place, motherhood out of wedlock was still socially unacceptable. In order to find "better" parents, adoption agencies often pushed single pregnant women to give up their children and told potential adoptive parents that these children were unwanted.

Reading firsthand testimonials from birth mothers of this period,

I am saddened that an unforgiving society forced these young unwed mothers to surrender their children. Many of these women never recovered from this trauma. Though Leda was not a kid at the time of our birth and was clearly unable to raise us, I cannot help but see Leda through the many stories of young unwed mothers.

For these women, the term *biological mother* seems to reduce their role in the birth to a merely biological function. If they are called anything at all, they prefer it to be *natural mother*. Though I consider Lynn my natural mother, I would like a better word to describe my relationship to Leda. Suddenly it occurs to me that Leda is not my mother, she is *our* mother.

· | ·

Since Pam told us that Leda is our mother, the lawyer who hung up on me back in May must indeed be our birth uncle. We're guessing that David Witt is not anxious to hear from us again, so Paula and I write him a letter explaining our situation, reassuring him that we are not looking to disturb him or his family. In case he's concerned that we're after money, we acknowledge that we're aware that according to New York State law, we are not entitled to any inheritance from our birth family. We let Mr. Witt know that we have already learned about Leda's mental illness and early death. He doesn't have to fear upsetting us.

"All we are hoping to gain are some stories or photos of Leda," we write. "In return, perhaps we may be able to offer you some comfort that your sister's children are doing well."

In the letter, we include bios, which depict us as worthwhile members of society, not psychotic maniacs. By describing our professional and personal accomplishments, we hope to show Mr. Witt that we are leading stable, happy lives. Perhaps he'll be curious to meet his sister's daughters, thirty-seven years after their birth.

PAULA: After two weeks and no response from Mr. Witt, Elyse and I can't wait any longer. Elyse takes the bus over to my apartment, where we hole up in Jesse's room to make the call. We've decided to phone him at home. When a woman, presumably Mrs. Witt, picks up the phone and realizes who is calling, she sets down the phone. I'm not sure if she's hung up, but I wait.

After several minutes, Mr. Witt grunts into the receiver, "Don't call here again. Thank you!"

Elyse and I shake our heads in shock and embarrassment. No doubt, it must be painful for him to dredge up the past, but did he have to be so gruff?

"What are we, stalkers?" I ask Elyse rhetorically. Mr. Witt's rejection stings. Not so long ago, I was the one who didn't want to be found; now I'm the intruder. Perhaps he doesn't realize that we're not expecting him to play the part of doting uncle. We just want some answers about Leda that only he can provide.

"This wasn't a good day to quit smoking!" says Elyse. She seems determined to quit cold turkey on the first try.

"You can say that again!"

ELYSE: Now that we know we can't ask David Witt to answer our questions about Leda, I am even more desperate to find someone who can. In between errands and e-mails, I routinely type Leda's name into search engines until one day I'm surprised to see it turn up under a link for the prestigious Bronx High School of Science. The graduating class of 1957 is organizing its fiftieth reunion and Leda Witt's name appears under "In Memoriam."

Maybe one of Leda's classmates will share reminiscences with us. But how should we present our story without creating further mystery? We certainly don't want to divulge the circumstances of our conception to her classmates. In the worst-case scenario, we can traipse up to the Bronx and get an old yearbook from the library. In the meantime, Paula and I write a concise e-mail to the organizers of the reunion mentioning that we are looking for information about a relative.

I'm thrilled when one of Leda's former classmates, Marsha, immediately responds that she and Leda often ran into each other on the Broadway bus on their way up to Bronx Science. Every tidbit fills me with joy. We are finally able to fill in some of the pieces of Leda's life.

Marsha recalls a "devastating accident in Italy" in which Leda was badly injured. "She joked how she was lying in a hospital bed under a crucifix, with very negative thoughts on the subject." Hearing about that one incident helps me to form a mental picture of Leda, who apparently had the same dark sense of humor as Paula and me.

This new information allows us to constitute a time line. In 1955, at age fifteen, Leda visited Italy. Both Paula and I visited Italy when we were fifteen, unknowingly following in her footsteps. Leda graduated from high school in 1957 and dropped out after a year of college. She was first institutionalized two years later, at age twenty. Eight years later she gave birth to us and surrendered us.

Looking at the Bronx High School of Science Class of 1957 reunion website, I pore over old pictures Marsha has posted of her and her classmates on graduation day. I scroll and scan through the beaming faces of the young graduates in their billowing white dresses and corsages, anticipating that I will spot Leda in their midst.

I shiver when an e-mail message from Marsha appears in my inbox. Though unaware of the exact nature our relation to Leda, Marsha had promised to scan Leda's yearbook photo for us. Recalling the frightening description of Leda given to us by the adoption agency, I am filled with trepidation that she will look like a werewolf.

Behind the fuzzy pixels on my computer screen, a faded image of an attractive young woman materializes. I immediately see myself in the contours of her face and in her dark, inquisitive eyes, and I am mesmerized. The woman in the picture exudes intelligence and sensitivity, and I imagine her as a misunderstood poetess.

What happened behind the facade of Leda's innocent expression that led to her institutionalization two years later? Knowing what tragic fate will befall her in the coming years, I yearn to warn the seventeen-year-old. Unable to tear myself away from the picture of our mother, I stare at my computer screen until my eyes ache.

PAULA: When Elyse forwards the e-mail and I first glimpse Leda's yearbook picture, she looks completely foreign to me. Only when I take a second look do I notice anything remotely familiar. Then suddenly, as if I have put on a pair of corrective lenses, her features come into focus and the resemblance turns uncannily clear. She's got the same thick, coarse, wavy hair. The same mischievous glint in her almond-shaped eyes. The same high forehead and oval face. The longer I stare at the grainy black-and-white photo, the more uncanny the likeness becomes. I scurry downstairs to locate my high school yearbook. When I place Leda's senior year photo side by side with mine, the resemblance is undeniable.

Less than three years ago I had no inkling I would ever reconnect with my origins and now I am looking at a picture of my birth mother.

She was not a big bad wolf after all. In fact, she looks like a sweet young woman with soft, attractive features. Could her appearance have changed so dramatically by the time she gave birth to Elyse and me? Although she is my mother, in the picture she is still a child. Seeing her, my maternal instincts kick in and I want to protect her from what's to come.

"There's nothing in Bartlette's for me," reads Leda's quote by her yearbook photo, suggesting that the famous book of quotations couldn't offer anything to adequately reflect her feelings. Her quote—or rather, lack of one—reflects her wit and intelligence, but also her sense of alienation. Maybe I'm reading too much into it, but her misspelling of Bartlett's makes her seem especially vulnerable and human. If Leda had known then that her twin daughters would one day pore over her yearbook for a glimmer of insight into her personality, she might have strained to come up with something more expressive.

Looking deeply into Leda's eyes, I try to imagine what she might have been thinking about when the picture was taken. Perhaps I'm projecting too much into every detail, but I sense that she was a sensitive young woman who, like Elyse and me, felt things too strongly.

"I miss her more now that I see her picture," says Elyse when I call her to compare reactions. "I wish she were here so she could know that her daughters turned out okay."

"And that we found each other," I add. The quest to find Leda ends here, with this digital reproduction of a vintage yearbook photo.

Chapter Twenty-one

ELYSE: "Guess what!" I exclaim, on the phone with Paula moments after opening the mail. "We got a letter from David Witt." According to the postmark, Mr. Witt sent the letter August 8, the day after he hung up on us, ordering us never to call him back. Paula and I had assumed we would have to content ourselves with the grainy copy of her yearbook photo, which we received only yesterday. The sudden hope that we will learn more about Leda buoys my spirit.

What to make of Mr. Witt's sudden change of heart? Perhaps he needed time to mull over the situation and was planning to call us on his own. Our last phone call might have goaded him into action, since he clearly didn't want us calling his house again. Maybe his curiosity got the best of him.

I read to Paula from the brief handwritten note, which sounds like a formal business letter:

"Dear Ms. Schein and Ms. Bernstein, I am willing to meet with you and answer any questions you may have about Leda, to the extent that I can," he writes cryptically in scrawled script. He adds that he will contact us as soon as he has plans to visit New York from his home in Delaware. There is no return address.

I have already composed a long list of questions to ask him. Some will be awfully hard to phrase. How do you ask someone, "How did your sister die?"

Mr. Witt didn't give us any indication of when he was planning to come to New York, so we must respect his boundaries and wait for him to contact us. Expecting him to call at any time, I program his telephone number into my cell phone so his name will pop up if he does. I wouldn't like to be caught off guard if Mr. Witt calls me while I'm waiting tables or am at home watching a movie with Wells.

· | ·

Though we've talked to fellow separated twins about their experiences, oddly enough Paula and I have never spoken with adult identical twins who were raised together. By meeting local twins Louise Crawford and Caroline Ghertler, perhaps we'll gain some insight into what our relationship might have been like had we been raised together.

Louise, a Park Slope writer/mom who we recently crossed paths with at a book reading, lives just two blocks from her twin sister, Caroline, a set designer and new mom. When Paula and I meet them for brunch at a patisserie on Seventh Avenue, the four of us look as if we could be waiting to audition for a Doublemint commercial. We sit across the table from one another, scrutinizing similarities and differences. In their late forties, the twins look remarkably similar, yet they are distinctive enough that we can easily tell them apart. They both wear their straight brown hair down to their shoulders, but Louise styles hers in a side part and Caroline has bangs.

"So what was it like growing up with your twin?" Paula asks and we all laugh at the absurdity of the question. They are the oddities for a change.

"We were sort of the anti-twin twins," says Louise, who seems to be the more outspoken of the pair. "We never traded places or played jokes on our teachers."

"Did you each play different roles?" I ask.

"Yes, definitely. Caroline was the artist and I was the musician.

For Christmas, Caroline was given an art box and I was given a guitar," Louise says.

Obviously, even identical twins who were raised together aren't exactly alike. It stands to reason that the parts of their environment they don't share—different friends, different life experiences, even different placements in the womb—must count for something.

"Did people ever confuse you?" I ask.

"Our parents never dressed us alike, and early on they did our hair differently," says Louise. "Also, for most of our childhood, we went to different schools."

"I was jealous of her friends. I thought she was more popular and did everything better," confesses Caroline. "She was the star. Then she got married much earlier than I did and had kids before I did, so that was hard."

"What's the best thing about being twins?"

"You have a shared history. You know each other so well that you can follow every reference," Louise says. "I'll call Caroline and just talk to her as if we were continuing a conversation. I don't have to explain myself to her."

"Are you ever irritated by each other? Is it hard to see your expressions on another person?" Paula asks.

"Yes, I don't like seeing Caroline angry because I see myself. I know now what I look like when I'm yelling at my husband and I don't like it," admits Louise.

I recall how irritated I used to get watching Paula make one of my expressions. Was it because of my possessiveness of my individuality or because I didn't like what her expression revealed about me? Probably both. Maybe Paula simply exaggerated her expressions in reaction to my own.

"And then it bugs me how Caroline is always fixing my hair or critiquing my outfits."

"I'm glad that you don't tell me how to wear my hair or what to wear!" Paula exclaims to me. "That would drive me crazy." Caroline and Louise smile, obviously getting a kick out of us. "But it is nice to hear that even twins who grew up together get on each other's nerves!"

"One occupational hazard of being a twin is that it makes your relationship with your spouse more challenging," explains Louise. "You expect them to understand you when you speak to them in shorthand the way you do with your twin."

"Not having grown up together, at least we don't have to worry about that," I say.

As the check comes, Caroline and Louise look back and forth at us as if they're watching a tennis match.

"You don't look identical," Louise pronounces. "The basic bone structure and features are the same, but you have very different"— she grasps for the right word—"styles,"

"That's funny, because I could imagine wearing what Elyse is wearing," Paula says, checking out my simple gray polo shirt and red cardigan.

"No," Louise explains, "it's more than that. You have different energies. I know it sounds new-age, but there's just an inexplicable difference between you."

"Do you ever wish you weren't twins?" I ask Louise and Caroline.

"Yes! Sometimes I wish I could just go far away, but I can't because we are so connected. Whatever decision I make is intrinsically linked to Caroline." Louise says this as if it were a great burden.

"She's an extension of me," says Caroline. "There are no boundaries between us."

"Like an appendage that you can't get rid of," I add, trying to comprehend the closeness of their relationship. Louise nods back affirmatively.

"Could you imagine not growing up together?" I ask.

"I can't imagine!" Louise says. "I wouldn't trade it for anything." Caroline nods in agreement.

Paula and I will never be able to compensate for losing out on a shared history, but now that she is part of my life I realize that, as with Louise and Caroline, there is an undeniable link that has united us. From now on, I will consider Paula and her family in whatever decision I make about my future.

PAULA: "Hang on," an attractive middle-aged woman softly commands when I lose my balance on a packed subway train. Heading into Manhattan to meet Avo for an early lunch in SoHo, I hadn't anticipated hitting rush hour.

I cling to her velvet jacket like a young child. As the train wobbles through the subway tunnel, I realize that serendipity—or rather, public transportation—has bound us to each other for the next ten minutes. We start chatting.

By profession, this stranger is a worker's compensation judge, but her real passion is chanting the Lotus Sutra. "I only found true happiness once I began to chant," she tells me. I generally pooh-pooh such spiritual claims, but this woman's big blue eyes gaze at me with maternal acceptance and suddenly I don't care how far-fetched it sounds.

To blow her mind, I briefly recount the story of Elyse and me.

"You had to go through the life you led to get to this place," she tells me. She's like a monk parceling out wisdom; in her words, I was destined to be born as Leda's daughter, be adopted by my parents, and marry Avo in order to find out at age thirty-five that I have a twin. There is no way that Elyse and I could have been raised together, because fate didn't have that in store for us.

Although I don't believe in reincarnation, I momentarily allow myself to pretend that this Zen stranger is Leda's representative on Earth. Even though it's not her stop, when we reach Fourteenth Street, the Buddhist judge steps off the train so she can give me a proper embrace. She calls after me, "Have a happy life!"

Emerging from the subway into Union Square, where the green

market is in full swing this fall morning, an irrepressible smile
breaks out on my face and everyone I pass seems to smile back. It
strikes me that I haven't popped an Ativan in weeks and I'm not a
complete wreck.

When I take out my wallet to pay for a cup of hot apple cider,
I notice that my cell phone is ringing.

"Hello?" I chirp.

"This is Mr. David Witt. I said I would call you when I'm coming to town."

Two months have passed since Elyse and I received Mr. Witt's
letter and we were beginning to get antsy. Just a few days ago, when
we celebrated our third birthday together, we wondered whether he
would ever contact us.

"Meet me at ten a.m. on December sixteenth on the southeast
corner of Seventy-seventh and Amsterdam, near where Leda grew
up," Mr. Witt commands.

"I'm looking forward to meeting you," I begin to say, before Mr.
Witt cuts me off.

"Good-bye."

I suddenly remember that I have bought tickets for Jesse and me
to see *Annie* that same day. I never could have predicted that *Annie*
would take on such mythic significance in my life.

I call Elyse to share the news.

"He called me too—I just got off the phone with him!" she exclaims. "Did you realize today would have been Leda's birthday?"

ELYSE: On a crisp, clear Saturday morning, the first day of Chanukah, I ride the C train uptown for our meeting with David Witt. Contemplating the bilingual health advertisements decorating the train, I am caught off guard when a familiar face approaches me.

"Hi," says Paula. Through the window speeding past like celluloid, Paula had caught a glimpse of me from the F train and had hopped across the platform to join me, though this wasn't our meeting place. On the ride uptown, we chatter about everything but our much-anticipated meeting with our birth uncle, including this year's Oscar contenders and the new phrases Ruby has concocted. We're so immersed in our conversation we almost miss our stop at the Eighty-first Street subway station. As we stroll past the American Museum of Natural History, I imagine Leda, who grew up just blocks away, wandering through its halls.

To calm our nerves, Paula and I nosh on a plain bagel, which we share at a bagel shop on Amsterdam Avenue. Meanwhile, we scope out the corner of Seventy-seventh and Amsterdam where Mr. Witt asked us to meet him. Taking surreptitious glances at the clock on the wall, at exactly ten a.m. we venture out to meet Mr. Witt.

"It's like we're in *The French Connection* and it's time to make the connection," Paula says as we bundle up and head outside.

I had anticipated that "Uncle David" would hide around a corner to confirm that we are not bag ladies before meeting us, but he is already at the corner across the street, looking up at us expectantly. Wearing khakis, an oxford shirt, a tweed jacket, and a cap, with a *New York Times* tucked neatly under his arm, Mr. Witt could easily pass for a professor. With his soft features, round face, and ruddy complexion, he doesn't resemble the hardened lawyer I had pictured or the man who barked at us on the phone.

"He's cute," I whisper as we cross Seventy-seventh Street, heading toward Mr. Witt. "I wish I knew what was going through his mind right now." Does he see his sister resurrected in us?

"He looks very distinguished," Paula agrees as we approach him.

PAULA: There are no warm embraces. Instead, we politely shake Mr. Witt's hand and obediently follow him around the corner. If I didn't know who he was, I don't think I would recognize him as a blood relative. But then again, I haven't met many blood relatives. I think of Mr. Witt as Leda's brother rather than our uncle.

I had expected a stronger reaction, maybe a hug or a look of surprise when he first spotted us. But Mr. Witt is strangely matter-of-fact. My nervousness dissipates as soon as he begins talking.

"This is where Leda grew up," Mr. Witt says, pointing at a nondescript brick apartment building. I stare at the turn-of-the-century edifice, as if it will reveal some secret about Leda's life. "When she lived here, there was a public school across the street," says Mr. Witt. He motions to a playground, which is abandoned on this brisk winter morning.

It seems odd to me that Mr. Witt uses the pronoun "she" as if he is a tour guide who was absent from the past he is depicting.

"And that's where she spent the last days of her life," he says, directing our attention to an upscale hotel across the street. "It didn't look so nice then. Back then it was the Benjamin Franklin, a single-room-occupancy hotel."

I shudder thinking of Leda living—and possibly dying—in a run-down SRO. At least the hotel was only a block away from her parents' apartment, so they would have been able to check in on her regularly. Since we just met Mr. Witt a few minutes ago, I restrain myself from asking how Leda died.

"Thank you for meeting with us," I say, trying to put him at ease. "Just so you know, we're prepared to learn the truth. You don't have to sugarcoat things for our sake."

I look to him for a reaction, but his face remains expressionless. He is cordial, but there is a clear, unspoken boundary between us.

Mr. Witt leads us a couple of blocks crosstown to the Viand Coffee Shop on Broadway, the same diner where I meet my parents for lunch whenever they're in town. As we settle into a booth at the back of the crowded restaurant, I picture my parents popping in to join us for dessert.

"Get whatever you want," he says, like a beneficent uncle taking his nieces out for Saturday brunch. I order a matzo ball soup, and Mr. Witt tells the Greek waiter, "I'll have what she's having."

I grin, as if his order is a sign of approval.

ELYSE: Mr. Witt takes out two manila envelopes and presents one to me and one to Paula. We excitedly open them and find pictures of Leda as a little girl. One is her kindergarten class picture from P.S. 87, taken in June 1945.

"Can you pick her out?" Mr. Witt asks, like a child playing a game.

"There she is!" I say proudly, spotting Leda immediately. Though there is no one characteristic that calls out to me, I know she is the nondescript six-year-old girl in a pinafore dress with a bow in her brown hair and her lips pursed together in a timid smile. So you can recognize family after all.

"These were all I could find," Mr. Witt says apologetically. I wonder if he's simply trying to spare us the disturbing image of Leda in her later years.

As Paula and I study the photos, Mr. Witt launches into Leda's story.

"During her first year of college, she was okay, but during her second year, she had a mental breakdown. She couldn't function. Mother had to go out and clean up her room, which was in quite a state, and bring her home," he says. Paula and I nod our heads, urging him to continue.

What exactly did Leda do to destroy her room? Did she just let newspapers pile up or was it a more dramatic gesture, like wrecking the place? I'm not about to ask Mr. Witt for the gruesome details. He looks to us for approval before continuing. "What we've imagined is probably worse than the reality," Paula says, urging him not to spare us the harsh truth.

"There were periods of functioning," Mr. Witt continues, "and then she would be hospitalized. When she wasn't in the hospital, she saw a psychiatrist. She never was able to work." Mr. Witt pauses for a moment, straining to remember before adding, "These are not things on which I've dwelled in recent years."

"Of course, we understand," I say sympathetically.

"Mother and Father would drop in on her periodically to make sure she was okay," Mr. Witt comments. "They did their best."

Hearing that Leda's family cared for her is a great relief. After we'd imagined her living on the street, this doesn't sound so awful—she had a regular place to live, and regular visits from her folks. I think of my brother Jay's dependence on our family and how we try to make his life as comfortable as possible.

"What was she like before she got sick?" Paula asks, looking up from her soup.

"She was pleasant, cheery, and active before she became ill. She was a good student. She was smart, like you guys," Mr. Witt says, looking up at us.

"She didn't become heavy until after she became sick. It was a combination of the depression and the medications. She liked to draw and paint, but I didn't think she was very good at it."

We laugh awkwardly at his honesty. "Neither am I," Paula says.

"Did she like music?" I ask, wondering if she ever did cross paths with Bob Dylan.

"No, she wasn't interested in popular music. Actually, she was pretty square," Mr. Witt says, grinning. So she might not have been the hip rebellious chick I imagined, but square can still be pretty cool.

PAULA: Each fact brings us slightly closer to knowing Leda. Her nickname was Dede. Devoted Brooklyn Dodgers fans, her family rooted for Jackie Robinson, the first African American to play on a Major League baseball team. Her parents spoke some Yiddish around the house.

"Our family was not religious at all," says Mr. Witt. "By heritage, we were Jewish, but I'm not even sure if Leda ever set foot in a synagogue."

"Really?" I'm incredulous and a bit disappointed.

Since all I had known about my birth mother was that she was Jewish, I somehow imagined that spending my junior year in Israel and learning Hebrew brought me closer to my biological heritage. As Reform Jews, my family didn't keep kosher or Shabbat, but we dutifully attended synagogue on the High Holy Days and celebrated Chanukah and Passover.

"Do you want to see pictures of my daughters?" I ask Mr. Witt.

Without waiting for an answer, I whip the pictures out of my bag and proudly present them to him. He studies a photo of Jesse and Ruby grinning for the camera in my parents' oversize Jacuzzi, sun streaming down on them from a skylight. I wait for Mr. Witt to comment on a family resemblance or to remark on their cuteness, but instead he silently hands the photos back to me. Jesse and Ruby would have been his sister's grandchildren, his great-nieces, but judging by Mr. Witt's reaction, he could just as well be looking at pictures of the waiter's kids.

"So did Leda have any friends?" I ask, changing the subject.

"Yes, she had a number of friends in her network," says Mr. Witt.

"You mean other mentally ill people?" I ask, wondering if "her network" is a euphemism for "other crazy people."

"Yes," he admits.

"So what was her diagnosis?" asks Elyse.

"She was diagnosed as schizophrenic, but I believe there was a large component of depression," says Mr. Witt. "It was painful for the family."

"Was she paranoid? Did she have delusions or hallucinations?" I ask. I want to pinpoint what was wrong with her. This may be the only chance we have to meet with Mr. Witt and get the real story.

"Not that I knew about," says Mr. Witt. "As far as I know, there was no other mental illness in the family."

So she was not a raving lunatic after all. While we'll never know for sure, it seems that our hunch was right: Leda primarily suffered from depression.

"Your mother was quite rational and intelligent," he adds.

Hearing Mr. Witt refer to Leda as our mother jolts me.

"I don't think of her as my mother," I say. "I prefer to say 'biological mother.' "

"I know you have other parents, but from my point of view, Leda was your mother," Mr. Witt responds.

ELYSE: "When did you learn she was pregnant?" I ask.

"Not until after you were born," he responds.

"So you didn't know about Louise Wise?"

"No, I'd never heard of them." If he's never heard of the agency who handled our adoption, surely he knows nothing about the twin study.

"I remember when she told me she had given birth to twins, we were sitting in our parents' living room," Mr. Witt continues as he transports himself back to 1968. "You know what she named you?" Mr. Witt asks with a grin.

"We know. I was Marian, and Paula was Jean," I say as Mr. Witt tries to visualize who is who.

"She said happily that she had named you Jean after Father's sister and Marian after a friend of the family. I had the impression that she was happy to have had children, but unhappy to have to give them up."

I smile at the notion that our birth made Leda happy, but I can't help but think that Mr. Witt is simplifying what must have been a painful, complicated situation.

"What was your parents' reaction to the pregnancy?" I ask.

"They felt it was sad, but there was no question she had to give you up. She knew she couldn't take care of you. She couldn't take care of herself."

"Did you know who the father was?"

"Leda never told me who the father was and I didn't ask. I wasn't judgmental about it. I hoped she had had a loving relationship." So we'll never know who our birth father was. In any case, there's a good chance that he was an acquaintance from her circle, a mentally ill friend. Like Mr. Witt, I sincerely hope that Leda had love in her life.

PAULA: "It's a relief to hear that she had a place to live and that she was cared for," I say, trying to be upbeat.

"She was loved as much as anyone could be," Mr. Witt says. "As a result, her illness was a real blow. Our parents were very fond of her, but they didn't know what to do."

Tears stream down my cheeks as I imagine how devastated my parents would be if I succumbed to a serious mental illness and died at a young age. I take my glasses off and pat my eyes dry, consoling myself with the knowledge that Leda was loved.

"So how did she die?" Elyse asks solemnly.

"I think she had a heart attack," he says. "She was found in her hotel room."

I turn to Elyse, who gazes back at me sympathetically. It sounds so bleak.

"Do you think it was suicide?" I ask.

"There were occasions when Leda took too much medication, but they seemed to be cries for help. I was never told she died of an overdose, but I can't rule it out."

We'll never know for sure how Leda died. Would that particular piece of information give us a greater understanding of who Leda was and how she lived? In the end, I decide it doesn't really matter.

Sitting in this coffee shop on the Upper West Side of Manhattan with our biological uncle, it strikes me that our journey ends here. Two and a half years after Elyse found me, my past is no longer shrouded in mystery.

ELYSE: Since Leda was cremated and there is no grave to visit, our pilgrimage consists of a visit to an old SRO converted into a tourist hotel on the Upper West Side, a stroll down Broadway, and a Greek diner. I am struck by the overwhelming realization that Paula and I are the last remnants of Leda's time on earth.

Now that our official interview with Mr. Witt is over, he seems more at ease and begins to chat about the old New York of his childhood. "Now it's all chain stores and Starbucks," he says forlornly.

"I share your sentiments exactly!" I say.

"Where are you two off to?" he asks casually as we stroll down Broadway to catch a cab.

"Well, I'm off to see *Annie* with my daughter and Elyse is going to see *La Bohème* with her boyfriend tonight," Paula says.

"Ah, *La Bohème!* How enchanting!"

When I admit that I don't know who's singing tonight, and that this will be my first time to see this opera, Mr. Witt reacts incredulously.

"You'll have to listen for 'Mi chiamano Mimi,' " he says with a glint in his eye.

Rifling through the pages of my CD booklet, I chirp back to him in my bad Italian.

"No, no, it goes, 'La storia mia è breve.' Mr. Witt sings excitedly and I am momentarily flooded with the fantasy of him as our doting, cosmopolitan uncle schooling me for a night at the opera. We shake hands and thank Mr. Witt for meeting with us. Though gracious and warm, he has made it clear that this will be our only meeting.

"It's good that you never got to meet her," he offers. "You would have been sad."

As we turn and begin to walk away, Mr. Witt calls after us, "She was a nice person."

· | ·

Paula and I climb into a yellow taxi and speed down Broadway.

Racing through the streets a-blur with last-minute holiday shoppers, the taxi stops abruptly at a busy corner near Madison Square Garden, at Paula's command. We exchange a hurried good-bye before Paula rushes into the coffee shop to meet her friend, who is waiting with Jesse and her own daughter in tow. With hours to spare before my date with Wells, I escape the overrun midtown streets and head back uptown. Now that Paula and I have come to the end of our shared quest, our paths diverge. What comes next will be invented by both of us.

Epilogue

Seven months later

PAULA: The following June, at the end of her last day of pre-K, Jesse is greeted by her mother, her little sister, and a surprise guest— her aunt Elyse. Elyse boosts Jesse up on her shoulders so she can watch the world from a grown-up's point of view. Looking at Jesse riding triumphantly aloft her aunt's shoulders, I see unadulterated joy.

After a celebratory lunch, the four of us stroll to a nearby playground, where the girls romp in the sprinklers. Squealing with delight, Jesse gleefully dumps water over Ruby's head as Elyse and I do our best to stay dry.

"This reminds me of a vacation I took with Gramma and Pop-Pop and Uncle Steve when I was little," I say to my daughters.

"And Aunt Elyse, too," Jesse adds, pointing at Aunt Elyse, who is patting Ruby dry with a towel.

"Well, actually, no, she didn't come with us," I say.

"Why not?" asks Jesse, scrunching up her nose.

"Because I didn't know her when I was a kid."

Jesse silently tries to make sense of my words. "But you're twins," she says, as if she's telling me something I don't already know.

"You're right. We were born at the same time to the same parents, but I was adopted by Gramma and PopPop and she was adopted by Marty and another mommy. Then, when we were grown-ups, we met each other for the first time."

Jesse looks down at her sandals.

"It's confusing—most grown-ups don't even understand it," I reassure her. "It's a very strange situation."

Jesse lets the subject drop, but I continue to contemplate the meaning of family as we walk home.

· | ·

When I was younger, I believed that blood connections were insignificant. But that changed after I met Elyse. I initially resisted the pull of our bond, but it is now impossible to deny.

Having lived our lives apart for so long, we have no need to differentiate ourselves. But as different as we are, we come from the same stock. In each other, we recognize a kindred spirit. Getting to know our twin and seeing the life we might have led has made us more certain of who we are. Although we don't always fit together neatly, we are missing pieces to the same puzzle.

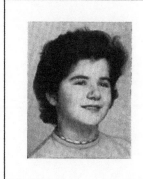

LEDA WITT
160 W. 77 St.
TR 7-5493
Forum, Mt. Sinai Hospital Vol.,
Office Sq., Lunchroom Sq., Art
Sq., Jr. Achievement.
*There's nothing in Bartlette's for
me.*

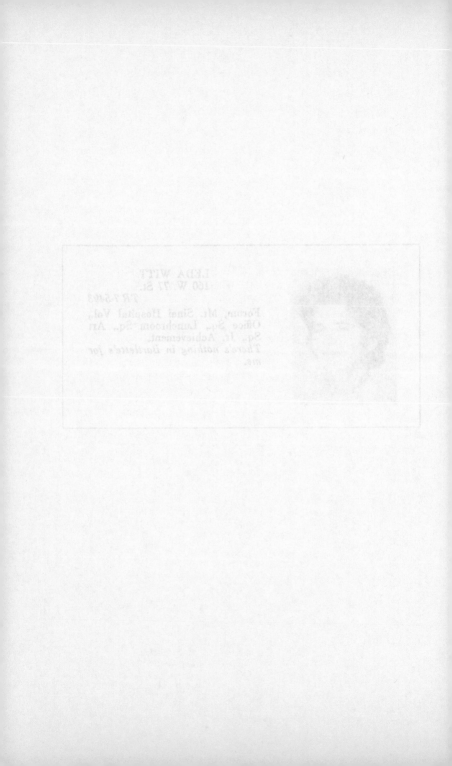

Acknowledgments

PAULA: Deep appreciation for the support of good friends: Blair Miller, Dori Fern, Andrea Sobrino, Rebecca Baer, Lauren Greiner, Amanda Aaron, Anne Mette Lundtofte, Christina Knight, Nancy Appel, Shannon Timms, Meirav Reuveni, Alexis Sheldon, and, for her insight into raising twins, Deb Heicklen.

Much gratefulness for the advice and camaraderie of my fellow writers at Brooklyn Writers Space. For granting me the time to write, I owe a great deal to Carol Cardinal and Elke Van Dyke.

Heartfelt gratitude to Steven Bernstein for being a friend as well as a brother.

Most of all, thanks to Avo, Jesse, and Ruby, who remind me of the meaning of family every day.

ELYSE: Profound thanks to Wells Crandall for his emotional support during the writing of this book and for being part of the story.

My sincere appreciation to Claire Brofman, Ken Cohen, and Charlotte Hodes for their recollections.

I thank Jaime Bley and Mario Courbis for sharing their story.

For being my readers and friends, I thank Patricia Bley, Jean-Claude Gaubert, Catherine Toussaint, Veronika Valentová, and Glenda Zumwalt.

For making me feel at home everywhere, I thank Joshua Bley, Laurent Bourdon, Jiří Brynda, Annie Cartoux, Juliette Col, Sylvie

Crochet, Max Farr, Hugh Harsh, Joseph Hill, Kateřina Krusová, Tracey Kucszinski, Fabrice Loiseau, Philippe Nathan, Claudia Ruf, Kelly Spain, Birgit Van Gestel, and Mischas Vernay.

With love I thank my parents, Martin and Toni Schein, and my brother, Jay Schein, for their willingness to share the story of our family.

I am forever thankful to my mother, Linda Schein, for watching over me.

PAULA AND ELYSE: We are eternally grateful to Peter Steinberg, our friend and agent, and to Jennifer Hershey, our inspired editor, who helped usher this book into the world.

For her editorial guidance and enthusiasm, we thank Laura Ford. For their keen professionalism, we thank Carol Schneider, Jynne Dilling Martin, Laura Goldin, Muriel Jorgenson, Dana Isaacson, and Porscha Burke.

For facilitating our research and guiding us along the way, we thank Ronny Diamond; Martin Juman; Sarah Saffian; Stephen E. Novak at the Columbia University Health Sciences Library; Patricia Kollappallil and Discovery Communications; Pam Slaton; Marsha Dennis; Nancy Kahn; David Kellman; Robert Shafran; Dr. Maggie Carpenter; Marla Berg; Helaine Olen; Jerome Feniger; Bruce Feniger; Stacy Horn; Dr. Dorothy Krugman, Stephanie Saul; Dr. Terence A. Leingang; Dr. Nancy Segal; Dr. Thomas Bouchard; Dr. Lawrence Perlman; Lawrence Wright; David Lanser; and Dr. Perry Ottenberg at the Viola Bernard Foundation.

A special thanks to Maria Pari-Keener, Louise Crawford, and Caroline Ghertler for sharing their experiences of growing up as a twin, and to all the separated twins.

Finally, our deepest gratitude to the Witt family for allowing us to tell this story.

IDENTICAL
STRANGERS

A MEMOIR OF TWINS
SEPARATED AND REUNITED

ELYSE SCHEIN | PAULA BERNSTEIN

A Reader's Guide

A Conversation with Paula Bernstein and Elyse Schein

Random House Reader's Circle: Why did you decide to write the book?

Elyse Schein: As separated identical twins, we found ourselves in the unique position of being able to examine the question of nature versus nurture firsthand. We thought that writing the book as it happened would put readers in our shoes and help them imagine, "What would it be like to meet my identical twin for the first time?" It's a common fantasy to have a twin, yet the relationship is more complex than one might think.

Paula Bernstein: Writing the book happened very organically. When I first got the phone call from the agency telling me the news that I had a twin, my initial instinct was to write. It was a way for me to remain grounded by reality and make sense of the puzzling situation. As soon as Elyse and I began exchanging e-mails, we realized that a narrative was unfolding. It became apparent that writing a book together was a way for us to explore our relationship and to find some answers to the mysteries of our origins.

RHRC: Why do you think the public is so fascinated by twins?

PB: Being a twin really forces you to answer the question, "What does it mean to be me?" If everyone is a unique individual, how is it possible that two people can be so alike?

Also, there is so much twin-based mythology and cultural lore that elevates twins to a special level in our society. On the other hand, twins are also viewed as nature's freaks.

ES: So many people come up to us and say, "You're so lucky. I wish I had a twin!" I think the idea is that a twin will be an ideal companion; someone who will understand you better than anyone else can. There seems to be a narcissistic element involved: "If only my partner could be just like me!" People seem to really enjoy comparing twins and pinpointing their similarities and differences.

RHRC: What memoirs inspired you during the process of writing the book? Were there any that influenced the way you conceived of *Identical Strangers*?

ES: As we prepared to embark on telling our story we found it necessary to study the genre, so we did a survey of all the most known memoirs, especially those that deal with similar themes. Since they both deal with the theme of a sudden shift of identity, Stephen J. Dubner's *Choosing My Religion* and Helen Fremont's *After Long Silence* stand out. It was also helpful to look at how Caroline Knapp's *Drinking: A Love Story* and John Colapinto's *As Nature Made Him: The Boy Who Was Raised as a Girl* integrated research into their narratives.

PB: I was also influenced by *Like Family: Growing up in Other People's Houses* by Paula McLain, *Borrowed Finery: A Memoir* by Paula Fox, and *Ithaka: A Daughter's Memoir of Being Found* by Sarah Saffian. In all of those books, the protaganists struggle to redefine "family." I related to Saffian's story in particular because, like me, she was found by biological relatives.

RHRC: How did you decide on the book's dual narrative?

PB: Since our individual stories were so different, when it came time to determine the structure of the book, we knew that we couldn't write in one unified voice. It seemed only natural that we would each write from our own perspective. We had no idea how our sections would piece together or if they would fit at all. We began by mapping out key events we would cover, then set off to write on our own. Exchanging chapters, we were often astounded that we chose the same words to describe things. Other times, we were surprised that we viewed the same situations quite differently. Still, without much editing, our separate sections effortlessly complemented each other's.

RHRC: How responsible do you think your environment was for the choices you made in your lives?

PB: Since I met Elyse, it has become clear to me that genetics plays a huge role in shaping our characters. It's not just our taste in music or books; it goes beyond that. We share the same basic personality. Elyse and I are variations of the same theme. We were each editor-in-chief of our respective high school newspapers and then went on to study film theory. But although we share many of the same interests and personality traits, it's a relief to discover that we're distinctly different people.

ES: I think we were both troubled by the thought that our identities might have been interchangeable. We each wondered, "If I had been raised by your parents and you had been raised by mine, would I be you and would you be me?" It took three and a half years of our getting to know each other to realize that that is not the case. Identity is not simply genetics plus environment.

RHRC: What was the writing process like? Was it difficult working together?

PB: At times, writing the book together was emotionally grueling, but it was also therapeutic. As challenging as the process was for me on a personal level, the editorial process went surprisingly smoothly. We seemed to share the same vision of the book.

ES: We knew that for the book to work we would have to be brutally honest, which was difficult because we were both concerned about hurting each other's feelings. It was often challenging not to edit the other's perspective but rather to accept that although we were writing about the same events our views might be extremely different.

RHRC: What is your relationship like now since the book came out?

PB: Writing the book definitely brought us closer together. It was very cathartic to work through so many of our conflicts. Now, Elyse lives just a short bike ride away in Brooklyn and she comes to babysit her nieces regularly. Also, we have become not just sisters, but friends. We have the same taste in movies, so it's easy to go see movies together. We also exchange favorite books.

We have come to trust each other and to understand each other; we respect each other's differences and no longer assume we'll always agree.

ES: It's true. I don't think we'd be as close now if we hadn't collaborated on the book together. It really forced us to confront a lot of issues that we might not have discussed otherwise. It ended up being easier to tackle difficult topics through writing. We are still getting to know each other. Our story is a work in progress.

RHRC: Have you discovered more similarities and differences between your personalities as time has passed? Have you noticed that you've become more alike?

ES: Now that I'm less defensive about our similarities I do notice them more. Sometimes Paula and I will choose the exact same phrase to express ourselves. It's becoming clearer that a large component of language is inherited.

Coincidentally, our hair length is the same now. Paula has started wearing her glasses more often and she now has the same wrinkle in her brow.

We are both naturally empathetic people so the more I get to know Paula the more I am in tune with her emotions, which is good and bad. If I'm not careful, I absorb her mood.

Even when we talk about something as straightforward as travel plans it's hard not to ask myself, "Would I go there? Would I do that?"

RHRC: Are you still angry with the psychiatrists who decided to separate you?

PB: We do not believe that Dr. Bernard and Dr. Neubauer were evil, nor do we think they set out to do harm. But we do think they were terribly misguided. How could they not have considered the ramifications of their decisions?

Still, as angry as we initially were with them, we have chosen to move on with our lives. We will never be able to make up for the thirty-five years that we missed, but we have the rest of our lives to try. We do not want that time to be marred by anger.

ES: We wish that Dr. Neubauer had at least conceded that they might have been off base with their theory (that twins would fare better separately), and had recognized that early separation might ultimately have been detrimental to the twins and triplets.

RHRC: Have there been any new developments since the last scene in the book? Did you learn more about the twin study? Have you heard from other separated twins? Learned more about your birth family?

ES: We're disappointed that the archives of the study have not been made accessible to us and others. We're hoping we'll gain access one day—even if it means waiting until we're old ladies when the records become public in 2066.

Dr. Neubauer died just four months after the hardcover publication of *Identical Strangers*. Paula and I are relieved that we had the opportunity to come face-to-face with him before he died. It is still difficult to understand how he didn't express any remorse about his involvement in the twin study.

Since the publication of the book, Paula and I haven't heard from David Witt or other members of our birth family. We respect their right to privacy. We've accepted that we may never know the full truth about our birth mother.

RHRC: How did meeting your twin and writing the book together change your lives?

ES: In countless ways. The story of my life was literally transformed the instant I learned I had a twin. Not only did I "have" a twin, I *was* a twin, which altered my sense of self. All the self-analysis I did while writing made me aware how important being in a relationship was for me. I had been living in a self-imposed exile of sorts and this discovery brought me back home and opened me up to the possibility of love.

PB: In a very concrete way, I gained a sister and my daughters have gained an aunt. In more amorphous ways, the experience challenged my own preconceptions about nature versus nurture and the idea of what makes a family.

RHRC: What has most surprised you about the response the book has received?

PB: We're surprised and gratified that so many people—not just twins or adoptees—have told us that they can relate to our story. Again and again, we've heard from people who, later in life, discovered surprising things about their family that caused them to rethink their sense of identity and their definition of family. Also, it's prompted friends who are parents to question the role of nature versus nurture in raising their children.

RHRC: Do you have any plans to write another book together?

PB: We are each working on separate projects—mine is another nonfiction book and Elyse's is fiction—but we are certainly open to the idea of working on another book together someday.

ES: Since we wrote the book as the events were unfolding, it might be interesting to revisit this period in a follow-up book in say ten or twenty years. Who knows where we'll both be then?

Questions and Topics
for Discussion

1. *Identical Strangers* delves into the age-old question of nature versus nurture. What conclusions does the book draw, if any? Has it changed the way you view the issue?

2. Paula and Elyse discuss the ways in which twins receive special attention in our society. Do you think twins have a special relationship? Why or why not would you want to be a twin?

3. Viola Bernard felt certain that twins would develop better senses of identity if they were raised separately. Even if you don't agree with her, do you think there is any validity to her claim?

4. "Thank God she is not my carbon copy" (p. 51). When they first meet as adults, Paula and Elyse are both relieved that they are not exactly identical in appearance or personal-

ity. How do you think you would react meeting your double for the first time?

5. Paula and Elyse each deal with the news of discovering she has an identical twin differently. How do you think you would react if you were in their situation?

6. "Once we separate today, I worry that my twin will vanish again" (p. 68), Paula writes after their first meeting. Soon after, she writes "I sometimes wish that [Elyse] hadn't found me" (p. 128). Can you understand Paula's ambivalence about her relationship with Elyse?

7. "I would like a better word to describe my relationship to Leda," writes Elyse. "Suddenly it occurs to me that Leda is *not* my mother, she is *our* mother" (p. 244). Do you think there is an adequate word to describe the sisters' relationship to Leda?

8. Mr. Witt seems reluctant to meet with Paula and Elyse. Can you understand his hesitance? Do you consider him to be their "uncle"?

9. Has *Identical Strangers* changed your views on adoption? If so, how?

10. Were you surprised by how well Paula and Elyse's families got along when they met? How do you imagine you'd

react if you found out your adopted child was a twin? What action would you take, if any?

11. Project into the future. How do you think Paula and Elyse's relationship will develop after the story ends?

ELYSE SCHEIN is a writer and filmmaker. Her short films "I Steal Happiness" and "Private Dick" have been shown at the Telluride Film Festival and at cinemas in Prague and San Francisco. A graduate of Stony Brook University, she studied film at FAMU, Prague's Film and TV School of the Academy of Performing Arts. She has also worked as an English teacher, photographer, and translator. Schein lives in Brooklyn.

PAULA BERNSTEIN is a freelance writer whose work has been published in *The New York Times, New York, The Village Voice,* and *Redbook,* among other publications. Formerly a reporter at *Variety* and *The Hollywood Reporter,* Bernstein has also been a regular contributor to CNN. A graduate of Wellesley College, she has a master's degree in cinema studies from New York University. Bernstein lives in Brooklyn with her husband and two daughters.

Join the Random House Reader's Circle to enhance your book club or personal reading experience.

Our FREE monthly e-newsletter gives you:

• Sneak-peek excerpts from our newest titles

• Exclusive interviews with your favorite authors

• Special offers and promotions giving you access to advance copies of books, our free "Book Club Companion" quarterly magazine, and much more

• Fun ideas to spice up your book club meetings: creative activities, outings, and discussion topics

• Opportunities to invite an author to your next book club meeting

• Anecdotes and pearls of wisdom from other book group members . . . and the opportunity to share your own!

To sign up, visit our website at
www.randomhousereaderscircle.com

 When you see this seal on the outside, there's a great book club read inside.